AF305210

INVESTING IN AMERICA

ANTONY BUGG-LEVINE

INVESTING IN AMERICA

EXPANDING ACCESS TO FINANCE TO SOLVE OUR SHARED CHALLENGES

WILEY

Library of Congress Cataloging-in-Publication Data:

Names: Bugg-Levine, Antony, 1974- author
Title: Investing in America / Antony Bugg-Levine.
Description: Hoboken, New Jersey : Wiley, [2026] | Includes index.
Identifiers: LCCN 2026010608 (print) | LCCN 2026010609 (ebook) | ISBN 9781394432776 cloth | ISBN 9781394432790 adobe pdf | ISBN 9781394432783 epub
Subjects: LCSH: Investments—Social aspects—United States | Finance, Personal—United States | Economic development—United States | United States—Economic policy
Classification: LCC HG4910 .B84 2026 (print) | LCC HG4910 (ebook)
LC record available at https://lccn.loc.gov/2026010608
LC ebook record available at https://lccn.loc.gov/2026010609

Cover Design: Wiley
Cover Image: Victor_69/Getty Images
Author Photo: Elise Campbell
Printed and bound by CPI Group (UK) Ltd, Croydon, CR0 4YY
C9781394432776_260526

For Ahadi, who makes my life and work better.

And for Aza, who makes it matter.

Legal Disclaimer

This book is intended to educate and inform, to help readers understand the evolving world of impact investing. It's not here to tell readers what to do with their money.

This book does not aim to provide, and it should not be read as providing, investment advice, legal guidance, tax strategies, or any other kind of professional counsel. I am not suggesting that any reader buy, sell, or hold onto anything I mention in this book. When I write in this book about a company, a fund, or a financial product, I am not making an endorsement or a recommendation. The examples and stories in these pages are meant to illustrate ideas, not to serve as a blueprint for your investment portfolio.

I have done my best to get things right in this book, but I cannot promise that every detail is perfectly accurate or complete, and neither the publisher nor I can be held responsible for any decisions a reader makes based on what he or she reads here.

Contents

Contents

Disclosures

I have funded, financed, worked for, and worked with many of the investors and companies described here. For transparency, I disclose those named in the book whose success I have an ongoing financial stake in and those who the company I work for is formally advising: American Pride Bank, Homium, ImpactAlpha, Lafayette Square, and TrimTab. I have also received sponsorship support from Gary Community Ventures.

I highlight them in the book, not because I work with them. I work with them because they are inspiring. The desire to share their stories, and the stories of other investors and leaders I know, is what initially motivated me to write this book.

ChatGPT 5.1 and 5.2 were used to identify specific details about the history and the organizations and individuals profiled in Chapters 2-11, and to identify additional sources for background research. AI-generated data points were reviewed, validated against original sources, and cross-checked for accuracy. AI did not influence my decisions about which organizations and history to highlight or the book's synthesis and conclusions.

1 | Why Invest in America?

When I completed high school, I was able to get a loan to pay for college. Later, I became a homeowner because the company I worked for had a deal with a bank that provided a loan to cover my down payment. The day I moved into my house, I drove a new car home without paying the dealership anything or any interest for the next five years. My company also made it easy for me to buy stocks through a tax-advantaged retirement account.

I did not have the cash to make these investments. I needed someone to provide the financing that could enable me to invest in a better future. Access to timely and fair financing has been crucial in propelling my family onto a trajectory of opportunity and financial security.

But what happens to the people who cannot access this type of fair financing? Almost half of the people in the United States cannot come up with $400 for an emergency without tapping credit cards, predatory loans, or family and friends for help. They certainly cannot pay upfront for a house, an education, or a car that is often crucial to get to work.

And what about the entrepreneur with a bold, new idea that requires spending money upfront before the business takes off? Or the health clinic or food bank that could expand their services, but only gets paid after they have delivered them? Or the local government that could provide better services in the future if able to access money to invest in improving delivery now? Today, too many of them are shut off from pathways to security and success because they cannot access fair and affordable financing. They are competing in an economy rigged to favor the people, companies, and communities with access to money to invest when opportunities arise.

Despite the myriad ways we are divided, Americans broadly agree that our economy is not providing enough hardworking people with a path to success and economic security. Expanding access to finance alone will not solve this problem. But solving it will be impossible unless we increase these financing opportunities.

What Is Investing in America?

Picture loans and equity investments like a river running through a valley. Capital follows the contours of the land, flowing to where there is least resistance downstream: large established companies, familiar financial products, mortgage applicants with high credit scores buying homes in middle-class and wealthier neighborhoods, small business owners with personal assets to pledge as a guarantee for a loan. Investments flow where investors can access the best data, the longest track records, the deepest relationships, and the lowest transaction costs.[1]

This investor behavior concentrates wealth and opportunity in the hands of too few people and communities. Beyond the banks of the river, and the lakes of capital it creates, many Americans live on parched land where the seeds of their hard work and ambition will not bear fruit because they cannot access the investment needed to nourish them.

Investing in America is about bringing the water of fair finance to that parched land. While sometimes investing in America is about finding ways to invest in specific overlooked places, it is about more than geography. It is often about investing in ways that help make the promise of America more real for more people, honoring the idea that we are a country that offers opportunities to hardworking people and gives everyone a fair chance at success.

Fortunately, across the United States, inspiring people are investing in America, bringing investments to where they have not been or back to places capital retreated from. They are expanding access to the loans and investments that will enable families and communities to work successfully for a better future. And they are helping to solve the national challenges that most Americans, from a wide range of political beliefs and backgrounds, agree we need to fix.

The chapters that follow begin with a title that expresses an aspiration about our economy that most Americans would agree with. Each chapter outlines the challenges we face in achieving that aspiration and then provides brief profiles of leading innovators helping to expand who gets access to fair financing to solve those challenges.

- How can we ensure that full-time work leads to financial stability and retirement security?
  - In El Paso, Texas the workers at a commercial landscaping company are growing their retirement accounts after they secured a loan to buy their company from its retiring owner.
- How can we make rent more affordable and home ownership more accessible?
  - In Detroit, first-time homeowners are partnering with investors to purchase homes with lower down payments and monthly mortgage costs through a new fund working closely with government and local donors to expand who gets to be a homeowner.
- How do we expand American energy production so that everyone can access reliable and affordable energy services?
  - In southwest Utah, an energy company is using fracking technology to create carbon-free energy, building the world's largest geothermal power plant, fueled by investment from a fund focused on financing new energy sources.
- How can we enable people to pay for the education and training they need to advance their careers without bankrupting them?
  - In Ohio, workers are getting trained and certified as diesel technicians through a loan they will only have to repay if they find and keep a good job after graduation.

- How can we create a healthcare system that is affordable and accessible and focused on helping us stay healthy?
  - In Tippecanoe County, Indiana, almost two thirds of county workers have reversed their Type 2 diabetes and are saving more than $3,000 in annual prescription costs after working with a startup company, backed by an impact-focused venture capitalist, that supports people to get healthier and lose weight.
- How can we enjoy our country's abundant land, waters, and wildlife and pass them on to future generations?
  - In Oregon's Rogue Valley, crews are clearing brush and thinning trees to reduce the risk of catastrophic fires on national forest and private lands, as part of a collaboration between a firm that arranges financing for fire resilience interventions, a local nonprofit, and Tribal leaders.
- How can all Americans access technology that is safe and improves our lives?
  - In the rural North Carolina town of Enfield, community members are enjoying the benefits of rapid internet broadband service that costs less than their old dial-up connections, after a nonprofit investment fund financed a local entrepreneur to build an internet provider focused on reaching households large companies ignore.
- How can we ensure that who you are and where you live do not limit your ability to secure an investment?
  - In the Wood Basket of Northern Minnesota, in an old timber mill town, small businesses are borrowing from a local foundation to invest in the upkeep of their stores to help preserve the beauty and vitality of their commercial district.

These are just a few of the inspiring examples of people and organizations investing to expand opportunity in America. From Alaska to Florida and Maine to California, determined and creative investors are broadening investment access and reviving the American Dream.

What does this mean for you? I hope you draw inspiration from these examples. But I also hope you are moved to take action. Investing in America need not be a spectator sport. You can use your powers as a voter to back government action that supports those who are investing in America, often a more efficient way to solve our challenges as Chapter 10 shows. And the final chapter describes how you can invest in America with just a savings account or $1 and an internet connection.

What Does It Take to Invest in America?

Having collected stories from across the country and across a wide range of issues, a few common themes stand out about what it takes to invest in America:

Buy-In, not Bail-Out: The people and institutions profiled in this book are not looking for handouts. They are trying to create a level playing field of capital access. They are working to make sure that the people creating more opportunity for more Americans can access credit on the same terms as those looking to perpetuate the status quo, where too many opportunities are hoarded by too few. They are equipping workers with the financing they need to compete with private equity investors when the chance arises to buy their company. They are setting up cooperatives so that family fishermen can compete with massive conglomerates to purchase the right to catch fish in Alaska. They are financing developers who put renters on a path to own their homes instead of buying out homeowners and turning them into renters. Part of America's economic genius has been its ability to steer capital to the best people with the best ideas. Investing in America is about making that truer for more people.

Bridge Builders: The people profiled in this book are remarkably diverse but share one common trait: they invariably excel at working with all kinds of people to get the job done. Many have taken wide-ranging career paths that allow them to draw on different skills and approaches themselves, like the Wall Street banker turned AME minister who is helping churches invest in their local communities, the Army veteran turned real estate developer buying old hotels to turn into permanently affordable supportive housing for veterans, the former nonprofit leader turned Goldman Sachs banker now lending to Dallas area public schools to invest in career counseling for high schoolers. Others have formed unusual partnerships to bring necessary skills together, such as the conservation nonprofit and global bank that formed an investment company to buy and preserve forests in Appalachia and around the country.

Pragmatism over Purity: The best investors in America are driven by a clear and unwavering moral vision about what this country can be. In service to that mission, they do not hesitate to work with people they do not always agree with. This seems to be an increasingly scarce mentality and skill. At a time when too many people choose purity over impact, the people in this book seek ways to collaborate with traditional and unexpected allies to achieve common goals.

First Steps: A multi-billion-dollar community bank in North Carolina began with start-up capital from a bake sale with goods donated by a local baker the founders had helped. An investment firm that has invented a new financing tool to fund national forest fire prevention began as a pitch in business school. An investment fund buying companies on behalf of their workers began in discussions about purpose among two friends in a college dorm room. It's easy to forget that many breakthroughs, like marathons, begin with a single step. What conversations are happening now that will become major contributors to this work in a decade?

Government as Wingman: The investors in this book solve national challenges in ways the mainstream investment markets have ignored. Sometimes that's because mainstream markets are mispricing risk or missing opportunities. Other times, the investments might be profitable eventually but will take too long for most investors to wait. In these cases, private markets can match the right investor to the right opportunity.

Sometimes these investments will simply not be as lucrative to investors as alternatives, even when they create substantial value for their borrowers and for America. Government has stepped in before to make financial incentives work for private sector investors to expand this type of lending, most notably with the creation of the 30-year fixed-rate mortgage market as we see in Chapter 3. Many of the investors profiled here collaborate with government in similar ways. They work with government to invest in nuclear energy production in Idaho, extend student loans in Illinois, and expand home ownership in Detroit. They know that investing in America sometimes requires working alongside our government, not trying to replace or circumvent it.

From Sea to Shining Sea: When you buy a red car, you start to see red cars everywhere. When you invest in America, you start to see examples everywhere. This book includes examples of investors operating in every state and describes specific work in 42 states and Washington, DC. Investing in America is not just a game for so-called Coastal Elites or for Red States. The challenges this book describes show up everywhere. Fortunately, so do the problem solvers.

Why I Wrote This Book

One of the greatest blessings of my work is the opportunity to meet so many inspiring people. I wrote this book so that more people can learn about them. Most of us who do this work cannot explain to our families what we do for a living, seeking to make profitable investments that also solve social challenges. But that also brings us closer. This has remained a remarkably collaborative and generous group, despite the financial stakes and growing competition.

I am honored to highlight the ways that practical problem solvers are making a difference, freed from old ways of thinking about the separate roles that government, investors, and nonprofits must play. I did not set out to be an investor. Like many people, I used to believe that advancing social progress required working for nonprofits or government and that investors should only seek to maximize profits. But through experience in Africa and across the United States, I have come to see the power of what we now call impact investing: the simple idea that for-profit investment could be a legitimate and effective tool to help solve social challenges.[2] I hope these examples make clear what a difference this work can make in communities across our country.

I hope the book helps more elected officials and voters see the potential in policies that expand access to fair finance across America. I am one of the few people I know who remains optimistic about the work of Congress and who enjoys spending time on Capitol Hill. Most of the elected officials and their staff members, from both parties, with whom I have discussed these ideas are excited to work on ways to bring more private investment to solve the pressing challenges their constituents face. Chapter 10 describes many of the tools the US government has and has used in the past to invest in America. There is real, bipartisan momentum for these initiatives.

Finally, I hope this book increases interest in investing in America among anyone who can make or advise on investments. The final chapter describes how anyone with a savings account or $1 and an internet connection can invest in America. Impact investing is too often portrayed as an indulgence of Coastal billionaires, attracted to an idea that can make them feel good without having to give their fortunes away. By contrast, this book shows how impact investors are deploying capital across the country to solve pressing national challenges.

What This Book Is Not

This book is not a "Best of . . ." list. Like a Bruce Springsteen concert set list, I could swap every example here with a different one and have just as many compelling stories to tell. I chose examples to convey the incredible range of people investing in America and the range of places where this is making a positive difference. I hope this allows you to draw inspiration for your own life and work.

This book is not exhaustively comprehensive. A strong case could be made to include a chapter on the need to finance a revolution in caregiving so that taking care of children and parents does not bankrupt a family or pull people, especially women, from the workforce. That chapter would highlight the work of venture capital funds like Magnify and the caregiving REIT created by Mission Driven Finance. There are also fascinating stories to tell about investors backing the revival of domestic manufacturing. Finding ways to invest in the systems, services, and products that could address the opioid crisis is another area most Americans agree needs attention. I hope others pick up where this book ends and share those stories.

This book does not focus on trading stocks and bonds and the considerations that investors make when determining what stocks and bonds to buy and sell on secondary, public markets. Investing in America is about making investment capital available directly to families, companies, community organizations, and local governments to turn capital into services and products and homes that expand opportunity.

This book is not a contribution to the debate about ESG, DEI, or "woke capitalism." Investing in America is bipartisan and spans both federal and local solutions. Leaders from both major political parties support much of the work described here, from the reddest and bluest places to everywhere in between. These are challenges that we can agree are worth solving, and solutions that most of us can get behind. In fact, the idea that all Americans should have access to fair financing that empowers them to invest in a better future for themselves and their families is a part of our nation's origin story. As you will learn in the next chapter, one of our Founding Fathers set up a fund in his will to invest in America, setting a precedent others are building on now.

This book is not making a naïve argument that more lending to more people is always good. Expanding access to financing can be exploitative. There are many visible, recent examples, especially from mortgage and student loan lenders, of companies that took advantage of people locked out of mainstream solutions to foist unaffordable loans and fees that stripped their borrowers of their assets. To invest in America, as this book describes it, is not only to find ways to extend financing to those who have been locked out, but also to do so in a way that leaves your customer better off. The innovators this book highlights are building scalable solutions that also support their customers to improve their financial security. The book uses "fair financing" as shorthand for what they do to control pricing, limit hidden fees, preserve borrower flexibility, and right-size investments to customer needs. There are easier ways to make money in this market. These innovators work harder to make a better future for their customers and communities.

This book is not a critique of what is wrong with America. It is a celebration of the inspiring people working to help America live up to its founding ideals. Each chapter begins with grounding, and often sobering, facts. I share them so that we can understand why these challenges demand innovative solutions and how expanding access to fair finance can make a meaningful contribution. I also know many readers will see in these sobering facts opportunities to build solutions that will strengthen the American Dream.

A More Perfect Union

Investing in America can reconnect people around shared goals and actions. This book shows how people from different communities, perspectives, ideologies, and economic status are advancing a broad movement that helps build a country that is better for all of us. They are patriots who work hard every day to make the promise of America more real for more people. Their ability to figure out how to collaborate in service to a common purpose is an important lesson that we could usefully apply to other areas of our lives.

This book is one grateful immigrant's 250th birthday gift to the country that has given my family and me so much. At a moment when Americans are dangerously divided, we face two urgent tasks: building a fairer economy that expands opportunity and learning how to live together productively and safely. In a small but hopeful way, this book aims to help by shining a light on the people who are investing in America's future and in the possibility of a country that can work better for all of us.

2 | Everyone Should Be Able to Earn Their American Dream

A global media mogul grew up in Boston, the youngest son of a large, middle-class family. As a teenager, he worked for his older brother, laboring long hours in a print shop before moving to Philadelphia to start his own business. He knew firsthand the difference between working for someone and working for yourself. He also knew that talent and effort alone were rarely enough to make that leap. Workers might have the skills to run a business, but without startup capital they remained stuck, selling their labor while others accumulated assets.

He wanted to change that. So, in a provision added to his will near the end of his life, he set aside a portion of his estate to create revolving loan funds to help young workers in Philadelphia and Boston become small business owners and build durable financial security for their families.[1] Each borrower could borrow enough to buy tools, inventory, or a stake in a small business. The loans would come with a 5% annual interest rate and be payable in 10 years.[2]

The will set out that the loans would revolve for 100 years, making loans to new workers when borrowers paid off previous ones. At the end of that first century, the trustees were instructed to spend part of the accumulated funds on public projects in each city, while preserving the remainder to continue lending for another 100 years, eventually making the full amount available to the cities' residents.[3]

Who was the media mogul who understood the need to finance workers to become owners? Benjamin Franklin: famous as a US founding father and lesser known as an impact investing O.G. By 1990, when the 200 years were up, thousands of workers had become business owners and Philadelphia had $2.3 million and Boston twice that to use for public purpose.[4]

For many American workers in the mid-20th century, a single job could support a family, buy a home, and allow for modest savings and a dignified retirement, even for people without a college degree. Work was not merely a source of income; it was the primary on-ramp to economic security and asset ownership.

For too many people, that opportunity has unraveled.

Today, millions of Americans work full time and still live on a knife's edge. Despite decades of economic growth and rising productivity, the financial condition of the typical worker has grown more precarious. Adjusted for inflation, average wages have barely moved in 40 years. Over the same period, worker productivity surged, but gains flowed overwhelmingly to company owners rather than workers.[5]

As of the late 2010s, 4 in 10 Americans could not cover a $400 emergency without borrowing or selling something.[6] More than half of US households have less than three months of emergency savings.[7] Between one-third and three-fifths of Americans report living paycheck to paycheck.[8] Even near retirement, the picture is grim: nearly half of households have no retirement savings at all, and the shift from pensions to do-it-yourself 401(k)s has left millions exposed to risks they were never equipped to manage.[9]

Wealth inequality compounds the problem. Median White household wealth is roughly 10 times that of Black and Latino households, reflecting generations of unequal access to homeownership, retirement plans, and capital.[10] And while the country is in the midst of the largest intergenerational wealth transfer in history, the vast majority of that inheritance will accrue to families already at the top.[11]

Work alone is no longer enough.

Insecurity is structural. Over the past half-century, the US economy has systematically shifted risk away from employers, institutions, and government and onto workers, a phenomenon economists have called the "Great Risk Shift."[12] Benefits eroded just as housing, healthcare, education, and childcare costs rose faster than wages.

Looking ahead, emerging technologies could improve economic productivity but also threaten to deepen these divides. Automation and artificial intelligence are accelerating productivity gains that make investors richer while wages lag behind. Since 1979, productivity has grown several times faster than typical worker pay, and research suggests automation explains a majority of the rise in wage inequality.[13] Without broader ownership, AI risks widening inequality.

If the American Dream is to remain something people can earn through work, it must be rebuilt on new foundations.

As Benjamin Franklin understood, more workers must own a meaningful stake in the companies they help build. Ownership determines who benefits when capital becomes more productive than labor. Employee ownership reconnects pay to productivity and creates durable pathways to retirement security.[14]

Second, good jobs must be accessible to more people. Too many Americans are locked out of stable employment because of criminal records, caregiving responsibilities, or lack of credentials.

Third, jobs must do more to address workers' financial insecurity directly. Wages matter, but they are not enough. Employers increasingly need to provide benefits such as emergency savings tools, affordable credit, healthcare access, and predictable schedules to help workers manage volatility. This is both good for workers and can drive productivity and business profitability.[15]

None of these shifts happens without financing.

Specifically, investors will need to answer three core questions to find ways to unlock financing to expand financial security for American workers:

- How can workers access capital to buy their companies and compete with private equity investors backed by the largest banks and pension funds?
- How can businesses that improve the financial security of their workers convince a skeptical market that this ultimately generates better financial returns for their investors as well?
- How can the start-ups that can improve job quality for all workers, not just the most well off, get the start-up and growth capital they need from investors without being steered toward serving people who least need their help?

Who will finance a revived American Dream? This chapter highlights dedicated fund managers financing employees to buy their companies, lenders using loans as a vector to improve the financial security of the workers in the companies they lend to, and nonprofits making venture capital investments in the innovative companies improving job access and quality. More than 200 years after Benjamin Franklin set the precedent, they point to the possibilities of investing in an American Dream for more people.

Building Wealth, One Buyout at a Time

"This could change people's lives."

That's how Joe Aguilar, a 30-year veteran of Accent Landscape Contractors in El Paso, Texas, described what it meant to the company's 130 workers to become the 100% employee-owners of their company in 2022. Aguilar, who started at Accent in 1989 as a job estimator and later became president, explained that most employees "pretty much live on their salaries," and had never expected to build real wealth from their jobs. For him and more than 100 colleagues in El Paso, the ownership transition represented not just job stability, but a transformative opportunity to accumulate long-term financial security.[16]

How could workers without savings afford to buy the company? Because Apis & Heritage, a new kind of investment firm, provided 100% of the sales price through their pioneering Employee-Led Buyout (ELBO) product. Modeled on the mechanics of a leveraged buyout, A&H raises investor capital to purchase companies from founders. But instead of delivering the business to private equity, A&H transfers 100% of the equity to workers through an Employee Stock Ownership Plan (ESOP) trust. The workers pay nothing. As the company's future profits repay the financing, employees accumulate shares over time. Workers can sell their shares when they retire.

ESOPs were first created in 1974 by a federal law that gave substantial tax breaks to owners who sell to their workers and to the workers themselves. ESOP-owned companies avoid federal corporate tax[i] and the selling owner can defer capital gains taxes. Almost 15 million Americans have a stake in an ESOP, while ESOP trusts hold $1.8 trillion of retirement wealth.[17] The typical worker with 10+ years in an ESOP-owned firm has $315,000 in retirement savings,[18] in contrast to the reality for half of all American workers who have no retirement savings at all.[19]

Despite this traction and the tax breaks, growth in ESOP formation has stalled. One major reason: the lack of lenders willing to give workers the loans they need to buy their company. Without this, owners face a choice between selling to private equity or a competitor for cash today or often waiting years and sometimes decades for their workers to pay them out of company profits. Few owners will wait that long, even those who would prefer to see their workers take over.

Solving this challenge is especially urgent as America's small- and medium-sized businesses face a "Silver Tsunami," with the impending retirement of 2.3 million Boomer business owners. Given how many businesses fail or get shuttered when these retirements occur, the Tsunami threatens one in six American jobs.[20]

Todd Leverette and Phil Reeves co-founded A&H to remove the financing barrier to worker ownership. Friends since attending Morehouse College together, they launched the firm in 2021 after its incubation at the nonprofit Democracy at Work Institute. A&H's first fund closed at $58 million in 2022 and financed five employee-led buyouts, transitioning

---

[i]ESOPs write down federal taxes as a share of their ESOP ownership: 100% ESOPs pay no federal taxes while partial ESOPs can write off the share of their tax bill equal to the ESOP's share of the company.

more than 400 workers into ownership. Impact investors rallied to help A&H launch. Groups like Philadelphia's Spring Point Capital Partners, drawn to the potential of this approach to improve financial security for American workers, not only made early investments but also supported the founders in raising additional capital from others. With the insights and credibility from their first fund, and motivated to support more workers, A&H set out to raise a $250 million fund in 2025, approaching more mainstream investors with the case that they are a financially attractive part of the private credit asset class.

A&H is not alone in solving the financing gap for worker owners. North Carolina-based Mosaic Capital Partners applies a more traditional private equity model, financing workers to convert companies into ESOPs while also taking equity shares that they can profit from.[21] Common Trust offers another twist on employee ownership. They finance and advise business owners to sell to their workers through a range of products, including an Employee Ownership Trust that provides workers with profit sharing and immediate equity rather than focusing on building retirement wealth.[22] The 135,000 workers of Consumer Direct Care Network, a national in-home care provider, now enjoy ownership benefits through a Common Trust-advised sale in 2025.[23]

Large, incumbent investors are also recognizing the value of supporting workers to benefit from the success of the companies they work for. Most notably, private equity giant KKR has implemented a profit-sharing plan for workers in all the US companies they buy, typically setting aside 3–5% of the equity of the business for a pool to be shared with workers when KKR sells the company or takes it public. KKR leader Pete Stavros has been particularly vocal about the moral imperative and financial advantage of giving workers a financial stake in the businesses they work for.[24] Ownership Works, the nonprofit he started to spread the practice throughout the industry, encourages and supports other investors to take up the approach with a goal of generating $20 billion of wealth for American workers in 10 years.

Together, this work seeks to build an economy where millions more American workers—landscapers, factory workers, drivers, technicians—benefit as owners in the businesses they sustain.

"Employee ownership shouldn't be exceptional," Reeves says. "It should be normal."

Loans as a Wedge to Improving Worker Financial Security

Amid the din of lunch hour, a college cafeteria worker in Western Massachusetts stares at her phone, seeing the $500 quote from her body shop to fix her car. Like more than 40% of all Americans, that's more money than she would have typically set aside for emergencies. A year earlier, she would have been forced to borrow from a payday lender whose fees would have cost more than the loan, leaving her digging out from that trap for months.

But now she has another option. She has built up $500 in a savings account through a partnership that her employer, Genuine Foods, has with Sunny Day Fund, a provider that helps companies offer emergency savings programs as a standard employee benefit. And the company partly covered the costs of this service because their lender, Lafayette Square, offered them a discount on the interest rate of their loan of up to 0.25% (which can add up to $125,000 per year on a $50 million loan).

Why would Lafayette Square, a commercial lender committed to providing their institutional investors with market-rate financial returns, make that offer? Because of their fundamental belief that supporting companies to help improve their workers' financial security is good business for everyone.

Lafayette Square was founded in 2020 by Damien Dwin, who grew up in a working-class Washington, D.C. neighborhood where people felt every economic downturn first and recovered last. Dwin built Lafayette Square to do something bold: use private credit to strengthen midsized businesses and the workers who power them. He raised a $100 million founding commitment from Morgan Stanley, and operating capital from the impact-oriented investment group Capricorn and others, as well as large pension funds to kickstart the work.[25]

Middle-market businesses, those with roughly $10 million–$1 billion in annual revenue, employ more than 50 million Americans and anchor communities across the country. They often sit in a financing "dead zone": too large for community banks or Small Business Administration programs, too small or too specialized for megabanks. Lafayette Square steps into that gap, supplying flexible credit paired with a systematic investment in worker financial security.

Dwin recruited Don Baylor, Jr., a community activist and foundation program officer, to build Worker Solutions, a service provider that helps companies identify policy changes and benefits that can measurably improve the financial security and health of workers. Worker Solutions contracts with service providers who can set up benefits that drive financial security such as emergency savings (Sunny Day Fund), student loan repayment (Candidly), and Honeybee (no-fee, no-interest loans). Lafayette Square provides an interest rate discount to their borrowers who implement these changes or offer one or more of these services to their workers. In another pioneering move, Lafayette Square reports its mission targets and specific impacts in its formal investment filings to the Securities and Exchange Commission, ensuring these results receive the same scrutiny and legal standing as reports on financial return.[26]

Lafayette Square could profit from this approach in ways that exceed the revenue it gives up when borrowers access the impact discount:

- Lafayette Square has secured large investment commitments from investors who also care about impact, such as the $5.6 billion Catalyst Fund of the British Insurance company M+G and from the impact-focused investment manager Capricorn. Lafayette Square has also accessed multiple pools of long-term, low-cost loan capital from the US government's Small Business Administration. And some of their borrowers provide rate discounts to Lafayette Square if they meet agreed impact targets.
- Signaling their interest in helping companies support their workers also helps Lafayette Square win business and overcome the skepticism and distrust that many business owners feel toward commercial lenders with Wall Street backing, especially businesses outside major financial centers like New York and San Francisco.
- Indirectly, outside research shows that workers with greater financial security are more productive and more likely to stay with their employer. That would increase the likelihood of the borrowers' financial success and ability to repay their loan to Lafayette Square.

Other investors are pursuing a similar belief that investing in worker financial security and health is good for business as part of a broader "good jobs" movement. HCAP Partners is a private equity firm that has developed a methodology for assessing and improving the financial health of workers at the companies it buys, intending to prove this will make them more valuable when resold. A holding company focused on proving that treating workers better will make businesses more financially valuable, NineDean launched in 2025, led by private equity veteran Aren LeeKong. LeeKong secured the largest-ever direct investment from Ford Foundation's Mission Investment Fund to implement this approach.[27] For its part, Lafayette Square spun out its Worker Solutions program as an independent company in 2025 to serve this growing market of investors looking to work with investees to improve the financial security of their workers.

The work is in its early days at Lafayette Square. In its Annual 10K filed for 2024, they reported 2,547 workers have used Worker Solutions services, and 4,651 workers have access to new zero-interest loans, coaching, or savings tools.[28] But by showing how a loan can be a vector to improve job quality, and reporting results transparently, they are showing how commercial private credit can help more American workers gain the financial security for their families that full-time work should deliver. And they are raising the bar for other lenders, many of whom have dismissed the potential to influence job quality as something only private equity investors with an ownership stake can attempt to do.

Back in Massachusetts, the college cafeteria worker starts her shift with a repaired car and a sigh of relief. Lafayette Square is out to show that companies full of workers like her, more stable, supported, and resilient, are precisely the kinds of companies worth lending to.

New Kinds of Investors Making Work Work

In Colorado, a job seeker named Alejandro had been locked out of work for months. Despite having skills and experience, his criminal record meant applications stalled or offers disappeared. That changed when his probation officer referred him to Honest Jobs, a fair-chance hiring platform backed by JFFVentures. Through the platform, Alejandro connected with an employer committed to giving people with criminal conviction history a fair shot at a job and soon secured a job as a forklift driver in Aurora.[29]

Companies like Honest Jobs reveal a truth about the US labor market: improving job quality and worker outcomes often requires rebuilding the systems that connect people to work, not just creating more openings. But businesses designed to reduce exclusion, modernize hiring, or create new pathways into good jobs frequently struggle to attract conventional venture capital investors, who are wary of often-complicated revenue structures and longer-term payoffs.

That gap has created space for a growing group of investors who understand that durable financial returns can coexist with better outcomes for American workers. Two influential examples, the venture capital fund JFFVentures and the investing arm of World Education Services (WES), come from unusual places, born out of workforce development and economic integration nonprofits that decided to make for-profit investments to diversify their revenue and activate new levers of impact.

Founded in 1983, Jobs for the Future (JFF) built its reputation as a national nonprofit shaping workforce policy, partnering with employers, and designing programs to improve outcomes for people facing structural barriers to opportunity. Over time, JFF's leadership accepted that while policy and programs could demonstrate what worked, they too seldom changed how labor markets actually operated at scale.

By the late 2010s, JFF concluded that capital itself had to become a tool for workforce reform. That insight led to the creation of JFFVentures, an impact-investing platform designed to back early-stage companies building new systems for hiring, advancement, and skill recognition. JFF hired Yigal Kerszenbaum to lead the effort, drawing on his background in impact investing and education and workforce technology. The fund attracted a mission-aligned group of initial investors from workforce-focused foundations to the American Council on Education.[30]

JFFVentures backs companies that target specific failures in how US labor markets connect people to quality jobs.

- Based in Texas, Honest Jobs focuses on expanding employment access for the 70 million Americans with a criminal record. Their jobs board connects them with employers adopting "second chance" hiring approaches that make it easier for qualified applicants with conviction histories to apply successfully. This JFF investment complements JFF's grant-funded policy work through its Center for Justice and Economic Advancement that works to break down employment barriers for people with criminal convictions.

- In Wisconsin, FactoryFix addresses chronic hiring bottlenecks in manufacturing and the skilled trades, helping employers identify and engage workers with relevant skills more efficiently.
- And in California, ChargerHelp! operates at the intersection of workforce development and the clean-energy transition, combining EV-charging infrastructure services with technician training programs that create new pathways into technical jobs tied to the rapidly expanding electric-vehicle economy.

What makes JFF's approach distinctive is not only the portfolio, but the institutional choice behind it. It remains unusual for a large nonprofit to operate a venture investing arm designed to attract private capital. JFF believes durable improvements in job quality require durable business models and that nonprofit expertise can reduce risk for early investors by supporting the investment team with deep labor market insight.

World Education Services (WES) arrived at a similar conclusion from a different starting point. WES launched as a nonprofit over 50 years ago to help immigrants, refugees, and international students translate credentials from their home countries to pursue education and qualify for better jobs in the United States and Canada. Over the years, WES built this service into a profitable business generating substantial income to fund its nonprofit operations. But leadership recognized that credential recognition alone was insufficient to achieve their vision of a workforce open to all and a world where anyone can thrive anywhere. Workers also face financial risk when pursuing education due in part to limited access to capital that supports mobility.

In response, WES used $30 million of operating reserves in 2019 to launch the Mariam Assefa Fund, initially to give grants to nonprofits operating to advance economic opportunities and integration for refugees and immigrants. A year later, it made its first impact investment, driven by a belief that achieving its mission requires supporting companies and shaping capital markets to extend opportunity and economic mobility for workers who mainstream investors overlook. Now committed to investing all its assets aligned to its mission, it invests impact-first capital into companies and funds across diverse impact themes, geographies, and asset classes.[31]

The move was notable not just for what the fund supports, but for what it represents: like JFF, a nonprofit choosing to align its assets with its mission. CEO Esther Benjamin has emphasized that WES's resources belong to the communities it serves and should be used to generate long-term, regenerative impact, while Smitha Das, who leads the WES's investment team, has helped build impact investing into a permanent institutional capability.[32]

With its investments, WES supported organizations improving credential portability, reducing the financial risk of education, and strengthening workforce pathways for immigrants. It invested in Apis & Heritage's first fund, helping to rally other impact investors to follow. It also made a lead commitment to Mission Driven Finance Capital Partners, which focuses on channeling capital to under-resourced communities and inclusive economic development.[33]

Taken together, JFF and WES demonstrate how mission-driven organizations are pushing beyond grants and advocacy to reshape labor markets from the inside. By using investment capital to align incentives among employers, educators, and workers, they show that improving job quality requires more than good intentions. It requires systems that reward advancement, reduce risk for workers, and make equity durable.

Very few American workers have cash to buy the company they work for. And very few have the cash to self-finance a start-up that could improve worker pay if only it can get through its early stages to financial stability itself. That is why expanding the ways investors make capital available will be crucial to reviving the simple idea that a lifetime of hard work should create economic security for all Americans.

Beyond work, the other single most reliable engine for long-term financial security and inter-generational wealth transfer in the last 100 years in America has been home ownership. And just like the workers who need financing to buy their company, most Americans need a mortgage to buy their home. Unfortunately, for many Americans, the engine of home ownership has stalled amidst a housing crisis that is leaving many people unable to invest in their future when they struggle to make the rent.

The next chapter shines a light on the investors who are finding new ways to finance both first-time home buyers and the developers looking to make rental housing more affordable.

3 | Everyone Should Be Able to Afford to Live in a Decent Home and Have a Realistic Path to Home Ownership

A major city faces a severe housing crisis. Many people cannot afford decent housing, even if they have a full-time job, and instead crowd into unsafe and unsanitary apartments. Recognizing the situation is both a moral crisis and a threat to their business interests and social stability, a group of wealthy businessmen and bankers come together to help solve it. Instead of relying solely on charity, they set up a new housing company with a twist: investors in the company will have their financial return capped at 4% annually. This allows the housing company to offer decent homes to working-class families with amenities typically only available to rich households at a rental price that the working-class families can afford.

The initial investment is quickly raised after a public meeting of investors that a local newspaper describes as "willing and even anxious to contribute their capital towards a scheme, which while yielding a moderate and safe return, will largely tend, not only to improve the dwellings of the poor, but also reduce the high rates now paid for the minimum of accommodation."[1] Two years later, the first residents move in. Within a decade, the company houses 4,000 people with evidence they are living healthier, longer lives.

That might sound like a modern impact investing initiative. But it's actually the 140-year-old story of the creation of the Four Per Cent Industrial Dwellings Company in London, led by banker and philanthropist Nathaniel Rothschild. And its legacy lives on as the Industrial Dwellings Company (renamed in 1952) owns and operates ~1,500 buildings across the London region.

The United States is in the midst of our own housing crisis. Rents are increasingly unaffordable and homeownership out of reach for too many people. It is hard to see a way forward to solving so many other national challenges without finding ways to make more housing more affordable and more accessible to new owners. The inflation crisis? The affordability crisis that is partly driving populist politics from the right and left? The crisis of isolation? Historically delayed family formation? All at their root cannot be solved without addressing the housing crisis.

Broken capital markets are not the only cause of this crisis, just as investment alone will not solve it. But investment has to be part of the solution because almost no one in America can pay for a home or real estate development project upfront in cash. Fortunately, as they were in London in the 1880s, savvy and committed investors are collaborating with communities and government to expand financial access to solve this challenge now.

The Housing Affordability Crisis

The housing crisis has two faces. For renters, rental costs have surged faster than wages in recent years. Nearly half of all US renters, more than 22 million households, spent more than 30% of their income on rent in 2022, a threshold commonly used to define housing unaffordability.[2] More than 12 million renter households were *severely* cost-burdened, devoting more than half of their income to housing.[3] There is no state, metropolitan area, or county where a full-time minimum wage worker can afford to rent a modest two-bedroom apartment at fair market rent without being financially burdened. With rent taking up so much of a family's income, renters earning less than $30,000 annually had a median of $250 left after housing costs each month.[4] Unaffordable rent also undermines other family prospects. One in five US college students are parents; when they are evicted their likelihood of completing college falls precipitously.[5] Homelessness has also reached record levels; more than 778,000 people were unhoused on a single night in January 2024.[6]

Homeowners and those who aspire to home ownership face similar strains. Almost two-thirds of American families own their own homes, a figure that has stayed relatively stable in recent decades. But servicing a mortgage is an increasing cost burden for many. With prices and interest rates up, the median monthly mortgage payment doubled from 2019 to 2024.[7] The median home now costs five times the median income (up from 3.2× in the 1990s)[8] while mortgage rates, taxes, and insurance costs have gone up for most families.

Average rates of home ownership also mask the inaccessibility of home ownership for many people. For decades, home ownership rates for African American families have lagged national averages. The gap between Black and White home ownership rates is now higher than it was in 1960,[9] with only 40% of Black families owning their own home, while Hispanic ownership rates are only slightly higher. Young people are also increasingly trapped out of home ownership by high rents that prevent them saving to cover high down payments. For the first time, the median age of first-time home buyers reached 40 in 2025 (after steadily increasing from 28 in 1991).[10]

At the root of both problems lies a persistent shortage of housing supply. Widely cited research estimates a shortfall of nearly 3.9–4.9 million homes nationwide.[11] Since the 2008 financial crisis, homebuilding for affordable rentals and entry-level homes has been particularly sparse while costs have soared in many previously affordable neighborhoods. Adjusted for inflation, units renting for < $1,000/month fell by more than 30% from 24.8 million (2013) to 17.2 million (2023).[12]

What's to Be Done?

To address the housing crisis will require policy reform and local efforts that make it easier to build new housing. That housing will have to be financed. At $50 trillion, the US residential housing market is the biggest asset class in the world. The government-backed 30-year, fixed-rate mortgage, with 20% down payment is an almost 100-year-old financial innovation that has served millions of people.[i] And developers putting up high-end rental homes can still secure affordable financing in most markets.

But what about the people and places overlooked and underserved by these products?

To help solve the housing crisis requires answering three core questions:

1. How can we finance affordable home purchases for families for whom the standard mortgage does not work?
2. How do we ensure that developers building or preserving affordable housing have access to financing so they can compete with developers seeking to increase the cost of home purchases or rents?
3. How can investors partner with government to make limited housing subsidies support more families?

---

[i] Prior to the creation of the Federal Housing Administration in 1934, Americans either bought their homes upfront or financed them with 50% down payments and principal and interest due after five years. The 30-year fixed rate amortizing mortgage became possible when the federal government committed to buy mortgage balances from banks. It helped turn home ownership into a significant contributor to wealth creation and inter-generational wealth transfer and to the creation of the broad American middle class (though notoriously excluding African American borrowers who were ineligible to receive government-backed loans in most places).

Across the country, investors are showing answers that are possible, and the hope and opportunity that can bring, often in collaboration with government and private donors.

- In Detroit, first-time homebuyers now have access to affordable mortgages through a program that allows them to share the cost and benefits of their home equity.
- In Liberty, Missouri, and across the country, tens of thousands of residents of manufactured home communities are accessing the debt and expertise they need to buy the land where their homes sit.
- In Charlotte, hundreds of families are moving into apartments in a vibrant community born from an abandoned manufacturing facility, financed by local investors motivated by a new national tax incentive program.
- One of the first community finance development institutions has financed its 1 millionth affordable home building on the 50-year-old legacy of three churchgoers in Washington, D.C.
- In Colorado, impact investors are bringing private capital into housing projects that enable a voter-approved annual housing subsidy to support more families.
- In Jacksonville, formerly homeless veterans are moving into apartments bought and repurposed for their use by a fund built to compete successfully with private developers to acquire scarce properties.

The examples highlighted in the following pages are just a sample of the many ways investors are expanding opportunities for people to own and live in affordable homes.

Raising the Roof on the Mortgage Market: Partnering with Government to Expand Shared Appreciation Mortgages

In Detroit, as in many US cities, home ownership is increasingly out of reach, especially for young people and others without savings to make a down payment. Rising rents have made it difficult for families to save for a down payment on their first home while the monthly costs of paying a mortgage have risen rapidly, a result of rising house prices, interest rates, and insurance. But in December 2025, a schoolteacher and single mother was able to purchase her first home while reducing her monthly housing costs by 25%, grabbing onto the US home ownership ladder. She is among the first participants of a new housing initiative piloting an approach developed by the housing finance innovator Homium that could significantly extend the wealth-building engine of home ownership to more Americans.

The fulcrum of this partnership is a shared appreciation mortgage (SAM), a financing tool through which investors pay part of a home purchase cost in return for sharing in the profits the homeowner makes when they sell their home. The basic math behind a shared appreciation mortgage is simple: homebuyers purchasing a $300,000 home, for example, can take out a $180,000 first mortgage with little to no down payment (program sponsors may want borrowers to retain some skin in the game with a 3% down payment) when investors put up the remaining $120,000 in return for 40% of the home's equity. If the owner refinances or sells the house for $450,000 in 15 years, they will keep $270,000 (minus the balance of the first mortgage) and pay the SAM investors $180,000 for their 40% share of the home's value. In the first months of the Detroit program almost all the initial homeowners saw their monthly cost of housing go down compared to their previous rental bills while they own at least 60% of the equity of their homes.[13]

Shared appreciation mortgages are not new, but they remain barely used for the ~4 million annual US home purchases. They primarily exist in relatively small government-backed programs like California's Dream for All program that made ~2,000 shared appreciation loans in 2024–2025, with ~10 applicants for each homebuyer the state-run program was able to support.[14]

Why have mainstream investors not stepped up? Investors into start-up companies demand higher rates of return than the relatively slow and steady average increase in US home prices. To achieve the returns necessary for these investors, certain lenders offer shared equity loans with complex contracts that seek to avoid mortgage regulations and extract a high price from borrowers by demanding repayment of multiples of the share of the equity they put up often off a discounted initial home valuation. They also charge ongoing fees and pick markets where home prices are expected to rise rapidly. These have limited the application of SAMs, their reputation, and their ability to help more people build wealth through home ownership.

In contrast, Homium has built its product around the constraint that it will not charge interest, fees, or take more in a home sale than the percentage of home value borrowed at origination. Once it achieves scale, and has data to show that a portfolio of SAMs is a low-risk asset, it could raise large pools of low-cost capital from institutional investors such as pension funds and insurance companies, increasingly seeking stable, inflation-protected assets and eager to tap into the $50 trillion US residential real estate market.[15]

To build a bridge to that future, Homium is organizing capital stacks that include government subsidy, private donations, and impact investments. In Detroit, that stack has taken the form of the Tobias Harris Homeownership Initiative, launched in September 2025, and anchored with a grant from NBA star Tobias Harris and investment by the Michigan Housing Development Authority. The Initiative makes Homium SAMs available to working-class, first-time homebuyers in affordable and stable neighborhoods, increasing the likelihood homebuyers will generate wealth through homeownership.

For the philanthropist and housing agency, working with Homium offers a way to support many more families than they could by providing typical down payment assistance grants directly. Other pilots in the pipeline will bring a similar combination of private and public donations and investments with a network of impact investors and state and local Housing Finance Authorities. The shared appreciation mortgage has the particular political appeal of being a pathway to make home ownership more affordable without requiring home prices to fall, something that would be unappealing to the 60% of Americans who own their own home.

Homium's leadership reflects this two-part strategy. Former CEO and current Board member, Tommy Mercein, brings deep relationships and insights into what it will take to raise low-cost institutional capital; while current CEO Marcus Martin draws on a career in both institutional capital markets and community banking to put together the impact capital and partnerships for the proof-of-concept phase.

A pivotal backer of Homium is Utah-based Jim Sorenson, founder and chairman of the Sorenson Impact Group, who led Homium's $10 million Series A equity round and has been instrumental in helping Homium launch a second pilot program in Utah. A successful entrepreneur, Sorenson has long championed financial innovation that aligns profit with purpose, advancing a wide range of efforts to extend the power of private markets to support more people.[16]

In addition to providing equity financing and leadership through his seat on the Board, Sorenson has also helped Homium to build relationships with state and federal government officials necessary to advance innovation in the highly-regulated mortgage market, including a move to give shared appreciation mortgage similar tax treatment to municipal bonds if they meet standards for fairness to the homebuyer.[17]

With the 30-year fixed-rate, 20% down mortgage no longer affordable for too many families, Homium and Sorenson are showing how combining flexible impact investing capital, strategy grounded in capital markets insights, and government engagement can extend the opportunity for homeownership to more people.

Level Ground: How ROC USA Helps Residents in Manufactured Home Communities Compete with Wall Street to Turn Precarity into Power

Residents of Liberty Landing in Liberty, Missouri, have a rare sense of security since they banded together to buy the land their 185 manufactured homes sit on in 2021. As the residents' first cooperative Board President Holly Waugh explained: "We don't have to worry about the land being sold out from underneath of us anymore."[18]

Manufactured housing, often referred to as mobile homes, offers one of the most affordable paths to homeownership in America, particularly for low-income and rural households. Approximately 22 million Americans, roughly 7% of US households, live in manufactured homes, which constitute 15% of rural housing stock. Their residents have a median household income of $30,000.[19] These factory-built homes, constructed offsite and transported to their locations, often cost nearly half per square foot compared to site-built housing.[20]

Yet for most residents, the affordability of manufactured housing comes with a catch: they own their home, but not the land beneath it. That land is typically part of a "land-lease" community, commonly known as a mobile home park, where residents pay monthly lot rent. Relocating a manufactured home can cost thousands of dollars, so many residents find themselves effectively trapped when rent spikes.

Increasingly, private equity firms and out-of-state investors have been buying up this land, raising rents and fees, and in some cases redeveloping the land altogether.[21] Nationally, institutional buyers accounted for roughly 23% of manufactured-housing community purchases in 2020–21 (up from 13% in 2017–19). In Michigan, for example, private equity investors now own more than one in four communities.[22] These investors often maximize financial returns through rapid rent hikes, pass-through fees, and deferred maintenance.[23]

ROC USA was created to provide residents with a different path. Founder Paul Bradley began organizing residents in manufactured home communities in New Hampshire in the late 1980s. He launched ROC USA, "Resident Owned Communities," out of the New Hampshire Community Loan Fund CDFI in 2008 to help residents buy the land as a cooperative, finance the acquisition, then support them to govern and maintain the community. Bradley sought to replace precarity with agency, with a vision that homeowners should not have to live at the mercy of landlords or distant investors.[24]

Through this model, residents form a nonprofit cooperative that owns the land and operates the business. Each household buys a membership share, gets one vote per home, and elects a board of directors. Families continue to own their homes individually, but now also own an equal share of the land under the entire neighborhood through the co-op. Monthly site fee profits (after debt service and reserves) are reinvested in the community, and technical assistance providers in the ROC USA Network coach boards on budgeting, maintenance, reserves, and capital planning. Resident-owned co-ops typically raise lot fees far more slowly than commercial owners (around 0.9% annually vs. the roughly 4–6% industry norms), helping preserve long-term affordability while improving infrastructure.[25]

For this model to work, residents need a lender who will finance their collective purchase of the land. ROC USA launched a dedicated CDFI to provide acquisition and improvement loans to the co-ops, complemented by bank lenders and impact investors. Recent pools include a $47 million National Acquisition Loan Pool backed by foundations, banks, and impact funds (for example, Robert Wood Johnson Foundation, JPMorgan Chase, Charles Schwab Bank, Ceniarth, ImpactAssets, Mercy Community Capital, and Enterprise Community Loan Fund). These funds let resident groups compete on timing and certainty.[26] With this approach, ROC USA has supported 356 resident-owned communities to preserve 24,342 homesites across the country. No resident-owned community has ever reverted to commercial ownership.[27]

This approach works best for stable and well-kept-up communities where residents have time to organize to buy with ROC USA's support. More sellers now bring multi-park portfolios or properties with heavy capital expenditure needs to market on tight timelines; deals that residents do not have the capital or time to compete for. To address this challenge, Bradley has explored new financing vehicles that can act as a bridge owner, acquiring and stabilizing hard-to-place communities, addressing deferred infrastructure, and preparing a path for a future co-op purchase, essentially "buying time" for residents to line up for community ownership.[28]

Because that bridge role is different from financing a resident co-op's immediate acquisition, it requires different capital: patient equity and flexible acquisition debt that can hold risk for several years while improvements are made and governance capacity is built. In 2025, the CDFI Community Vision financed a $3.4 million loan to acquire and revitalize an 84-site community in Tuolumne County, California, preserving 54 homes with plans to grow to 92 and positioning the property for eventual resident takeover.[29] Raising this type of equity financing is difficult and substantial work and new partnerships remain necessary to bring it to scale.

Beyond capital, ROC USA has joined national policy advocacy efforts to pass state laws that require owners to give current tenants the right of refusal to buy the community land when it goes up for sale. Together with new sources of capital, this policy change could help ensure many more people throughout the United States enjoy the relative security of the cooperative owners of Liberty Landing in Missouri.

From Model Ts to Mixed-Use Dreams: How Policy-Incented, Patient Capital Helped Revive Charlotte's Camp North End

On a crisp Fall Saturday in Charlotte's North End neighborhood, a 76-acre real estate development hums with life. Children dart between a mini-pitch soccer field and a popsicle stand. Couples browse artisan stalls housed in repurposed military warehouses. And residents are moving into apartments with a range of sizes and price options. It's hard to imagine that just a few years ago, this was a shuttered industrial site, after a storied life as a Ford Model T factory in the 1920s, a WWII military depot, a missile plant, and a pharmaceutical distribution center, before falling silent in 2016.[30]

The rebirth of Camp North End began in 2016 when developer ATCO purchased the property with a vision to create a "live-work-play" district.[31] But transforming 76 acres of rusting industrial infrastructure into a thriving neighborhood would take more than good design. It needed patient investment capital willing to back a project that would unfold over a decade. That's where Ross Baird and his firm, Blueprint Local, came in. In 2022, Blueprint invested in Kinship, the first multifamily housing at Camp North End: 301 units integrated into the mixed-use community.

Ross Baird launched Blueprint in 2018 after a career focused on closing capital access gaps. As co-founder of Village Capital, he helped rethink early-stage investing by putting funding decisions in the hands of entrepreneurs themselves. Baird led Village Capital to invest in more than 100 start-ups in dozens of communities worldwide. Reflecting on that work, he explained, "I saw how a single transformational investment could reshape the story a community tells about itself, and I wanted to bring that same spark to how communities reimagine their future."[32]

Blueprint's mission is simple: make real estate investments that build wealth for investors while helping communities thrive. Central to Blueprint's capital raising strategy is the federal Opportunity Zone (OZ) program, created in 2017 to channel investment into low-income neighborhoods by offering investors capital gains tax breaks in exchange for long-term investments. The policy was a rare bipartisan initiative, championed by Senators Tim Scott, a Republican from South Carolina, and Cory Booker, a Democrat from New Jersey.[33]

Blueprint has raised more than $250 million to invest in Opportunity Zones, supporting more than 6,000 housing units in cities like Charlotte, Austin, and Dallas. These projects deliberately target the "missing middle": developments too large for local investors to finance but too small to interest giant institutional players. And they seek to create neighborhoods where "the whole is greater than the sum of its parts," according to Baird, places where residents can live, work, and connect in ways that strengthen the local economy and culture. For example, Baird collaborated closely with Blueprint's advisory board chair, NBA legend and seasoned real estate investor David Robinson, on a redevelopment in downtown San Antonio with similar ambitions to Camp North End.

Blueprint's investors include a mix of family offices, community banks, mission-driven foundations, and local high-net-worth individuals. Nearly half of Blueprint's investors are based in the regions where the firm invests. Most were initially interested in the tax breaks rather than social impact, but have become motivated to harness their capital for community development, especially those investing in their local communities.[34] This motivation is crucial for projects in historically overlooked neighborhoods where progress and profits can take a decade or more to unfold.

The Opportunity Zone program has grown into a major source of financing for real estate development in many low-income neighborhoods. Since 2018, more than $100 billion in private capital has flowed into Qualified Opportunity Zone investments.[35] According to an analysis by Economic Innovation Group, the thinktank that championed the initial bill, those investments have helped generate more than 313,000 new homes, roughly doubling the rate of housing supply growth compared with similar neighborhoods outside OZ boundaries. OZ capital has become a critical supplement to strained public funding for housing and economic development in cities such as Charlotte, Birmingham, and Cleveland.[36]

Critics warn that OZs can become tax shelters for projects that would have happened anyway, offering windfalls to wealthy investors without meaningful local benefit, displacing local residents, and ignoring the places most overlooked by mainstream investors.[37]

Aware of this challenge, Blueprint seeks to steer capital into projects that drive positive community outcomes. Blueprint and its partners adopt a 10-year hold period, focusing on raising the value of real estate throughout the areas where it invests. As in Camp North End, Blueprint has steered its capital into projects that have not displaced existing residents.

With the Opportunity Zone program made permanent in 2025, developers can plan multi-phase, decade-long transformations like Camp North End without fear that their tax benefits will expire mid-project. For Baird, this stability offers the chance to make "patient capital permanent," creating a capital market where investors can afford to think like builders rather than speculators.

Today, Camp North End has become a vibrant destination, hosting art festivals, small-business pop-ups, and community events. Kinship residents inhabit not just new apartments but a revived piece of industrial history, proof that when vision meets patient capital, the ghosts of America's manufacturing past can anchor more inclusive, modern prosperity.

The Architecture of Inclusion: Building America's Affordable Housing Market Through Public-Private Finance

Jubilee Housing began in 1973 when three women from Washington, D.C.'s Church of the Saviour, Terry Flood, Barbara Moore, and Carolyn Banker, made a non-refundable deposit to purchase 90 apartments in two buildings in the Adams Morgan neighborhood despite their lack of real estate development experience or financing commitments to complete the purchase.[38,39] Impressed by their audacity and resolve, legendary real estate developer Jim Rouse and his wife Patty helped secure $625,000 to complete the purchase and $125,000 for repairs.[40] By 1978, Jubilee Housing had expanded to 5 buildings totaling 165 units. Between 1973 and 1976, Jubilee residents and volunteers logged roughly 50,000 hours tackling code violations.

Inspired by the Jubilee example, in 1982 the Rouses founded Enterprise, a nonprofit real estate organization built to help other groups like Jubilee Housing access private investment, design expertise, and development capacity. Toward its vision that every American should be able to live in a decent, affordable home, Enterprise has since mobilized more than $80 billion of financing to build or preserve 1 million homes. And it is not alone. A broader industry of Community Development Finance Institutions has built up around the opportunity to channel capital into underserved and overlooked people and places, financing affordable housing, small businesses, and community facilities. More than 1,400 CDFIs, including the Enterprise Community Loan Fund, now hold more than $400 billion in assets.[41]

Funded with an initial $1 million investment from the Rouses, and a grant from the Ford Foundation, followed by additional loans from Ford and MacArthur Foundations, Enterprise's trajectory exemplifies how affordable housing in the United States has coupled private action with government support. CDFIs have been an important conduit for financing affordable housing for decades, serving as a nexus of government policy, donors, and investors, spurred by three landmark laws.

- The Community Reinvestment Act (CRA) (1977) required federally insured depository institutions to help meet the credit needs of all segments of their communities, aiming to tackle the historic redlining that had withheld finance from primarily Black neighborhoods in cities.[42] Rather than make loans directly, over time many banks met this requirement primarily by investing in CDFIs that originated qualifying loans.[43]
- The Low Income Housing Tax Credit (1986) provided developers who build or rehabilitate rental housing and restrict a portion of units for low-income residents with the ability to sell tax credits to help pay for those projects.
- The CDFI Fund (created in 1994) regulates, provides subsidies to, and organizes financing for CDFIs with a history of strong bipartisan support in Congress.

These programs enabled private organizations, typically nonprofits, to build the financial base to access additional financing for affordable housing. HUD data shows LIHTC credits have been mobilized in more than 50,000 projects with 3.7 million homes now bringing $18-20 billion of investment annually.[44] CDFIs have played a crucial role in implementing the program. First, they have served as syndicators or intermediaries, pooling LIHTC equity and allocating it to mission-aligned housing developers in geographically underserved markets. In addition, they have provided gap financing (pre-development loans, bridge loans, subordinate debt) in LIHTC deals in neighborhoods that conventional banks avoided.[45] CDFIs have also continued to be a major tool for banks to meet their Community Reinvestment Act obligations.

Enterprise and other CDFIs have also innovated ways to bring new investors into this work. Enterprise created an SEC-regulated note offering in 2010 that has mobilized $100 million from retail investors.[46] Beyond innovations in how they finance, Enterprise and other CDFIs are also innovating what they finance. In 2004, Enterprise created the first standard for environmentally sound building of affordable housing and is now financing energy efficient retrofits and renewable energy production on affordable homes across the country.[47]

CDFIs have also begun to finance home ownership, recognizing the limits of the LIHTC regime that has focused efforts on affordable rent rather than wealth-creating ownership. In the early 2000s, Self-Help Credit Union made mortgages throughout the Southeast, managing the risk of lower down payment with borrower training and support.[ii] More recently, Enterprise's Renter Wealth Creation Fund supports renters in building equity without owning a home outright. Launched in 2022, the Fund rewards renters who pay on time with monthly cash back payments and, over time, allows them to participate in shared appreciation when the property is refinanced or sold. Other CDFIs finance land trusts, land banks, and community ownership schemes.

The history of CDFIs underscores how impact investors and large banks working with savvy intermediaries in a supportive regulatory environment can direct capital to communities that need it to turn their effort and vision into better neighborhoods and prospects for the families that live and work in them. Yet the lingering housing affordability crisis underscores the need to reinvigorate this work with new ideas and capital.

Making Affordable Investable: How a Colorado Foundation Uses Policy Advocacy and Impact Capital to Reshape Housing Finance

In Denver's Capitol Hill neighborhood, Tamika Cox, a psychology student at Metropolitan State University, stepped into her new bedroom in The People's Mansion, a 19-room, century-old house now reborn as a permanently affordable co-op. She pays less than $600 a month for her room, joining a community of artists, workers, and students committed to shared living and long-term affordability.[48] The project was financed through the Colorado Housing Accelerator Initiative (CHAI), a mission-driven fund

---

[ii]Shut down after the government housing agencies withdrew funding during the 2008 housing finance crisis, Self-Help's program became one of the efforts to extend home ownership blamed by some for causing the Great Financial Crisis by loading banks with imprudent mortgages. Subsequent analysis shows defaults rates in the program were not higher than those on loans made to borrowers with higher credit scores and 20% down payments.

that blends grants, impact investments, and government subsidy to help nonprofits and residents buy and keep properties affordable before market pressures push them out.

For Cox, it's a rare foothold in a city where rents have risen faster than wages for years. In addition to the benefits of affordable rent, CHAI provides Cox and other residents with support to build their wealth. They receive 2% of their timely rent payments back each month and share in CHAI's annual profits through their Tenant Equity Vehicle Program.[49]

The People's Mansion is a glimpse of the kind of systemic change that Gary Community Ventures (GCV) works to catalyze statewide. The Denver-based foundation is attacking Colorado's housing affordability crisis from multiple angles, combining grants, investments, and policy advocacy.

GCV's roots lie in its founder Sam Gary, a self-made oil "wildcatter" who built the Gary-Williams Company and later turned his entrepreneurial energy toward civic innovation. Gary believed that business discipline, philanthropy, and public policy should work together to expand opportunity. That philosophy animates GCV today, which describes its mission as "solving Colorado's biggest problems at the intersection of business, impact investing, and policy."[50,51] In its Denver headquarters, one conference room is named "The 33rd," reminding staff that Gary did not give up when his first 32 attempts to find oil failed.[52] And its intentional "impermanence," a plan to cease operations after 2035, focuses the team on urgent action.

GCV takes an "opportunity first; tool second" approach integrating grant making, impact investing, policy advocacy, and a venture team tasked with standing up rapid prototype solutions. It focuses on using impact investment to demonstrate new possibilities, recognizing that scaling solutions will often necessitate creating new incentives to harness mainstream investors.

For Gary, helping to address the housing affordability crisis was essential to realize GCV's vision for Colorado. As in many parts of our country, Colorado home prices have more than doubled since 2010, and roughly half of renter households spend more than 30% of their income on housing.[53] In the Denver metro area, the median home price hovers above $600,000 even after recent softening.[54]

GCV informed its housing work by talking with housing developers and financiers about where market gaps were most intractable. The Low Income Housing Tax Credit provided support to developers putting up deeply affordable housing (for residents earning less than 60% of the median family income). And financing was available for developers riding the housing boom to build apartments for upper-income residents. But financing was sparse for housing serving residents whose incomes were too high to qualify for LIHTC units and too low to pay for high-end apartments.

What would it take to enable developers serving this missing market to access financing they could afford? To answer this question, GCV applied its multi-tool approach, integrating policy, philanthropy, and investment to address the shortage of production financing, the lack of resident ownership pathways, and the difficulty of accessing the subsidized capital essential for developers to build affordable housing.

This approach has been evident in its work with CHAI. GCV provided a small grant to CHAI and made an investment in their fund in 2021. GCV's policy team then advocated for the passage of Proposition 123, a statewide ballot initiative in 2022 that dedicates one-tenth of 1% of state income-tax revenue, about $300 million annually, to a new State Affordable Housing Fund, providing a long-term source of subsidized debt and equity that GCV knew would be essential to create incentives for developers to build housing for the missing middle. The fund supports the production and preservation of affordable rental and for-sale homes, land banking, and down-payment assistance for first-time buyers.[55]

Even a $300 million annual government appropriation will not build enough housing unless it can attract private investment. (At $300,000/unit this total would only pay directly for 1,000 units, less than 1% of the 104,000 units the state estimates need to be built.[56]) So CHAI pools flexible, impact-first dollars from foundations, CDFIs, and individuals to multiply the power of the state subsidy.

In addition to affordable rent, GCV has used grants and investments to seed a range of experiments in "wealth-through-ownership" models that allow residents to build equity and stability instead of watching value flow to absentee landlords.

The People's Mansion's century-old walls now shelter a new generation of Coloradans who can afford to stay, study, and build futures in the heart of their city. Behind these new possibilities is a statewide infrastructure of policy, capital, and collaboration that Gary Community Ventures helped make possible, an example of the tangible difference investors can make in people's lives when aligned with advocacy, community power, and a clear-eyed understanding of what barriers limit investment flows and how to remove them.

Fast Enough to Win: How Mission-Driven Capital Is Helping End Homelessness

In Jacksonville, Florida, and cities across the country, more people are moving out of homelessness each month than entering it. As part of the national Built for Zero movement, Jacksonville's ambitions are greater: to end homelessness for all veterans on the way to ending chronic homelessness completely.

What will it take to achieve this goal? Rosanne Haggerty has been pioneering answers to this question for decades. In the 1990s, Haggerty founded an organization that transformed abandoned buildings in New York City into supportive housing for chronically homeless individuals. The model worked, but she came to see its limits: fixing homelessness building-by-building wouldn't solve the problem at the population level.

In 2011, she launched Community Solutions, shifting the focus to systemic change.[57] The organization's flagship effort, Built for Zero, now involves more than 150 US communities working to make homelessness rare and brief through real-time data, shared accountability, and cross-sector coordination. Built for Zero communities have achieved measurable success, ending veteran homelessness in more than 14 cities and chronic homelessness in several others. In Jacksonville, for example, the number of people experiencing chronic homelessness dropped 35% since they joined Built for Zero in 2015.

But the work kept hitting a bottleneck: even with strong systems in place, many communities simply didn't have enough available housing for people exiting homelessness. By 2023, more than 650,000 people were homeless nationwide.[58] In overheated real estate markets, buyers intending to create affordable homes were routinely outbid by private equity firms or developers with more lucrative plans and the ready cash to buy up a property quickly. Government programs to create housing for homeless people often took years before they could house anyone in the face of community resistance and bureaucratic inertia.

To capitalize a more responsive, private sector solution, Haggerty and her team launched the CS Large Cities Housing Fund in 2022, anchored with their own $10 million investment, sourced from part of a major MacArthur Foundation grant.[59] To run the fund, they spun off a fund management company, BDP Impact Real Estate, led by Dave Foster, a US military veteran whose career spans more than 15 years of social-impact real estate development in for-profit and nonprofit organizations in the United States and abroad.

Large Cities Housing Fund focuses on "naturally occurring affordable housing" (NOAH)—apartment complexes that rent below market rates without subsidies—along with hotels and motels whose values declined during the pandemic. These properties can be purchased and converted far faster than new construction, which often takes years. Moving at the speed of the real estate market, the Fund can close on properties in the standard 60–90 days and start to house individuals exiting homelessness immediately thereafter. Each property is mixed income. Half the units are reserved for people exiting homelessness and half remain affordable for a typical middle-income renter. After acquisition, the Fund brings in third-party property management companies and onsite Resident Service Coordinators who together ensure the properties are managed with tenant stability and retention in mind.

By mid-2024, the fund had raised $135 million from a coalition of impact-minded backers, including Kaiser Permanente, UnitedHealth Group, Woodforest National Bank, Wells Fargo, the Ford Foundation, and the Leon Levine Foundation. While financial returns to investors are slightly below conventional market rates, investors are drawn to a range of measurable social impacts. The healthcare providers and insurers understand the health system savings that come when people have stable housing; banks received credit from their regulators for making this type of community commitment and community goodwill; and the private foundations recognize this as a high-impact investment opportunity. In its first two years, the fund acquired 1,100 units across Baltimore, Charlotte, Denver, Jacksonville, Nashville, and Phoenix, housing more than 340 people exiting homelessness.

The Fund plans to acquire 2,500 units, not enough to solve the housing shortage for people exiting homelessness, but large enough to demonstrate to other developers and investors the viability of this approach. In Jacksonville, for example, in early 2023, the Fund had acquired 175 units, leveraging a $10 million investment from Northern Trust. Through the coordination work of Built for Zero, the city knew 186 people on the real-time list of homeless veterans, 92 of whom had housing vouchers or subsidies but no place to spend them. By pairing those homes with the city's coordinated response system, people who had spent months, or years, on the streets could now move indoors within weeks.[60]

Homelessness isn't inevitable, but ending it requires strong systems, the right housing stock, and ready finance that moves at market speed. Haggerty and Foster have already launched a second fund, expanding the model to more cities and scaling a strategy that is proving effective. Their work shows what is possible when government, nonprofit leaders, and people experiencing homelessness can access capital that is fast, patient, coordinated, and aiming toward an inspiring vision.

The housing affordability crisis has been a major threat to the financial security of many American families for years. But now a secondary affordability crisis has landed in many American communities as rising energy prices are creating unsustainable bills for the electricity, oil, and gas Americans need to power our homes and stay comfortable in them. Solving this crisis will require rapid increases in electricity production and rapid adoption of cost-saving energy efficiency solutions. As with housing ownership and development, both are going to require new investors. And unlike housing, these investors are going to have to finance new technologies, helping small start-ups and massive utility companies get across the "valley of death" that too often stops good ideas reaching the scale where they can make a real contribution to solving our national challenges. The next chapter explores this challenge and the people who are solving it, adapting the lessons from decades of housing finance to build partnerships between investors, government, donors, and communities to create a future of reliable, affordable, American-made energy to power the next generation of American success.

4

Energy Services Should Be Affordable, Reliable, and Increasingly Made in America

Most Americans of all political views agree that when we flip a switch in our home the lights should turn on without creating financial stress for our families. Reliable and affordable energy is a prerequisite for economic security, public health, and national competitiveness. And yet for a growing share of Americans, energy is becoming less reliable, less affordable, and more precarious each year.

Household energy costs have climbed sharply in recent years. Nationally, average residential electricity prices have increased faster than inflation, and utilities continue to raise rates as grid investments, extreme weather, and rising demand push costs upward.[1] Those price increases land hardest on families already stretched by housing, healthcare, and food costs. For many, energy is no longer a predictable monthly expense but a volatile bill that can spike without warning.

Approximately 1 in 4 US households, 30 million families, are defined as energy burdened, paying more than 6% of their income for energy services. More than half of low-income households pay more than 8% of their income for energy, often forcing painful tradeoffs between keeping the lights on and paying for groceries, medicine, or rent.[2]

Affordability is only one facet of the problem. According to national survey data, more than one-quarter of US households reported experiencing a power outage in a given year and many of those outages lasted for hours due to severe weather, equipment failures, or grid overload.[3] Extreme heatwaves push grids past their limits. Wildfires, hurricanes, floods, and winter storms knock out transmission and distribution systems that were built decades ago for a more stable climate.

Absent major changes, these pressures are likely to intensify. Electricity demand is rising for the first time in a generation, driven by electrification of vehicles and buildings, reshoring of manufacturing, and the explosive growth of data centers and artificial intelligence that require vast amounts of always-on power. US data centers consumed roughly 4% of the nation's electricity in 2024 and are projected to grow to between 6.7 and 12% by 2028.[4] This new demand, on top of conventional load growth and climate-exacerbated seasonal peaks, is straining infrastructure that was not built for decades of rapid change.

How did we get here? For decades, the US energy system was optimized for centralized generation, predictable load growth, and long asset lifetimes. That model delivered affordability for a time, but it also discouraged experimentation and left little room for resilience, flexibility, or rapid innovation. Capital flowed primarily to large, regulated utilities and incumbent energy producers, entities well-suited to incremental upgrades but poorly positioned to pioneer new technologies or business models.

To be clear, those incumbents remain essential. Utilities and large energy companies will need to invest hundreds of billions of dollars in grid upgrades, generation capacity, and transmission. They will finance much of that work through traditional means: bank loans, project finance, and bond markets. These capital markets are deep and effective for projects with proven technologies, stable cash flows, and clear and supportive regulatory frameworks.

But ensuring that all Americans have access to reliable and affordable energy services will require more than scaling what already exists. It will require new companies and new technologies, from advanced nuclear and geothermal power to grid-enhancing hardware and software, to energy-efficient solutions that lower bills. These innovations are essential to delivering cleaner, cheaper, and more resilient energy. And they are precisely where mainstream finance struggles.

The problem is not a lack of ideas. It is a lack of capital willing to move early. High potential energy innovations often face first-of-a-kind (FOAK) risk: the uncertainty that comes with being the first commercial deployment of a new technology. Even when the underlying science is sound, early projects tend to cost more, take longer, and face regulatory or market hurdles that investors struggle to assess. Even technologies that reach a pilot phase often fall into the well-documented "valley of death," the long, underfunded stretch between early validation and bankable scale, when grants have run out and commercial investors are not yet ready to step in.

As a result, too little capital flows to the innovations that could lower costs, improve reliability, and strengthen American energy independence. Promising technologies stall because the financing structures needed to carry them to scale never materialize.

There is, however, reason for optimism. A growing group of investors is organizing around this challenge, aiming to take the kinds of smart, early risks that mainstream finance cannot or will not. One signal of this shift is the emergence of investor networks such as the nonprofit CREO Syndicate, co-founded by long-time climate investor Jason Scott, which brings together families, foundations, and individuals to share diligence, coordinate learning, and co-invest selectively in climate and energy solutions.

This chapter tells the stories of a wide range of investors who are investing to make American energy more abundant, cleaner, reliable, and affordable. They are answering three core questions to bring investment capital at the scale and urgency needed to drive energy production and access in the United States:

- How can investors capitalize projects that have a strong potential to be profitable but with a longer time horizon than mainstream markets are willing to wait?
- How can investors work alongside philanthropists and government to create the conditions where investors can support energy projects with substantial social benefit?
- How can investors responsibly finance first-of-a-kind projects despite their risk and the unglamorous "soft costs" for large infrastructure projects that leave many investors wary?

Together, these investors are reshaping how energy innovation gets funded and who benefits when it succeeds. Our ability to deliver abundant, clean, domestically produced, reliable energy will happen because investors like these figured out how to manage risk in service of resilience, affordability, and a more secure energy future for all Americans.

Put a Rig on It: Financing to Kickstart Next-Generation Geothermal Power

Just outside Milford, Utah, the scene could be mistaken for an oilfield: a tall drilling rig, heavy trucks, and crews in hard hats moving with the practiced rhythm of people who have spent years in shale country. Fervo Energy's Cape Station looks familiar on purpose. It uses horizontal drilling and hydraulic stimulation to engineer pathways in hot rock so water can circulate, pick up heat, and return to the surface as round-the-clock geothermal power. Many of the jobs at Cape Station are filled by oil and gas workers applying their expertise to a new energy system.

Cape Station is slated to begin delivering roughly 100 megawatts of electricity in 2026 and scale to approximately 500 megawatts by 2028.[5] At full buildout, that always-on power would generate enough electricity to supply approximately 400,000 average US homes and serve as a proof point for replication across the country wherever geologic conditions are favorable.[6]

Fervo's success would not have been possible without investors willing to take the risk on a new company with a new approach to establishing next-generation geothermal as a reliable, scaled energy source. Fervo Energy's earliest backers included impact-focused investors willing to underwrite technical and execution risk long before geothermal was commercially proven at scale. Those early investors included Elemental Excelerator, which supported Fervo through its initial technology development and pilots, as well as Breakthrough Energy Ventures, the climate investment fund founded by Bill Gates to back capital-intensive technologies with long time horizons. Together, these investors helped Fervo apply advanced oil-and-gas drilling techniques to geothermal, move beyond the lab, and demonstrate that enhanced geothermal systems could work in real operating conditions.

New York-based Capricorn Investment Group entered at the pivotal moment when Fervo needed to bridge from early validation to commercial viability. In April 2021, Capricorn led Fervo's $28 million Series B, marking its first investment and providing growth capital to scale drilling operations and advance toward utility-scale projects.[7] Capricorn then deepened its role in December 2024, when its Technology Impact Fund II led the corporate equity portion of a $255 million financing to support development of Fervo's Cape Station project in Utah.[8] By the time Fervo raised its $462 million Series E in 2025,[9] the company had crossed a key threshold: traditional infrastructure investors and project-finance capital were ready to step in.

Capricorn is built for this task. The impact-investment firm was founded to manage the wealth of Jeff Skoll, the first president of eBay, and the endowment of the Skoll Foundation.

"We've always believed that investment capital can be catalytic," said Ion Yadigaroglu, Managing Partner at Capricorn. "Fervo shows what's possible when you back transformative technology with patient, values-aligned capital."[10]

Fervo is a textbook example of the energy-innovation challenge: promising technologies often fall into the so-called "valley of death," the perilous funding gap between R&D and commercially scaled deployment, especially for capital-intensive clean energy infrastructure. By the Series E, Capricorn participated in the round but did not lead it, illustrating how Capricorn and other impact-oriented investors help companies traverse the "valley of death," leading when risk is highest and stepping back once commercial viability is in sight.

"Capricorn believed in us before geothermal was cool," said Tim Latimer, CEO of Fervo and a former drilling engineer turned climate entrepreneur. "They understood not just the climate case but the business case. Geothermal has the potential to provide baseload power that complements wind and solar, and investors like Capricorn are making that future possible."[11]

Capricorn's approach to impact investing is both mission-driven and pragmatic. It manages billions in assets, including the endowment of the Skoll Foundation, other foundations, and the assets of families and institutions. It also serves as an Outsourced Chief Investment Officer, guiding the investment strategies of those seeking impact alongside returns. Through its Sustainable Investors Fund and the Technology Impact Fund, Capricorn targets scalable climate solutions and transformative technologies. The Sustainable Investors Fund focuses on established market opportunities such as wind and solar energy technologies and resource efficiency while the Technology Impact Fund backs earlier-stage, high-potential breakthroughs. This dual-fund approach allows Capricorn to address different parts of the capital continuum, deploying the right kind of capital at the right stage.[12]

At the heart of Capricorn's strategy is Ion Yadigaroglu, Managing Partner since 2004. A physicist by training, Yadigaroglu was Jeff Skoll's roommate at Stanford when he was pursuing graduate studies in physics while Skoll was launching eBay. In the early 2000s, Skoll approached Yadigaroglu with a bold idea: invest his post-eBay wealth not just philanthropically, but as a vehicle for change. Together, they founded Capricorn with the goal of "beating Wall Street at its own game" by driving both financial returns and meaningful global impact.[13]

Capricorn's model combining long-term investment with technical insight is rare in venture capital, where investors often chase quick returns in software and AI. The firm doesn't just write checks; it persists through the commercialization journey. In addition to Fervo, Capricorn investments include Electric Hydrogen, which is developing clean hydrogen via electrolysis, and Twelve, a company transforming CO_2 into useful chemicals and fuels. These are foundational bets on building the industrial backbone of a carbon-free energy future.

While the Skoll Foundation provides grants to nonprofits focused on energy access and climate resilience, Capricorn pursues market-driven solutions. Together, they form a holistic strategy deploying grants, investments, and advocacy to advance their mission. With the US energy system strained by climate shocks and aging infrastructure, Capricorn's investments not only push clean energy forward but also enhance grid reliability and resilience.

By bridging the valley of death for companies like Fervo, Capricorn helps provide the finance necessary to turn ideas into infrastructure. And in doing so, they prove that investing in America's energy future can be good for the planet, good for people, and generate good financial returns.

Reaching Critical Mass: Financing Risk to Revive Nuclear Power

In a rugged stretch of the Idaho desert, a new nuclear power plant is taking shape on land provided by Idaho National Laboratory, one of the country's most storied centers of nuclear research. Built by nuclear start-up Aalo Energy, the facility is a demonstration of a small modular reactor designed to ship to data centers and other power-hungry locations, arriving with its nuclear core and safety systems sealed, requiring far fewer people on site to install, commission, and operate.

If it works as intended, Aalo's Idaho project will demonstrate how zero-carbon, American-made nuclear energy can be deployed faster, more flexibly, and with lower operating costs than traditional nuclear plants. The ambition is not just cleaner power, but a deployment model that treats nuclear power less like a bespoke megaproject and more like industrial equipment.

But milestones like this do not happen on engineering ingenuity alone. They require capital willing to take risks that traditional markets have long avoided.

Reviving nuclear power as a meaningful part of America's energy system requires overcoming two very different kinds of investment risk. For advanced and small modular reactors like Aalo's, the central challenge is FOAK risk. While the physics of nuclear fission is well understood, new reactor designs must still prove that they can be manufactured, licensed, deployed, and operated at commercial scale. FOAK projects often struggle to secure financing because they can cost more and take longer than expected when supply chains, construction processes, and regulatory pathways are being navigated for the first time.

A growing group of impact-oriented investors has begun to step into that gap. Aalo's early funding came from a range of venture capital firms focused on climate and deep-technology innovation, including Earth Venture Capital, a science-driven climate venture capital firm that participated in Aalo's $27 million Series A round backing technologies with large decarbonization potential.[14] That support expanded in August 2025, when Aalo closed a $100 million Series B led by Valor Equity Partners and joined by climate-aligned investors such as Kindred Ventures, a San Francisco–based early-stage firm backing foundational technologies, and Vamos Ventures, which invests in diverse founders building mission-driven climate solutions.[15] With this financing, Aalo is on its way across the FOAK valley of death to potentially access traditional project finance for scaleup.

The revival of nuclear energy in the United States is not just about small reactor innovation. Given the unmatched density of their zero-carbon energy production, large, utility-scale reactors could be an important part of America's future energy production mix too. But they face a different financing challenge. Their technology is proven and has operated safely for decades. Their barriers are political and financial. Politically, many communities fear nuclear power plants in their proximity. Financially, large energy companies no longer want to finance the earliest stages of nuclear power development on their own balance sheets as they did in the first decades of nuclear energy production.

The opportunity to close this financing gap has drawn in Charles Oppenheimer, the grandson of J. Robert Oppenheimer, the scientist who led the Manhattan Project to develop the world's first nuclear weapon. Having grappled with his grandfather's legacy, Oppenheimer has become an advocate for nuclear power as a climate and energy-security solution.

"When I looked into it," he recalled in a 2024 interview, "I was shocked that nuclear energy wasn't dangerous and was incredibly effective. It can and must be part of our clean-energy future."[16] His company, Oppenheimer Energy, and the affiliated Oppenheimer Project, are built around the conviction that nuclear energy is indispensable to meet surging electricity demand while slashing carbon emissions and that the bottleneck is not technology but finance.

Traditional financiers—banks, utilities, and infrastructure funds—rarely fund the riskiest early phases of nuclear projects: site selection, community engagement, environmental reviews, engineering studies, and the multi-year regulatory process. These "soft costs," which can total hundreds of millions of dollars per project, are too speculative for conventional lenders. Utilities prefer to buy power through long-term contracts once projects are permitted. Banks typically step in only after approvals are in place and cash flow is visible, similar to housing finance, where lenders finance construction and mortgages, but not the years of planning, permitting, and legal work that precede them.[17]

Nuclear energy remains complicated terrain for many mission-driven investors who sometimes operate under investment policies that prohibit involvement in the nuclear industry. Despite this constraint, Oppenheimer Energy is working to bring together investment groups willing to finance these soft costs, including impact investors concerned about climate change and energy security. These investors will be an essential part of getting new nuclear projects up and running.

Nuclear power, both advanced and conventional, is poised to answer America's call for reliable, affordable, and clean American-made energy that can meet growing demand. Mobilizing more investors willing to take on FOAK risk and finance soft costs will be essential to realizing its potential.

Grid, Sweat, and Tears: Financing Energy Affordability and Reliability

On a punishing summer afternoon in Phoenix, Arizona, the air-conditioning hummed steadily inside a mid-rise apartment building where many residents live on fixed or hourly incomes. Outside, temperatures pushed past 110 degrees. Inside, a cloud-based energy-management system quietly adjusted cooling loads, optimized ventilation, and reduced peak electricity demand without residents needing to change their routines or sacrifice comfort. The technology came from ENTOUCH Controls, a Dallas-based building energy platform designed to lower utility costs and improve reliability.

For residents, the impact shows up in lower monthly electricity bills during the most expensive months of the year. For building owners, it means reduced operating costs and greater resilience during extreme heat. And for Arizona's grid, stressed by rapid growth and rising temperatures, it reduces demand precisely when reliability matters most.

Along the way to growing its business to Phoenix and beyond, ENTOUCH had relied on venture funding, including from an impact-focused venture firm that has been investing in climate technology long before it became cool. SJF Ventures began in Durham, North Carolina, in 1999, when Dave Kirkpatrick and partner Rick Defieux launched what was then called the Sustainable Jobs Fund. Rooted in North Carolina's social-enterprise ecosystem, the firm was founded on a simple idea that venture capital, if structured with discipline and intent, could be a powerful tool for advancing environmental sustainability and economic opportunity at the same time.[18]

Kirkpatrick came to investing after years working in and around non-profit and mission-driven organizations in North Carolina, including efforts to promote recycling, renewable energy, and environmental job creation. That background shaped his conviction that grants and concessional capital were essential for experimentation but insufficient for building industries at scale.

In its early years, SJF raised capital to invest primarily from mission-aligned foundations, family offices, and individual investors willing to support a then-unproven idea: that market-rate venture capital could be a vehicle for job creation and environmental benefit. Over time, as clean energy and energy efficiency markets matured, SJF deliberately broadened its investor base to include pensions, funds-of-funds, and other institutional allocators while seeking not to abandon its impact discipline.

For SJF, that evolution was not about diluting mission, but sharpening it. Kirkpatrick has described the firm's discipline as generating "alpha in impact," asking whether a strong financial outcome can be paired with deeper, more measurable benefits for customers and communities.

ENTOUCH reflects that logic. Rather than relying on new construction or expensive retrofits, the company improves energy efficiency in existing buildings where energy costs hit tenants hardest and reliability is critical during heat waves. SJF backed the company early, recognizing that demand-side efficiency is among the fastest and most cost-effective ways to strengthen grids while lowering household energy burdens.

SJF's energy investments also extend to grid-scale infrastructure. In 2010, the firm led the Series A in Community Energy, helping prove that 100-megawatt-scale solar projects could be financed across multiple states. Over the following decade, the company developed gigawatts of projects before being acquired by AES in December 2021, accelerating solar's transition into a mainstream asset class.[19]

Similarly, in 2014, SJF led Nextracker's Series B round, ahead of its acquisition by Flex. The deal helped propel a single-axis tracking technology that increases energy output per acre, improving both the economics and reliability of utility-scale solar across the grid.

Across five funds, SJF reports having raised approximately $435 million and supported 86 portfolio companies since its founding. Its most recent fund, SJF Ventures V, closed at $175 million in February 2021 with a diversified limited-partner base that included foundation endowments, pension funds, family offices, funds-of-funds, and individual investors.[20]

SJF's impact reporting makes the household-level implications tangible. In 2023, portfolio companies delivered outcomes that translated directly into lower energy costs, improved building performance, and cleaner power in regions facing increasing climate stress. The through-line is affordability, reliability, and equity, ensuring that the benefits of the energy transition reach households historically excluded from clean-energy savings.

SJF has set out to show that a for-profit vehicle with market-rate expectations can expand the scale of impact by attracting durable capital. It anchored in energy and efficiency long enough and early enough to build expertise and was willing to broaden its impact focus from job counts to affordability, reliability, and system-level outcomes as the industry matured. Balancing financial performance and impact is never easy, but can be a powerful way to keep the capital flowing to energy innovators who can help keep American lights on and air cool.

From Grant to Grid: Philanthropy-Backed Investors Financing Energy Innovation

In neighborhoods across Massachusetts and New York, homeowners eager to install rooftop solar ran into an unexpected barrier: aging electrical panels that could not safely accommodate new solar, batteries, or EV chargers without costly upgrades. ConnectDER's meter-collar adapter solved that problem. Utilities including National Grid and Eversource began piloting the device, allowing households to connect clean energy systems without rewiring their homes.

To reach this point, ConnectDER had to raise financing to develop and bring their technology to market, a struggle for many companies developing new clean energy technology. Fortunately for them and their customers, they had found an early backer willing to build a financing bridge from an early grant converted to a Program Related Investment to support in closing their Series A commercial financing. That backer was Prime Coalition.[21]

Building this bridge from grant to scalable investment is precisely how donor-funded nonprofits help climate technologies cross the "valley of death," the funding chasm where many industrial and infrastructure-heavy startups fail.

Prime Coalition's founder and leader Sarah Kearney had built a career path from a family foundation to graduate research at MIT, where she studied how philanthropic capital could bridge nonprofit and for-profit innovation. In 2014, she launched Prime with a premise that philanthropy is uniquely positioned to take early risk that others cannot and "to do so in ways that unlock much larger pools of capital later."[22] Recognized as an Echoing Green fellow, Kearney built Prime to focus on industrial and deep-technology start-ups because they are often hardware-intensive and capital-heavy companies most overlooked by mainstream investors.

These companies face two related challenges. The first is FOAK risk, where financiers balk at unproven technologies. The second is the valley of death: the long, capital-starved period between early validation and commercial viability. Prime's model begins with grants from philanthropic sources such as foundations, donor-advised funds, and individuals that flow into Prime's nonprofit investment vehicles, including the Prime Impact Fund, or into its affiliated for-profit venture firm, Azolla Ventures. Prime then deploys this capital as equity, convertible notes, or other for-profit instruments into early-stage companies. If those companies succeed, financial returns flow back into Prime, where they are recycled into new climate investments or used to fund market-shaping research and tools. The result is a self-renewing pool of catalytic capital that allows donors' money to work twice: first to accelerate urgently needed innovation, and again when returns are redeployed for future impact.

By 2025, Prime had mobilized more than $315 million from philanthropic partners, supporting nearly 40 companies with the potential to cut gigaton-scale emissions.[23] Family offices such as Blue Haven Initiative have been among the long-term supporters of this work, backing Prime through grants and catalytic investments and helping strengthen the broader ecosystem for early-stage climate finance.

Dawn Lippert, founder and CEO of Elemental Impact, arrived at similar conclusions through a different path. With early career experience in conservation work in Puerto Rico and energy commercialization in India, Lippert saw firsthand that technology alone does not deliver climate outcomes without community trust and project execution.[24] These observations led her to believe that technology alone cannot solve climate change without risk-taking, early-stage capital, and trust with communities where that technology is deployed.[25]

Elemental blends grant funding with investment-like tools to help companies complete FOAK projects. Among these tools are SAFEs, the Simple Agreements for Future Equity commonly used in Silicon Valley early-stage venture capital deals, which allow start-ups to raise capital without setting a valuation, converting into equity at a later priced round. Elemental worked with the law firm Wilson Sonsini to adapt this structure into a Development SAFE (D-SAFE), designed specifically for climate infrastructure and hardware companies. Unlike a standard SAFE, the D-SAFE is tied to project-level development milestones—such as permitting, engineering, or site control—rather than product development alone, making it better suited to finance the soft costs that stall climate projects before traditional investors can step in.[26]

Over more than a decade, Elemental has supported more than 160 companies and more than 150 real-world projects across energy, transportation, water, agriculture, and the circular economy.[27] Its credibility has been reinforced by funders such as Emerson Collective, founded by Laurene Powell Jobs, which has supported Elemental since the late 2010s as part of a broader commitment to climate and systems change.

Prime Coalition and Elemental Impact address the same structural failure in climate markets: promising industrial technologies stranded between proof and scale. Together, they show how some opportunities require early nurturing from investors who raise grants that provide them with a risk appetite to match the opportunity to finance the hardest, earliest work to turn climate ambition into durable infrastructure.

Whether it's a family putting solar panels on their home or a company building a nuclear power station, energy financing is a clear example of investments that involve spending money now to build something that will create ongoing profits or savings in the future. As simple as this sounds, the challenge in securing that upfront funding, and the risk associated with the potential for those savings or profits not to materialize, can lead to underinvestment and lost opportunity for companies, families, and their communities.

That same dynamic is powerfully on display in the challenge many Americans face in making investments in their education and skills. If they work, these investments result in lifetime earnings gains and other benefits for the people who make them. But for some people they instead become a burden. For others, the opportunity passes them by when they cannot access financing to catch it.

The next chapter explores investment innovators who are expanding educational opportunity, shifting financial risk away from people least able to bear it, and providing public schools with the financing they need to invest in improved student outcomes.

5

Education Should Set Everyone Up for Success

Education has long been the fulcrum of the American Dream: work hard in your free public school, work your way through an affordable public college or invest in job training, and you can earn your way to financial security for your family.

Unfortunately, for too many people, that fulcrum is now broken at every level. Despite our government spending almost $1 trillion on our public schools, more than double the per-student expenditure in the 1970s,[1] US students perform worse than most of our developed nation peers on standard assessments of basic math and reading skills.[2] The lingering effects of pandemic lockdowns and social media distraction have made student outcomes even worse. Fourth-grade math scores have fallen back to levels last seen in the late 1990s, while eighth-grade reading scores have dropped to levels comparable to the early 1990s.[3,4]

These averages obscure even deeper challenges. Despite massive public expenditure, the education system continues to underserve the students who rely on it most for opportunity and mobility. Research from Stanford's

Education Recovery Scorecard shows that schools serving predominantly Black, Latino, and low-income students lost the equivalent of half a year to a full year of math learning during the pandemic, and recovery since then has been uneven.[5]

The crisis does not end at high school graduation. For those students who graduate and seek higher education, college is increasingly unaffordable. The average college costs $38,000/year and continues to rise more quickly than inflation.[6] Even for students at public colleges, the days when they could cover the cost of school with summer jobs and part-time work during the school year are long past. Those costs have grown much faster than median wages, forcing many students to delay enrollment, enroll part-time, or abandon college plans altogether.

For those who do enroll, financing higher education often means taking on substantial debt. Student loan balances in the United States now exceed $1.6 trillion, making education debt one of the largest categories of consumer credit in the economy. Tens of millions of borrowers carry student loans, with the median borrower owing between $20,000 and $25,000 years into repayment. This debt burden constrains household balance sheets and shapes life decisions well beyond graduation.

The long-term effects are increasingly visible. Student debt can delay homeownership, limit retirement savings, and reduce financial resilience in the face of economic shocks. And these effects are not only for people who sought college degrees. They are also burdening people who increasingly need to spend tens of thousands of dollars on training to participate in the more lucrative roles available in various trades.

Taken together, these trends reveal a structural failure rather than a funding shortfall. The system needs transformative innovation. But innovation often requires upfront investment in new ways of working that can be risky, something large bureaucracies like those that run the education system are reluctant to take on. Educational systems change requires innovative financing that answers three core questions:

1. How can we improve the performance of public schools by getting schools the money they need to invest in better outcomes for students and ensuring new, high-quality schools have the financing they need to expand?

2. How can we finance individuals to invest in their education and training in ways that do not bankrupt them?
3. How can we ensure early-stage companies whose technologies could improve educational outcomes get the capital they need to scale?

Around the country, investors, philanthropists, and government are working together to answer these questions.

- In Dallas, schools have accessed loans to invest in guidance counselors and other resources to help students stay on track for a successful post-school transition that they will repay from bonuses the state will pay them for this success.
- In Houston, a school has moved into a new building where their students can thrive, financed through bonds issued by a fund created to lower the cost of financing for high-performing charter schools.
- In Ohio, future diesel technicians are getting trained and accredited without having to pay anything upfront, eventually paying for their education only if they secure a good job.
- In Illinois, a student has accessed a loan that did not require her parents as co-signers, an essential ingredient to keep her on track to graduate.
- In New Hampshire, college counselors are responding to student mental health needs that would previously have been hidden to them after deploying a new online student chatbot, whose company received early financing from a workforce-focused venture capital fund.

They are just a few examples of how investors are providing the necessary fuel for the many people seeking to revive the American education system as an engine of opportunity that all Americans can access.

Educating for Results: Finance to Help Public Schools Invest in Student Success

What if public high schools could be paid more by the state if they successfully prepared their students to graduate into careers, college, or military service? That question may seem obvious, but it holds the kernel of an idea that could help reverse the trend in public schools where more spending is not generating better outcomes for students. Schools could spend more on ensuring student success if they knew they would receive more funding after those investments. That was the core idea behind a major school funding bill passed by the Texas legislature in 2019.

The Bill offered schools bonus payments between $3,500 and $7,000 for every graduate above a basic threshold who were CCM ready (meeting a set of criteria indicating their readiness for success in career, college, or military service).[7] For some high schools, this could translate into millions of potential dollars each year. But the state does not advance that money upfront; districts must invest first in counselors, advising systems, and data tools.

The new funding formula creates a financial opportunity but also a cash-flow challenge. Many school boards are reluctant to take on debt or shift spending to pursue the bonuses that are not guaranteed. And banks will generally not lend to a public school pursuing a bonus payment from a new state program without a clear track record to provide confidence that the investments the school makes will work. So, few schools answered the legislature's challenge to invest in student success. By 2024, the state paid out less than 20% of eligible funding.[8]

This Texas story shows how crucial finance can be to reorient systems like a state's public education around outcomes. But the story did not end with inertia winning. In 2025, Maycomb Capital announced a loan to Education is Freedom (EIF), a long-standing provider of postsecondary advising and student success supports.[9] Through this investment, EIF is expanding its advising model into three school districts in Dallas County expecting to reach more than 34,000 additional students. The financing covers the upfront costs of scaling guidance counseling services, allowing schools to implement the program without diverting scarce operating dollars. As participating districts improve college, career, and military readiness (CCMR) indicators, they will earn bonus payments that can sustain the advising services over time and repay the initial investment.

Maycomb Capital, named after the fictional Alabama town where *To Kill a Mockingbird* is set,[10] is a New York-based lender built specifically to finance this shift toward outcomes-based payments for social services like education. Its founder, Andi Phillips, had a wide-ranging career in nonprofit social service agencies managing large government contracts before joining Goldman Sachs' community investing unit. These experiences helped her identify how lack of financing would undermine the shift to outcomes-based funding and motivated her to found a firm to address the financing gap.[11]

Around the country, as in Texas, government typically pays for activities (staff time, tutoring hours, curriculum purchases), not outcomes (reading proficiency, credential attainment, graduation). Outcomes-based financing reverses this logic: public payors agree to pay only if measurable results are achieved. But service providers must invest upfront before outcome payments arrive, hiring tutors, adding pre-K slots, modernizing instructional materials. That timing mismatch is precisely the gap Maycomb Capital fills.

Maycomb has raised approximately $150 million across its outcomes finance and lending strategies since its launch in 2018.[12] Its Community Outcomes strategy had aggregated an initial $145 million in private capital by the end of 2025.[13] Investors include major foundations such as Kresge, Hewlett, and Kellogg, institutional investors such as Prudential, and individuals such as former Microsoft CEO Steve Ballmer and his wife Connie.[14]

Beyond Texas, Maycomb is financing other shifts to outcomes-focused educational spending by government. Deals include an $18 million financing enabling 3,000 high-quality pre-Kindergarten seats in Shelby County, Tennessee, flexible loans through the Educational Resources Impact Strategy to instructional materials innovators like Illustrative Mathematics and CenterPoint Education Solutions, and financing the "Hello Family" early-childhood outcomes initiative in Spartanburg, South Carolina, linking repayment to improvements in birth outcomes and early development.[15]

Across these projects, Maycomb's message has evolved: rather than describing themselves as pay-for-success or outcomes lenders, the firm now describes itself simply as a lender providing mission-aligned private credit specifically targeting lending opportunities where repayment will come from contracts that reward outcomes with revenue.[16] By focusing on this niche, Maycomb can become comfortable understanding and managing the risk of lending into these outcomes contracts in ways banks and other lenders have not. And Maycomb can identify and recruit investors who value this approach and expertise, expanding the money available to finance outcomes.

At a moment when American students face historic learning loss and widening inequities, this model represents a path to getting better educational outcomes for the money government spends, by aligning incentives, rewarding what works, and enabling districts to invest immediately in evidence-based programs.

AAA Bonds for A Students: Harnessing the Commercial Bond Market to Close School Financing Gaps

In Houston, at the Beatrice Mayes Institute, students once sat in classrooms without air conditioning, a real distraction in the Texas heat. The school's founder knew that crumbling infrastructure undermined education but lacked the money to pay for costly repairs upfront. Now, thanks to a loan from the Equitable Facilities Fund (EFF), the school is transformed. "EFF enabled Beatrice Mayes to build a proper facility, a transformation that moved teachers . . . to tears. This isn't just about construction but about fairness and opportunity," said Anand Kesavan, EFF's founder and CEO.[17]

EFF began with a question and a grant. The Arkansas-based Walton Family Foundation, established by the family of Walmart founder Sam Walton, had long focused on education reform and innovation, directing significant grant funding to advance the charter school movement.[18] Walton's grants supported everything from developing new school models to leadership training to helping charter schools secure and improve facilities.

By the mid-2010s, however, Walton leaders saw a structural barrier they could not dismantle with grants alone. Charter school operators, no matter how strong their academic record, often faced borrowing costs far higher than traditional public school districts. Banks and conventional lenders viewed charters as risky because they were relatively young, because each school was too small to justify the transaction costs of a bond offering, and because many operated in neighborhoods that traditional lenders considered too risky to prioritize.[19] Even high-performing charter schools could be denied loans or forced to accept high interest rates and burdensome fees.

Walton realized that building a new gym or science wing with grant dollars was helpful in the short term, but the need was far larger than philanthropy could cover. The strategic question: What would it take to create the conditions in which charter schools could access loans for buying and renovating their school buildings on the same terms that traditional public schools get when their towns issue municipal bonds for these purposes?

With that guiding question, Walton committed $200 million in grants to create EFF in 2017 and hired Kesavan to run it. After a successful finance career specializing in structured and municipal finance, he became the first CFO of a charter school in Austin, partly inspired by his mother's role in founding one of Michigan's first charter schools.[20]

To answer the foundational question, EFF adapted the concept of state revolving funds, commonly used to finance infrastructure such as water systems, to the needs of charter schools. By pooling multiple loans into larger bond issuances, EFF could secure investment-grade ratings and pass on the benefits to schools: lower interest rates, reduced fees, and elimination of reserve requirements that otherwise tied up scarce resources. With the grant money in hand, EFF committed to cover part of any potential defaults on the loans, reducing the risk to potential investors and helping to overcome their discomfort with charter school lending.

EFF's first bond issuance in 2017 received an 'A' rating from S&P, allowing the pension funds and insurance companies that typically buy municipal bonds to invest and securing a 3.3% interest rate, lower than the charter schools could get on their own. The bond also lowered transaction fees from industry norms around 4.5% of project cost to roughly 2%. EFF then used the bond proceeds to finance high-performing charter schools directly. For one school, that meant saving $3 million that stayed in the classroom rather than going to debt service.[21]

Beginning with a loan to a school in Memphis, by 2025 EFF had gone on to support 75 charter organizations in 23 states with $1.7 billion in loans that have saved the schools $320 million.[22] They reached a symbolic milestone in October 2024, when EFF issued $350 million in A-rated bonds priced on par with municipal bonds for school construction.[23]

EFF is no longer solely Walton-funded. Seventeen philanthropic funders and the federal government have contributed to its capital base, and more than 70 institutional investors have participated in its bond offerings including JPMorgan, Goldman Sachs, UBS, Vanguard, Wilmington Trust, and AllianceBernstein.[24]

At Beatrice Mayes Institute, the loan from EFF delivered more than air conditioning. It delivered dignity, comfort, and a physical environment in which teachers and students have a better chance to thrive. Across the country, EFF's model has transformed the facilities financing landscape for charter schools, creating equal access to financing in what was previously a chronic disadvantage.

Student Loans Without the Risk to the Students

Daniel Villalta enjoyed working with his hands and fixing things. Community college had been a poor fit for him and bouts of unemployment left him unable to pay for a traditional technical training course without a guarantee of employment. But the diesel technician program at ADTC in Columbus, Ohio, offered something compelling: a Career Impact Bond (CIB) that allowed him to enroll with zero upfront cost. Only if the training led to a solid job would he have to make modest, capped repayments of his loans. Within weeks of graduating, he was earning a decent wage inspecting and repairing trucks in Virginia with prospects for rapid advancement.[25]

Daniel's experience reflects a broader movement among impact investors to redesign education financing to shift financial risk away from students. The CIB emerged from Social Finance, the nonprofit that helped introduce "Pay for Success" financing to the United States. Inspired by the world's first Social Impact Bond in the United Kingdom, these models sought to shift social spending away from paying for outputs (such as hours spent in a classroom or even gaining a certification) to outcomes (e.g., a graduate earning a higher wage).

For decades, US students have shouldered almost all the risk of post-secondary school training programs that may or may not lead to upward mobility. Borrowers must repay loans whether or not they graduate or their education helps them earn more. Some of the worst effects of the student loan crisis are borne by people who incurred debt to get degrees they didn't finish. Pay for success financing avoids this trap.

Under a Career Impact Bond structure, donors and investors cover training costs upfront, and students make payments only if they land jobs that meet defined earning thresholds. This approach links the cost of education directly to the economic value it produces. Investors pay for the training upfront, taking on the risk the training will not produce expected income gains for students. They also have a clear financial incentive to fund only those training programs that help students raise their income, shifting resources over time to programs that work.

The ADTC Career Impact Bond, implemented between 2020 and 2022, invested almost $9 million in funding from Social Finance's UP Fund. More than 1,100 learners enrolled in ADTC's 300-hour, hands-on diesel mechanic program with no upfront fees.[26] The CIB covered tuition, room and board, and even a 193-piece professional toolset. Participants also received career coaching and financial literacy training designed to strengthen long-term economic stability.

The Career Impact Bond was structured as an Income Share Agreement. Graduates earning $30,000–$40,000 repaid $150 per month (or $187 including the toolset), while those earning above $40,000 repaid $280 (or $317 with tools) for 48 months. If they did not reach these salary thresholds, they paid nothing. The CIB enabled ADTC to expand capacity from serving roughly 350–600 students annually.

Even students who found good jobs often did not pay anything. Because diesel technicians were in high demand, major employers, including Penske Truck Leasing, Aim Transportation Solutions, and National Fleet Management, voluntarily assumed repayment obligations for the graduates they hired. Initially, more than half of all participants had their training fully covered by employers, and in the second tranche of investment that share rose to 83%.

In addition to shifting risk away from students, this approach also recruited employers to share in the cost of training the skilled labor that helps them to generate profits. The CIB demonstrates how employer co-investment can align incentives, reduce debt burdens, and support equitable access to career pathways.

While the CIB may be the clearest example of incentive-aligned education finance, several other initiatives are working to reduce student loan burdens. The Student Freedom Initiative, backed by successful financier Robert Smith, offers income-contingent financing as an alternative to costly Parent PLUS loans, ensuring students at Historically Black Colleges and Universities repay only when they achieve sustainable wages.[27] Social Finance has also launched "Pay it Forward Funds" in New Jersey, California, and Massachusetts whose participants receive no-interest loans for career-linked education, repaying only if they succeed in finding work at higher incomes.

Income Share Agreements are not new. They have historically failed to take off because of the dangers that borrowers and policymakers see in their potential to exploit workers (by demanding a high share of potential earnings). And some ISAs have been promoted by companies uninterested in the long-term financial health of their borrowers.

But in the hands of impact investors, innovating around the needs of workers to improve their financial prospects through training, these innovations can advance the core idea that students should not bear all the risk of education, especially when employers and the broader economy benefit from a skilled workforce. By realigning financial incentives through income-linked repayment, employer co-financing, and mission-driven credit products, impact investors are creating opportunities for more people to be able to improve their prospects through education without having to take on destabilizing risk.

Degrees of Debt: Fixing How We Finance College

Higher education remains one of the strongest predictors of lifetime earnings, civic participation, and intergenerational mobility. Yet the way the United States finances college increasingly undermines that promise. Student debt has shifted from a bridge that helps families manage tuition to a structural feature of the system, one that shapes who enrolls, who persists, and what life choices graduates can make.

The scale of the student debt crisis is well documented. More than 40 million Americans hold student loan debt totaling more than $1.6 trillion.[28] The consequences are especially severe for borrowers who did not complete a degree and for students from low-income families and communities of color, who are more likely to borrow, borrow more, and struggle longer to repay.[29]

This crisis reflects fundamental changes in the economics of higher education. A generation ago, many students could attend public college, work part time, and graduate with little or no debt. Over time, per-student state funding declined, colleges raised tuition to fill the gap, and household incomes failed to keep pace.[30] Federal policy expanded access to loans faster than grant aid, normalizing debt as the primary way to pay for college.[31] Even modest unmet need can increase dropout risk: roughly 2 million students face an average annual shortfall of $7,000 that threatens their ability to stay enrolled.[32] Financing failures now affect access and persistence as much as repayment.

A better financing system must address two challenges: making borrowing and repayment more affordable for those who rely on loans, and expanding responsible access to credit for students shut out of the private student loan market.

The size of the problem has drawn innovators and impact investors. Companies such as Sixup, Better Future Forward, and Vemo experimented with income-based repayment models that tied payments to earnings rather than fixed schedules. Many struggled, however, due to regulatory uncertainty, limited patient capital, adverse selection, and competition from federal income-driven repayment programs.

Other efforts have focused on repayment support, particularly through employers. Candidly is a workplace financial wellness platform that helps employers support employees with student loan repayment and debt navigation. By enabling tax-advantaged employer contributions, Candidly turns student loan assistance into a strategic talent benefit, helping companies attract and retain workers while improving employees' financial stability and reducing long-term debt burdens.

Being shut out of credit can be as damaging as carrying debt. Atlanta-based Funding U addresses this gap by expanding access to responsible private student loans. Its founder, Jeannie Tarkenton, first saw the problem when she lent a college roommate $1,000 to prevent her from dropping out. She later observed similar barriers to college success facing students of a girls' school she helped found in Atlanta.

Today, more than 90% of private undergraduate student loans require a creditworthy cosigner, effectively excluding many first-generation, low-income, and credit-invisible students.[33] Funding U offers no-cosigner loans to students who have completed at least two years of a four-year degree and need support to close a "last gap" threatening enrollment. Using forward-looking indicators such as academic performance and degree progress, the company lends to students likely to repay relatively comfortably.

To scale the model, Funding U has raised capital from banks and impact investors, including $20 million from philanthropist MacKenzie Scott, Tarkenton's roommate who had needed the $1,000 loan. In her 2024 annual letter, Scott described her intention to invest capital for impact before giving it away[34]; her investment in Funding U reflects that strategy. Structured as subordinated debt, it helps the company attract additional commercial capital from banks.[35] Funding U also participates in the Illinois Student Empowerment Fund, a public–private initiative that uses state assets to support private lenders to expand access to student loans for Illinois students, including Funding U's lower-cost, no-cosigner option.[36]

Taken together, these examples highlight both the promise and difficulty of innovation in college finance. If higher education is to function again as a broad engine of mobility, fair financing will need to become available for more students. That means debt that is affordable to repay and accessible to students who can succeed but do not have family members who can help them secure affordable loans. Solving both sides of the problem is essential to restoring the promise of education and training as a widely accessible path to the American Dream.

Growth Capital for Education Innovation

After returning from the disruption of COVID-19 lockdowns, teachers in a middle school in Fort Worth, Texas, began noticing a pattern they could sense but not quite see: students who were quietly spiraling. One seemed unusually withdrawn; another was wrestling with self-harm. Four days after the school adopted Rhithm, a new mental health check-in tool, teachers were identifying and supporting students in distress in real time, connecting them to targeted counselors and helping a student feeling isolated connect with a buddy.[37]

Five years after its launch in 2020, Rhithm was serving 1.5 million students in 22 states. Helping to fuel its growth was an early investment from Reach Capital, a venture capital fund spun out of an education nonprofit. Reach Capital's genesis and trajectory is a good example of how private capital can complement donations to advance solutions with scale and impatience.

Reach traces its lineage to the NewSchools Venture Fund (NSVF), a nonprofit launched in 1998 by Silicon Valley supporters such as John Doerr, Brook Byers, and Kim Smith who set out to improve educational outcomes by providing funding to innovative leaders with new approaches. NSVF raised donations and gave grants to support public charter schools, nonprofits, and early-stage learning technologies. In 2011, it launched a Seed Fund to write small equity investment checks to companies supporting K–12 public school teaching and learning such as Newsela and BrightBytes, an experiment in marrying impact goals with market-driven tools.

By 2015, the Seed Fund partners recognized a structural limit to this approach. Relying on grants constrained their ability to make follow on investments in successful companies, attract mainstream co-investors, or recycle returns.[38] The Seed Fund partners believed that scaling the most effective learning tools required vehicles that could invest larger amounts of capital, stay engaged through multiple rounds, and bring in institutional co-investors. NSVF's leadership agreed. NSVF understood that certain innovations, especially technologies used by districts, families, and adult learners, needed risk-tolerant investment capital that grants alone could not provide.

NSVF approved the spin-out of the Seed Fund into a venture capital firm that would raise profit-seeking investment capital. NSVF sought to ensure the mission remained protected by retaining an advisory presence, helping to set Reach's early impact guardrails, and remaining a close collaborator in policy and ecosystem work. Reach's founding partnership agreement explicitly anchored the new fund's strategy in education equity and established impact reporting standards that tie back to the values of its nonprofit origin. Its four cofounders brought a range of complementary experience including teaching in public schools, scaling technology companies, and supporting systems change in education.

Reach launched in 2015 with a $53 million first fund that included the 43 Seed Fund investments. They went on to raise more than $500 million in total with three successively larger additional funds, one of the largest dedicated pools of early-stage education capital.[39] Since 2021, Reach has added a dedicated "Roadrunners" program to incubate new companies emerging from founder communities historically excluded from edtech investing.[40]

Traditional venture investors have long avoided early-stage education. District sales cycles stretch 12–24 months; procurement is cumbersome; margins are thinner than in consumer tech; and revenues depend on public budgets. Reach steps into this gap, deploying patient, mission-aligned capital to founders building for the complexity, not despite it. Its launch also coincided with the beginning of a profound technology-driven transformation of public education through the ubiquity of cellphones and social media among students. Reach's particular expertise and investment focus on the role of technology in education has enabled it to invest in companies seeking to harness this shift to improve student outcomes and mitigate harms.

Reach's team and track record has attracted investment from mission-driven organizations such as Sesame Workshop, the Ford Foundation, and Kaiser Permanente alongside mainstream allocators including Goldman Sachs and the Los Angeles Fire & Police Pension System. Their investments signal that education innovation can generate competitive returns while delivering measurable social outcomes.

Reach built a distinctive impact framework around three linked pillars: Access, Outcomes, and Equity. Access asks whether the company is reaching the learners who most need support, including schools in low-income districts, families unable to pay for supplemental services, or jobseekers without traditional networks. Outcomes focuses on whether the product demonstrably works, using real-world data rather than anecdotes. Equity emphasizes who benefits and whether historically marginalized learners gain disproportionately.[41]

Beyond investments in companies that seek to improve public school student well-being and performance, such as Rhithm and Paper, which provides tutoring services for public school students, Reach Capital has also made investments aimed at improving career success for college graduates such as Handshake, one of the most important on-ramps for first-generation college students into the labor market and Springboard, which helps working adults gain new skills to improve their career prospects.

From the Fort Worth teacher who used a check-in tool to save a student from crisis to the first-generation college student who landed her first internship through Handshake, the story of Reach Capital shows how a nonprofit's mission carried forward through thoughtful impact investment can widen how many people can turn a public education into a successful life for themselves and their families.

Investing When Grants Alone Cannot Shift the Educational System

Leaders at Dallas College confronted a familiar but underappreciated cause of student attrition. Many students were leaving not because of academic difficulty, but because small financial shocks—a missed paycheck, a car repair, an overdue bill—made continuing untenable. Emergency aid existed, but it often arrived too late.

To address this, in 2019 Dallas College partnered with Edquity, a new technology platform designed to identify students in financial distress and deliver financial support quickly. Through a short assessment, students could be connected to resources and, when eligible, emergency aid that often arrived within a day rather than weeks. By reducing administrative friction, colleges were able to intervene before temporary crises led to permanent withdrawal.

Within weeks of going live with Edquity's first deployment, tornadoes wrecked the neighborhoods where many Dallas College students lived. In the first 24 hours, 250 students applied for emergency aid. Then, months later, when the pandemic struck, Edquity helped the college and other institutions distribute emergency aid, moving tens of millions of dollars to students far faster than traditional systems allowed.[42] Now Edquity (subsequently rebranded Beam) works with more than 100 colleges, nonprofits, and government agencies across the United States, and has made more than 100,000 payments totaling almost half a billion dollars.[43]

To build the initial solution and then reach this scale, Edquity had relied on mission-aligned investors who provided almost $10 million in early investor funding rounds.[44] Among those investors was Indiana-based Lumina Foundation. The story of how a traditional education foundation became an edtech venture capitalist illustrates how important investing in America can be for organizations that understand what it takes to achieve impact at scale.

Lumina Foundation was established in 2000 as an independent private foundation when the nonprofit USA Group sold the operating assets of its student loan guarantor business. With an initial endowment exceeding $1 billion, Lumina focused on early grants that could increase college access for first-generation, low-income, and working-adult students. By the late 2000s, however, Lumina concluded that access alone was insufficient. Completion, credential quality, and labor-market value mattered as much as enrollment. In response, Lumina announced its signature Goal 2025: that 60% of US adults would hold a high-quality postsecondary credential by 2025.[45]

Progress toward that goal has been meaningful but uneven.[46] Recognizing the pace of change, Lumina extended its long-term ambition to 75% attainment by 2040 while doubling down on equity, adult learners, and workforce-aligned credentials.[47]

To accelerate progress, Lumina expanded beyond grantmaking into impact investing. A 2016 sector scan commissioned with the Kresge Foundation identified persistent capital gaps for ventures serving adult learners, alternative credentials, and student-success technologies.[48] Many promising solutions required flexible, early-stage capital rather than grants alone. Lumina began deploying both program-related investments that typically targeted below-market rate financial returns and market-rate mission-related investments to de-risk innovation, catalyze markets, and attract additional private capital.

Lumina's investment strategy focuses on expanding equitable access, improving student success and completion, and increasing the relevance and quality of credentials.[49] Its portfolio includes digital credentialing platforms, advising and analytics tools, and workforce-aligned learning platforms that create faster, lower-cost pathways into high-demand jobs. Across these investments, Lumina emphasizes equity, scale, and systems change, using data, convening power, and policy engagement alongside capital.[50]

Lumina is not the only education-focused institution to conclude that achieving mission outcomes requires coordinating multiple forms of capital. ECMC Foundation was established in 2000 in Minnesota as the charitable arm of ECMC Group, a major nonprofit guaranty agency in the federal student-loan system. For many years, the foundation focused primarily on scholarships, distributing millions of dollars to individual students. While meaningful, these awards did little to address the systemic barriers that prevent many low-income and first-generation students from completing college.

By 2014, ECMC Foundation's leadership recognized these limits and made a strategic pivot toward improving college success and career readiness by changing how the postsecondary system itself operates. This shift paralleled ECMC Group's transformation as it diversified into new education and workforce-aligned models.

In 2018, ECMC Foundation launched Education Innovation Ventures, a program-related investment initiative deploying loans, equity, deposits, and guarantees in mission-aligned organizations. ECMC also launched the Education Impact Fund, a $250 million pool investing in direct deals and fund managers across the learner-to-worker pipeline.

A core feature of ECMC strategy is providing the full range of capital. Together, grantmaking, PRIs, and market-rate investments form a coordinated capital stack aimed at improving postsecondary completion and economic mobility. Between its various entities, the ECMC group can provide grants to seed an innovation, PRIs when they are high risk and early stage, and a follow-on investment from the larger Impact Fund.[51]

Multiyear grants fund field-building initiatives and research while helping institutions adopt evidence-based practices; Program-Related Investments (PRIs) scale the tools those institutions rely on.[52] ECMC has found grantmaking particularly important for organizations where market forces cannot fully support the cost of serving the hardest-to-reach students and encourages organizations that do not meet specific financial return expectations for investment to apply for grants.[53] It deploys risk-taking, patient PRI capital through its Innovation Ventures Fund to support companies capable of reshaping institutional behavior, recognizing that this kind of systems change can take longer to pay off than a profit-maximizing venture capital fund would tolerate.[54]

Taken together, Lumina and ECMC point to a shared conclusion: the most effective way to improve educational outcomes is not to choose between grants, investments, or policy work, but to intentionally align all three. Grants fund experimentation and equity. Investments scale proven solutions and shape markets. Policy and data work create the conditions for adoption and sustainability. When coordinated, these tools reinforce one another, making progress toward educational attainment more scalable and enduring.

Many Americans experience education as a massive system with large institutions and forces beyond their control that often seem to be driving up costs without obvious benefits. That is also true for healthcare. As with education, healthcare costs are going up, as is the burden on many individuals to pay for them. As with education, to disrupt this trajectory requires financing for innovation and inclusion. People and companies that can improve how healthcare is delivered need financing to take on the status quo. At the same time, people and communities need financing just to keep local clinics and hospitals open.

Mainstream investors lack financial incentives to make this happen. Fortunately, innovative investors, highlighted in the next chapter, often working alongside government, are figuring out not only how to make healthcare more available and affordable, but also how to shift the system itself to focus on keeping people healthy rather than treating them when they get sick.

6

Healthcare Should Be Affordable, Accessible, and Keep Us Healthy

Healthcare costs have become one of the most destabilizing forces in American families' financial lives. Medical debt is the leading cause of personal bankruptcy and even insured families face overwhelming expenses.[1] In 2023, the average employer-sponsored family health plan cost more than $24,000 in total premiums,[2] and deductibles have tripled since the early 2000s. Out-of-pocket spending now exceeds $1,500 per person annually, and most Americans report delaying care because of cost.

We spend more on healthcare than any nation on Earth, approximately $14,880 per person in 2024.[3] Yet Americans die younger, experience higher chronic disease burdens, and report worse access to care than people in other wealthy nations. The typical American now lives four years fewer than the average resident of peer countries. Despite producing breakthroughs in specialized medicine, the system has failed to deliver basic health security to millions.

These national averages conceal deeper inequities. Black Americans live six years shorter on average than white Americans[4]; maternal mortality for Black women is three times higher[5]; and Native American communities face life expectancy comparable to lower-middle-income countries. Neighborhoods only a few miles apart can have life expectancy differences of 15–20 years, primarily driven not by access to advanced medicine but by social and environmental conditions such as housing quality, food access, environmental exposure, and community safety.

Geography deepens the divide: rural healthcare is in crisis. More than 150 rural hospitals have closed since 2010,[6] and hundreds more operate on razor-thin margins. Primary-care practices struggle to survive as reimbursements stagnate. Many rural counties have no obstetric unit at all,[7] and emergency care may be more than an hour away. As hospitals close, communities lose not only care but also major employers, economic anchors, and civic institutions.

Meanwhile, even urban areas with top-tier hospitals experience fragmented care, financial ruin driven by unexpected bills, and widening affordability gaps. Half of US adults carry medical debt.[8] A quarter skip prescriptions for cost reasons. Low-wage workers often face deductibles that exceed two months' take-home pay. The people who need care most frequently have the least reliable access.

Lack of financing did not create these problems, but it is making them worse. Traditional banks and venture capital or private equity investors rarely finance community clinics, rural providers, or prevention oriented start-ups because they cannot generate the same financial returns or require more risk than businesses serving richer communities. These healthcare providers also often get by combining customer payments with government programs that can be hard to decipher or rely on. They also can take longer to reach financial sustainability than traditional investors have come to expect.

Improving health outcomes and affordability will require new businesses, inventions, government actions, and community mobilization. It will also require expanding who gets access to finance. We need to figure out:

- How can we scale up specialist lenders who understand how to lend prudently to hospitals and clinics that serve rural areas and low-income communities while relying on Medicaid reimbursement, low-margin primary care, community-rooted health models, and braided revenue streams?

- How can we harness investment capital from all the institutions that benefit from healthier communities, including healthcare and insurance giants and other large corporations?
- How can investors finance effective "upstream" services programs that keep people healthy when the health systems savings they produce can take years to materialize?

Across the country, a growing group of impact-oriented investors has begun stepping into this role. Community Development Financial Institutions are financing free and charitable clinics while rural-focused lenders are working with government programs to help rebuild primary care access. Hospital systems and health industry companies are bringing new investment capital for healthcare, using corporate cash to become healthcare investors. And, because of the centrality of healthcare in the daily economic life of employees and customers, other large corporations like big banks are investing in America's health with corporate venture arms backing prevention focused technology and companies advancing disruptive solutions to healthcare and health insurance. In their own ways, these investors are constructing the scaffolding for a healthier America.

This chapter highlights five examples from that group. Together, they show how investors are strengthening primary care, scaling technology that improves chronic disease management, expanding behavioral health capacity, and financing the housing and social support that improve and sustain health more than medical services alone. These investors are not just financing better healthcare, they are investing in health itself, helping build a system that is more equitable, preventive, and financially sustainable.

Checks for Check-Ups: How Community Lenders Partner to Support Community Clinics

In New Orleans' Mid-City neighborhood, patients walking into CrescentCare's new 64,000-square-foot health center find primary care, HIV services, behavioral health, housing navigation support, and a food pantry all under one roof. The transformation from four cramped leased sites to a modern consolidated campus was made possible through a $10 million loan from the Primary Care Development Corporation (PCDC), combined with financing from the Low Income Investment Fund and Reinvestment Fund, and supported by New Markets Tax Credits (NMTCs).[9]

CrescentCare is a Federally Qualified Health Clinic (FQHC), a health center that receives favorable reimbursement rates from Medicaid and other government supports in return for a commitment to serve anyone who walks through its doors. These centers must offer a sliding scale of payment and a broad range of integrated services, including primary care, dental, behavioral health, and preventive care. Many centers also provide enabling services rarely found in traditional medical settings such as transportation, translation, case management, and outreach.

Today, the FQHC system is one of the largest and essential parts of America's healthcare infrastructure. In 2023–2024, those centers delivered care to more than 31 million people, making them the primary care provider for 1 in 11 Americans and 1 in 5 rural residents.[10] There are roughly 1,400 health centers operating more than 16,000 service sites across the United States and its territories.[11]

Complementing the FQHC network, 5,000 Rural Health Clinics also receive government support to serve underserved communities, though with fewer restrictions than FQHCs. They often represent the only accessible outpatient care available when rural hospitals close. Together these systems of health clinics ensure that income and geography do not become destiny in determining who can access healthcare services.

Despite their importance, these clinics are typically shut out from traditional sources of finance. Where can they get loans to expand or renovate their facilities, hire staff, or improve their IT and medical technology? Usually not from banks that are generally wary of lending to these health centers that typically operate with thin margins, limited assets to put up for collateral, and complex revenue projections that rely on navigating government programs.

Instead, Community Development Financial Institutions (CDFIs) such as PCDC and the other lenders to CrescentCare in New Orleans have become essential financiers of community health centers nationwide. Often nonprofits themselves, they can structure flexible loans, have experience operating in chronically underinvested communities, and with organizations led by people more focused on serving a mission than generating a profit. They also have crucial experience from their work in housing and other areas in collaborating with government programs to raise subsidies that can make loans viable. They have become especially adept at placing financing from the New Markets Tax Credit (NMTC) program to cover the part of real estate projects that health clinics cannot afford to cover through loans.

PCDC, founded in 1993, has leveraged more than $1.7 billion for primary care expansion.[12] Since 2008, it has deployed $377 million in NMTC tax credits across 42 health facility projects.[13] Other national CDFIs are also crucial to provide financing to health clinics. Momentus Capital (including Capital Impact Partners) has financed more than $780 million in community health centers and aging-in-place models nationwide.[14] As of 2024, it had received $792 million in NMTC allocation, supporting 94 community facility projects, including clinics in rural Texas, Detroit, and California's Central Valley.[15] The Community Health Center Capital Fund, the lending affiliate of health clinic advisor Capital Link, is another specialized institution supporting facility projects for FQHCs and other safety net providers. Beyond NMTC, CDFIs mobilize other government funding to support this work, such as Mississippi-based HOPE Enterprises' $40 million partnership with the US Department of Agriculture that included loan guarantees for health clinic lending in the Mississippi Delta.[16]

Regional CDFIs also support health clinic expansion. BlueHub Capital has financed multiple community health providers in Massachusetts, including Lowell Community Health Center, one of the largest and most diverse FQHCs in New England.[17] Reinvestment Fund has supported several Philadelphia-area clinic projects, reinforcing how place-rooted lenders address local needs that national actors may miss.

CDFIs can also offer flexibility that traditional lenders would not. Nonprofit Finance Fund used a loan and NMTC credits in 2017 to finance the 11,500-square-foot La'i 'Opua Health Center on the Big Island in Hawaii. Sitting on Hawaiian Crown Land, the project would have been difficult for a bank to finance with its standard approach to securing real estate as collateral for the loan.[18]

The unique health clinic system needs lenders who can understand how to make investments work for providers caring for underserved communities. CDFIs have stepped up to the challenge, navigating government programs, offering flexible loans that regulated banks would struggle to approve, and developing expertise in the real vs. perceived risks these loans involve.

In rural parishes, Delta towns, Pacific islands, and urban neighborhoods alike, CDFIs are financing the physical infrastructure of better health for more people one clinic at a time. For Americans living in inner cities and remote rural areas, this partnership between health clinics and CDFIs manifests as shorter drives, earlier screenings, accessible behavioral health services, and providers rooted in community life.

Investing for the People Who Need It Most: How Venture Capital Is Backing Health Solutions for Underserved Communities

In the race to develop a vaccine for COVID-19, Moderna stunned the world by producing one of the first successful candidates in under a year. Behind this historic breakthrough was Flagship Pioneering, a life sciences venture firm whose long-term, high-risk investment model illustrates how visionary investors can help solve national health challenges.

Boston-based Flagship Pioneering isn't a typical venture capital firm. Rather than just investing in promising biotech start-ups, Flagship creates them. Founded in 2000, it assembles interdisciplinary teams that explore radical ideas in biology and launch companies to bring them to life. These "venture creation" efforts are funded initially from Flagship's own money, often before a company is ready to raise outside capital or even has a product road map.[19]

In 2010, one of those efforts became Moderna. Over the next decade, Flagship committed hundreds of millions of dollars to Moderna, deploying capital from major university endowments, pension funds, foundations, and sovereign wealth funds seeking long-term, outsized returns.[20] The US government also played a catalytic role in Moderna's journey, particularly through the Defense Advanced Research Projects Agency (DARPA) that awarded Moderna $25 million in 2013 and the Biomedical Advanced Research and Development Authority (BARDA) that committed nearly $1 billion to support clinical trials and secure vaccine doses under Operation Warp Speed.[21]

Moderna's success story is not just about scientific ingenuity. It also highlights how investment, both public and private, can be essential to accelerate breakthroughs. Flagship's patient capital and venture creation model enabled the early development of transformative technologies. Government investment de-risked early stages and enabled rapid scaling. Together, they formed a pipeline for innovation that proved invaluable during a global crisis.

As the COVID-19 vaccine revealed how venture-backed science can serve humanity in moments of crisis, venture investors are also helping to address the crisis of US healthcare system cost and access. The massive US healthcare market attracts no shortage of venture capitalists looking to back companies that can expand quickly. But these investments tend to focus on companies serving wealthier people with health insurance. In contrast, a new generation of venture investors is directing capital, talent, and innovation toward the people and communities long ignored by mainstream healthcare markets.

Town Hall Ventures (THV) is an example of this movement. Its co-founder, Andy Slavitt, previously served as a senior government official managing Medicare and Medicaid where he helped lead drives to shift spending toward preventing rather than treating illness. His experience in Washington convinced him that lasting transformation requires new business models built for Medicaid beneficiaries, low-income seniors, and other underserved populations. Venture capital, Slavitt concluded, is essential to testing and scaling such models.

THV's mission can be seen in its investment in New York-based Cityblock Health. Although decades of public health research have shown that community based, preventive interventions can keep people healthier at lower cost, no company had cracked the business model needed to scale such work. Cityblock solved that problem by entering into value-based, at-risk contracts with Medicaid and Medicare Advantage plans, earning revenue when its multidisciplinary care teams keep members healthier and out of the hospital.

Building such an integrated model required enormous up-front spending: neighborhood clinics, behavioral health staff, home visiting care teams, social supports, and the data infrastructure to tie it all together. Spun out of Google Labs, with support from early stage investors like TMV and then

Town Hall Ventures, CityBlock has grown to take on more mainstream private equity and is poised to grow through a public offering.[22]

Also having figured out how to drive revenue and profits from improving health outcomes, San Francisco–based Virta Health supports clients to reverse Type 2 diabetes, a chronic condition that disproportionately afflicts low-income communities. It too has scaled to the point where it is now on the verge of an IPO. But the bridge from a powerful idea to a scaled business required early venture capital investment from groups like Bronze Capital, an investment fund founded by Stephen DeBerry around the simple thesis that the opportunity gap in underserved communities creates a market inefficiency where smart, early capital can generate both outsized returns and meaningful social impact.

Similarly, Rhia Ventures focuses on one of the most underfunded areas of American healthcare: reproductive and maternal health. Maternal mortality in the United States far exceeds peer nations, with Black women facing mortality rates two to three times higher than white women.[23] Rhia's venture fund, RH Capital, invests in products and services often ignored by traditional investors, such as companies building solutions across contraception, maternal health, doula care, and postpartum support. RH Capital draws heavily from philanthropic and mission-aligned capital, enabling it to take risks aligned with long-term social outcomes rather than short-term returns.

In Illinois, Impact Engine represents another model: a multi-asset-class impact investment platform deploying venture, growth equity, and private credit capital. Its health-equity strategy focuses on companies improving access, affordability, and quality of care for underserved communities. What makes Impact Engine distinctive is its institutional investor base of foundations, family offices, and increasingly larger private-market investors who combine financial analysis with rigorous impact measurement that treats health equity as a core performance metric.

Foreground Capital illustrates the rise of specialist VCs targeting specific inequities. Foreground invests exclusively in behavioral-health solutions addressing unmet needs among low-income and marginalized populations. At a time when the commercial mental health boom has largely focused on affluent, well-insured users, Foreground backs companies expanding culturally competent, affordable behavioral care for those the market has overlooked.

These investors are funding the innovations and companies building new care models for people the health system has historically failed: Medicaid members, low-income seniors, pregnant people, individuals with chronic illness, and communities facing structural barriers to care. They show how venture capital, when intentionally directed, can be a powerful tool for equity by shifting incentives toward prevention, designing care around patient needs, and proving that serving vulnerable populations can be both impactful and financially sustainable.

The Great Conversion: How a Wave of Hospital Sales Created a New Class of Investors in Community Health

Roots Community Health began in East Oakland, California in 2008 as a grassroots response to the exclusion of some of the city's most vulnerable residents, particularly men returning from incarceration and others routinely shut out of the healthcare system. Starting as a community-based organization delivering services wherever they were needed, Roots was built on the belief that health equity required meeting people where they are, with culturally grounded care and trust at the center.

As demand grew, that vision required permanent space and scale. In 2018, Roots secured a $1.4 million loan from the $20 million Healthier California Fund, a fund investing in health clinics and run by Capital Impact Partners with anchor investment funding from The California Endowment (TCE). Roots used this financing to purchase and renovate a 6,456-square-foot clinic facility in Oakland, significantly expanding capacity for integrated medical, behavioral, and wraparound services. Today, Roots serves more than 10,000 patients as their primary medical home and engages thousands more through navigation and community programs, operating multiple clinic sites in East Oakland and the South Bay alongside street outreach and mobile services that extend care across the region.[24]

The Healthier California Fund is a powerful sign of what is possible when traditional grantmaking foundations embrace investing as a complement to their grantmaking. Health conversion foundations, of which TCE is the country's largest, emerged in the 1980s and 1990s as waves of nonprofit hospitals, health plans, and health systems converted into for-profit corporations. State law required that the charitable value accumulated by these institutions be preserved for public benefit, leading to the creation of hundreds of independent health foundations. Today, more than 300 of these foundations collectively manage $40 billion in assets, providing more than $1 billion in annual grants.[25] Because of their typically local or state-specific mandate, they are a crucial source of funding for social services and healthcare in many places.

How can they support their mission beyond grantmaking? That question prompted TCE to tap its endowment as a source of impact investments. The California Endowment was formed in 1996 after Blue Cross of California converted into WellPoint Health Networks, a controversial transaction that ultimately resulted in the creation of two new statewide health foundations endowed with more than $3 billion. Today TCE holds more than $4 billion in assets and has become one of the country's most ambitious impact investors among health conversion foundations.

In 2024, TCE announced a landmark commitment to align its roughly $4 billion endowment with its mission of advancing health and racial equity across California, joining a small but growing group of foundations moving all of their assets toward mission-aligned investing.[26] This decision built on years of the foundation's use of impact investing to support community health centers and other frontline institutions, expand dental and behavioral health capacity in underserved communities, and strengthen community development financial institutions that serve low-income borrowers.[27] For TCE's president and CEO, Dr. Robert K. Ross, the logic was straightforward: achieving health equity requires mobilizing all of the foundation's assets, not only its grantmaking, to address the structural and economic conditions that shape health outcomes across the state.[28]

The Colorado Health Foundation (CHF), another major health conversion foundation, has pursued a similar investment evolution. Created from the 1995 restructuring of the nonprofit HealthONE hospital system and significantly expanded after the 2011 sale of its remaining HealthONE equity stake, CHF today manages ~$3 billion in assets.[29] In recent years, it has become a model for how foundations can pair grants with a flexible suite of investment tools to advance health equity such as investment in loan funds, recoverable grants, guarantees, and strategic deposits.

The Foundation emphasizes that traditional grantmaking is insufficient on its own to address structural drivers of health, such as housing instability, food insecurity, workforce shortages, community power disparities, and lack of primary care infrastructure. To complement its grantmaking, the Foundation increasingly deploys "patient, flexible, mission-driven capital to innovative and scalable solutions in affordable and healthy housing, primary-care infrastructure, health workforce development, and community-led economic and civic power-building."[30]

An example is the foundation's $6 million investment in a mixed-use affordable housing development in Denver's Globeville neighborhood, a historically industrial and Latino community facing displacement pressures. The financing supported a community-driven redevelopment led by the GES Coalition and local partners to create permanently affordable homes alongside commercial and cultural space.

This blending of health expertise, community partnership, and flexible capital makes health conversion foundations uniquely suited to impact investing. Their assets originate from the health system itself, yet their missions require them to invest in the underlying community conditions that produce or prevent illness.

For organizations like TCE and CHF, that responsibility now extends from their grant budgets to their balance sheets. And for communities like East Oakland or Denver's Globeville, the impact shows up not as abstract capital market innovations but as permanent clinics, safer housing, stable neighborhoods, and healthier lives. As TCE's former President Ross asks: Imagine what would happen if all $40 billion in health conversion foundation endowments were similarly mobilized for health impact?

Healthy Returns: Why Hospitals, Insurers, and Even Banks Are Investing in the Health of People and Communities

When Barbara King, an 82-year-old survivor of the devastating Tubbs fire in Northern California, moved into Laurel at Perennial Park, a new affordable senior housing complex built on the ashes of her destroyed mobile home community in Santa Rosa, her life and her health began to improve. Kaiser Permanente's Thriving Communities Fund provided critical early capital for the housing development: a $1 million low-interest loan and a $1.6 million fire-recovery grant.

"When I wake up in the morning, I'm very grateful and thankful," King shared. Having "a place to live," she said, allowed her to "recover" in more ways than one.[31] Her experience embodies a shift taking place across some of the country's largest health systems: a recognition that investing directly in the social conditions that shape health can improve outcomes more effectively and cheaply than treating crisis after crisis.

For decades, nonprofit hospital systems directed philanthropic dollars toward community programs. But Kaiser Permanente's affordable housing loan is indicative of a broader embrace of investment as a tool to improve health, and the bottom line. As a self-insured health system, Kaiser Permanente benefits financially when these projects work, as people with homes spend far less time in the system's emergency rooms, receiving care that is often not reimbursed. Health system investments in supportive housing often yield savings of $6,000 to $20,000 per person each year from reduced emergency and inpatient use.[32]

Their Thriving Communities Fund, initially a $200 million commitment in 2018, and now more than $400 million, invests in affordable housing, homelessness prevention, and neighborhood health infrastructure, resources Kaiser Permanente explicitly frames as "health interventions."[33] It generates financial return and also savings for the health system.

CommonSpirit Health has made similar moves through its Community Investment Program, providing almost $500 million in low-interest loans to projects that expand healthy food access, stabilize housing, support maternal health, and strengthen behavioral health infrastructure in low-income communities.[34] These initiatives represent a growing understanding: for hospital systems, investing in upstream social determinants is not ancillary to their mission, it is essential to improving population health and reducing avoidable hospital utilization.

Beyond pioneers like Kaiser Permanente and CommonSpirit, a growing number of hospitals are also recognizing the opportunity to act as anchor investors in their local communities, deploying their investments, not just their grant budgets, to strengthen the neighborhoods whose health outcomes they ultimately share. These systems are recognizing that economic vitality, stable housing, and local ownership are not "adjacent" to health but foundational to it and extending financing to community groups is an effective way to improve it.

Boston Medical Center is one of the clearest examples, having invested more than $6.5 million for local affordable-housing initiatives, including a $1 million zero-interest loan for a mixed-use redevelopment and an investment in the Healthy Neighborhoods Equity Fund, which finances transit oriented, health promoting development across the Boston region.[35] In Toledo, Ohio, ProMedica has taken a similarly integrated approach, opening and operating a full-service grocery store in a former food desert and providing grants and low-cost loans to the national CDFI LISC to create a $25 million loan pool for housing and commercial projects in the UpTown neighborhood.[36] In a similar move, Rush University Medical Center in Chicago placed approximately $1 million with the Chicago Community Loan Fund, capital earmarked to rehabilitate vacant buildings into affordable homes on the South and West Sides, projects that generate modest returns while strengthening the communities that rely on Rush for care.[37]

It's not just health systems. Other major healthcare corporations are investing in companies that can improve long-term health outcomes. Optum Ventures, the investment arm of UnitedHealth Group, backs companies such as Brightline, a pediatric and family behavioral health provider expanding access to timely care, and Akasa, which uses automation and AI to reduce administrative burdens that drive up system costs.[38] Rhode Island-based CVS Health Ventures has likewise expanded beyond its pharmacy roots, making a major investment in Carbon Health, a hybrid clinic and virtual care model that broadens access to primary and urgent care while lowering costs for payers and patients.[39] These investments reflect a broader industry recognition that improving population health requires shifting capital upstream to prevention, access, behavioral health, and data-driven coordination.

Beyond the healthcare sector, other large corporations are also investing to improve the US health system. Following an unsuccessful attempt to launch its own employer-based health insurance company, JPMorgan Chase shifted to making investments aimed at transforming employer-sponsored healthcare. The result was Morgan Health, a $250 million investment platform dedicated to improving cost, quality, equity, and outcomes in employer health plans. Exemplifying this approach, in 2022 Morgan Health invested

$30 million in Centivo, a health plan platform built around advanced primary care, simple benefit design, and lower costs for working families.[40] By focusing on companies that have already demonstrated the ability to improve outcomes and affordability, Morgan Health aims to generate competitive financial returns while reshaping the employer-sponsored market for its own 165,000 employees and for millions of workers across the country.

Taken together, these examples demonstrate how improving health outcomes through investment in social determinants and system transformation is an increasing imperative for large American companies. Hospital systems invest to reduce emergency use spikes and uncompensated care; insurers and pharmacy chains invest to improve member outcomes and to lower claims costs; employers and banks invest to strengthen workforce health and productivity. Together, they are investing in the promise of a new American healthcare system that helps more Americans maintain better health without having to bankrupt their families.

When an Ounce of Prevention Is Worth Pounds of Returns

Before he was investing in American workers to become business owners, Benjamin Franklin is famously cited for having written (in an anonymous letter to his own newspaper!) that "an ounce of prevention is worth a pound of cure."

Shifting from a health system that pays for cure to one that invests in prevention is not only a policy challenge but also fundamentally a financing challenge. In our current system, a hospital gets paid for the number of surgeries it performs, or the number of nights patients spend there. In a system oriented around helping people stay healthy, payments would flow after services have been delivered, when it's clear that those services worked. Or, more comprehensively, they would pay for people's well-being.

This should be attractive because it can create better outcomes at lower cost to people and government. There is solid evidence for the ability of many social services and public health interventions to generate far more in health system savings than they cost to deliver, including by delivering healthy meals to people suffering chronic health conditions, helping families with children with asthma to remove air pollutants and install purifiers in their homes, and supporting expecting and new mothers in raising healthy children, etc.

But the organizations best positioned to deliver these programs—community-based nonprofits, human services agencies, and prevention oriented health companies—rarely have the capital required to deliver interventions before payment. And most cannot access bank loans because outcomes contracts are still unusual and the organizations typically lack characteristics most lenders require such as predictable revenue, high margins, and assets to pledge for collateral.

A range of investors are now addressing this challenge. One family of tools enabling this shift is pay-for-success (PFS) and outcomes-based financing. Parallel to the earlier example of lenders supporting Dallas-area schools to invest in guidance counselors, in these models investors provide upfront financing that pays for prevention programs; governments or health plans repay only if outcomes improve, especially where these improvements save money. David Erickson, now at the Federal Resource Bank of New York, has for years worked to bring investors, community service providers, policymakers, and investors together to advance this type of work.[41]

Quantified Ventures' Health Outcomes Fund demonstrates how this works in practice. In 2020, the health insurance company Humana committed $5 million to expand Volunteers of America's Family Focused Recovery programs for pregnant and parenting women with substance use disorders in Kentucky, Ohio, and Indiana.[42] Investors financed the delivery of integrated addiction treatment, parenting supports, transportation assistance, and basic needs services. Humana paid for verified improvements, such as sustained recovery, reduced neonatal complications, and family reunification.

Similarly, Hello Family in Spartanburg, South Carolina, is a citywide prenatal and early childhood initiative offering nurse home visiting, parenting training, and early development programs. Its financing blends Medicaid dollars, city funds, philanthropy, and outcomes-based investments. The pay-for-success component was structured by Maycomb Capital (who led the financing of the Dallas school initiative), with support from the City of Spartanburg, The Duke Endowment, Blue Cross Blue Shield of South Carolina, and the Mary Black Foundation.[43] Subsequent expansion has attracted federal outcomes funding and large national funders.

In New York City, the Green & Healthy Homes Initiative is helping 850 children and adults reduce asthma crises. The four-year project combined investment from Northern Trust and GHHI itself with grants from JPB Foundation to pay for home visits, asthma prevention coaching, and remediation of environmental triggers delivered by local nonprofits. If the projects succeeds, it could save health insurer Affinity by Molina $6.5 million in Medicaid costs associated with emergency room visits and hospital stays which will cover repayment to investors.[44]

Nutrition is another frontier for upstream investment. The Food as Medicine movement has accelerated as research shows that medically tailored meals (MTMs) can reduce hospitalizations and annual healthcare spending. While large home meal delivery nonprofits have struggled to get pay for success deals from pilot to scale, venture backed for-profit companies are also entering the space. For example, ModifyHealth raised $13.5 million in late 2024 in a Series C round led by the Dohmen Corporation Foundation to scale its medically tailored meals programs and partner with health insurance payors on chronic disease cost reduction.[45]

However, evidence is increasingly clear that well-being is not created or sustained by individual medical, social, or environmental interventions, but by comprehensive combinations of them, supporting the person, their family/household, and their neighborhood. This reality creates an additional challenge for these issue specific outcomes-based payment approaches, where the outcome may well result from multiple factors beyond the control of any issue specific set of interventions.

To address this, the Investing in Flourishing initiative offers a glimpse of an even bolder vision for transforming health and social system funding around outcomes.[46] A cross sector effort launched with support from the Federal Reserve Bank of New York, the initiative aims to create a new model to finance the coordination and expansion of a full set of upstream health and social services for children, and their families and neighborhoods, that together can help set more young people for successful, healthy lives and reverse the tidal wave of chronic illnesses beginning in childhood that are driving overall health costs upward.

To coordinate the integrated delivery of, and payment for, these services, the initiative is convening local "Flourishing Councils" that will enter into contracts with a range of institutions in a community that would benefit from having more children, and their parents, flourishing and set up to be successful adults, including health programs (e.g., Medicaid), child welfare, school systems, criminal justice systems, and employers. The Council arranges loans from investors to pay for the expanded services upfront. The investors are repaid from the income generated by shared savings contracts between the Flourishing Council and downstream beneficiary organizations.

By stacking multiple shared savings (and revenue) agreements, community-led collaborations can generate substantial funding to invest upstream in family and community well-being, including covering principal and interest on loans. As the Initiative describes it, this work results in "children, families, and neighborhoods thrive without increasing government spending by tapping into commercial capital instead."[47] Supported by a national "Design Team," initial pilots (initially funded by philanthropy) are being developed in Cincinnati and Columbus, Ohio, Anne Arundel County, Maryland, and rural Upper Cumberland Valley, Tennessee.

As these examples illustrate, American healthcare cannot meaningfully shift toward prevention without investors willing to provide upfront capital for long-term health improvements. Whether through outcomes-based funds expanding nonprofit services, for-profit companies helping people stay healthy, or the flourishing council coordinating a range of interventions, investors are helping build the financial infrastructure required to shift the nation's focus from reacting to illness to preventing it.

While healthcare and the preceding chapters focused primarily on services enjoyed by people and families, investing in America can also be about investing to preserve a part of America we enjoy together: our abundant natural resources. As with issues like healthcare and education, the challenge is how we can get financing to the people who want to expand who can enjoy natural resources so they can compete on equal terms with the forces who want to exploit them.

This can be more difficult, as the few individuals who stand to benefit from exploiting natural resources tend to be more powerful and organized than the many people who will benefit from their preservation. But investors are finding innovative ways to get financing to farmers, loggers, fishermen, and forest clearing crews, so that they can benefit from and manage our abundant natural resources sustainably. The next chapter shows what is possible when investors can create pathways for people most likely to steward a natural resource to have control over it and for the people who benefit from natural resources to pay for part of the cost of preserving them.

7

We Should Be Able to Enjoy America's Abundant Land, Waters, and Wildlife and Pass Them on to Future Generations

A 2025 Senate bill proposing to sell 3.3 million acres of public land in the West achieved something few thought possible at the time: uniting an unlikely coalition of opponents from across a wide range of the political spectrum. From hunters and fishermen to hikers and climate change activists, the proposed bill revealed how passionate people are about preserving America's natural beauty and bounty.[1]

But much of our country's remarkable natural endowment—our forest lands and rivers, farmland and fisheries—is under threat from investors and corporations eager to maximize short-term profits regardless of long-term consequences. Policies created to preserve these resources can often have the unintended consequence of making it harder for community members with the greatest stake in preserving the resources to participate in managing them.

There are many ways to preserve our natural heritage while also sustaining jobs and economic development. But these often require upfront costs that few community members can afford, while generating long-term financial benefits they cannot wait for. These communities need investment partners who share the community's view that our natural heritage is worth more than just the dollars they can generate in the short term.

To harness private investment markets to the task of preserving land for future generations requires creative ways to make investment returns through preservation, not despite it.

- How can farmers secure the financing they need to cover the costs of transitioning farmland to sustainable production or for preserving water and soil health?
- How can investors find ways to get the water and electrical utility companies that benefit from living forests to pay for the cost of clearing them of the debris that fuels forest fires?
- How can small boat fishermen access financing to compete with industrial fishing companies to buy the quota necessary to stay in business?
- How can an environmental nonprofit partner with a major bank to create new platform for environmental investments?
- How can a timber company find ways to get paid for conserving forests rather than cutting them down?

The people and institutions this chapter highlights are answering these questions with models that can be expanded and replicated. This work is important and urgent because the relentless lure of corporate profit and the imperative to maximize financial returns will not go away, even as our lands and waterways become more vulnerable to development pressure and a changing climate.

Turning Seed Capital into Cover Crops: How a Foundation Harnesses All Its Assets to Finance Agricultural Transformation

On a crisp October morning in Hoffman, Minnesota, farmer Andrew Barsness crouches between rows of late-season maize, biting a kernel to test moisture. He manages about 900 acres, of which 270 are already certified organic with more in transition. As is typical in shifting to organic production, initially yields dipped, input costs rose, and for three years he earned no organic premium. Yet Barsness persisted because he was able to access financing designed to address this challenge. Through Mad Capital's Perennial Fund, he secured a flexible, five-year, interest-only loan to bridge the tough years of conversion.

"Taking this to conventional lenders felt frustrating," Barsness told the Rockefeller Foundation in 2024. "I was a novice, without a decades-long track record. And traditional lenders usually don't understand the switch to regenerative. I might as well have been growing bananas and oranges instead of corn and soy."[2]

Transitioning to organic or regenerative farming typically requires external financing. In the long term, an organic farm can benefit from premium pricing and lower input costs. But the short-term economics are punishing. During the mandatory three-year transition period, farmers must eliminate prohibited chemicals, often see yields drop, and shoulder new costs for equipment and certification. Revenues fall just as expenses rise. Traditional lenders, even the participants in the $500 billion US government-supported Farm Credit System, rarely step in, viewing these operations as too risky. As a result, many farmers cannot afford the transition, despite evidence that regenerative practices build resilience, sequester carbon, support biodiversity, and can help sustain family farms as viable businesses.

Mad Capital launched the Perennial Fund in 2020 to fill this financing gap. Supported with an operating grant from the US Department of Agriculture, the Boulder, Colorado-based nonprofit lender raised $10 million, mostly from mission-focused private foundation investors. The fund provides working capital loans and equipment or infrastructure financing structured around the "J-curve" of the transition: low or negative returns up front but growing profitability later. It aimed to prove that financing soil health can also generate durable financial returns.[3]

After supporting more than 30 farmers transition more than 100,000 acres through its first fund, Mad Capital raised Perennial Fund II (PFII). Initially targeting $25 million, PFII eventually secured more than $78 million by late 2025, with investors ranging from large family offices and foundations such as Sam Walton's grandson Lukas' Builders Vision, impact investors organized through the TONIIC network, and private foundations.[4] The new capital allows loans for farmland, infrastructure, and working capital tied to regenerative and organic practices across the United States.

One of Perennial's early, catalytic investors was the Woodcock Foundation, a New York-based family foundation established in 1996 whose mission spans democracy, economic opportunity, and environmental stewardship.[5] As a relatively small foundation with assets less than $100 million taking on massive challenges, the Foundation decided that it made sense to put all their assets to work for the mission. Over the last decade, Woodcock's trustees have deliberately aligned their endowment with their program goals, pursuing what they call "a portfolio where every investment has a positive impact."[6]

In 2020, Woodcock formally committed to work to achieving 100% mission alignment across its endowment. (By mid-2025, they reported 90% progress toward that goal.) Without the resources to hire a dedicated impact investing team, the Foundation revised its Investment Policy Statement (IPS) to give their outside investment managers a clear impact investing mandate: "We are committed to an impact-focused portfolio with the goal of leveraging our full asset base for both financial returns and positive social and environmental impact. . .Our intention is to combine grantmaking, PRIs/catalytic investments, and market-rate investments to further the mission of the Foundation."[7] To make sure their investment portfolio truly reflects the intentions of this revised IPS, the Foundation switched investment advisors twice to partner with the best-fit firm to achieve both their financial and impact objectives.

Regenerative agriculture is a central program area for Woodcock. It uses grants to support nonprofit groups that advance food-system reform, rural livelihoods, and environmental restoration. It has also invested in numerous agriculture and forestry funds that support regenerative land stewardship. By backing Perennial, Woodcock aligned its capital with the same systems change its grantees fight for.

Beyond financing the short-term costs of transitioning to organic production, other financing innovations are rewarding farmers who steward their land for future generations. The Soil & Water Outcomes Fund (SWOF) offers a leading example of how capital can reward farmers not just for what they grow, but for the environmental outcomes their fields deliver.

Managed by a subsidiary of the Iowa Soybean Association (ISA), in partnership with Quantified Ventures, SWOF uses an outcomes-based model that pays farmers for verified improvements in soil health, water quality, and greenhouse-gas reductions. Farmers are compensated for results generated by cover crops, reduced tillage, improved nutrient management, and diversified rotations, creating a new revenue stream tied directly to environmental performance.[8]

The model works by "stacking" buyers. Watershed utilities and public agencies purchase documented water-quality benefits, while food and beverage companies purchase emissions reductions to meet supply-chain decarbonization goals. Those outcome payments flow back to farmers through multi-year contracts, with average payments of roughly $30–$35 per acre, competitive with traditional cost-share programs.[9]

What began as a small Iowa pilot in 2020 has scaled rapidly. By 2023, SWOF enrolled more than 300,000 acres across 14 states, paying $10.5 million directly to farmers in a single year for verified outcomes.[10] By 2024–2025, the program had expanded to 1.7 million acres across 21 states, with more than $55 million paid to farmers and measurable reductions in nutrient runoff and greenhouse-gas emissions.[11]

Corporate commitments are anchoring this growth. In 2023, PepsiCo and Walmart announced a seven-year, $120 million collaboration explicitly citing SWOF as a vehicle for delivering regenerative outcomes at scale.[12] For farmers, the contracts make conservation pay. For investors and buyers, SWOF demonstrates how outcomes-based finance can align farm profitability with long-term stewardship of soil and water, turning environmental performance into a durable asset rather than an unfunded mandate.

For farmers like Andrew Barsness, Perennial's flexible loans make sustainable transitions possible. For investors like Woodcock, they exemplify how endowments can finance climate mitigation and land conservation directly without waiting for policy or philanthropy alone to do the work and how a small family foundation can harness all its assets to punch above its impact weight.

Burn Capital: Making Wildfire Prevention an Investable Asset

A pale morning haze lingered over the slopes of the Tahoe National Forest in California as crews began thinning dense understory and preparing prescribed fire breaks. In the past, such work would have waited until after a catastrophic blaze. Now, thanks to Blue Forest's Forest Resilience Bond (FRB), investors fronted the money to pay for this restoration work. It's a classic case of solving the "wrong-pocket" problem. What if those who depend on healthy forests—utilities, governments, corporations, and communities—could co-invest in their preservation?

The FRB idea was born among a team of finance and investment experts, scientists, and engineers at UC Berkeley's Haas School of Business in 2015. The Rim Fire, which tore across 250,000 acres of Stanislaus National Forest and Yosemite, was an ever-present memory, driving the team to find a solution to the catastrophic wildfire problem facing much of the Western United States. Among them was Zach Knight, a former Wall Street bond trader at Merrill Lynch, steeped in structured finance, securitization, and derivatives, who had left the trading floor to pursue an MBA focused on sustainability and impact investing. Together with classmates Nick Wobbrock, Chad Reed, and Leigh Madeira, they won the 2015 Kellogg-Morgan Stanley Sustainable Investing Challenge with the FRB concept, gaining validation and critical introductions to investors.

From that spark, Knight co-founded Blue Forest in 2015. Two years later, Blue Forest signed an MOU with the US Forest Service, and in 2018 launched the $4 million Yuba I FRB in Tahoe National Forest, protecting over 8,000 acres with thinning, meadow restoration, prescribed fire, and invasive species removal.

Why do we need a Forest Resilience Bond?

Nearly one-third of the 193 million acres of land managed by the USDA Forest Service faces high or very high wildfire risk. Restoring these priority areas to reduce fire risk is estimated to cost $65 billion, more than the agency can afford, and involve implementing complex science-based practices at scale.

However, the Forest Service isn't the only entity that relies on healthy, resilient forests. Water utilities, private landowners, and even corporate supply chains depend on them for water security, infrastructure protection, and wildfire risk reduction. But these stakeholders cannot invest in ways that match their incentives or timelines, leaving restoration efforts fragmented and struggling to keep up with rapidly expanding needs.

Blue Forest was created to help solve this problem, not by replacing public funding, but by designing financial tools that attract new capital and reduce risk for those who benefit from resilient forests. By pooling resources across public and private sectors, Blue Forest accelerates work that would otherwise stall due to funding gaps and positions restoration as an economically sound investment in water security, infrastructure protection, and climate resilience. In the $4 million Yuba I project, investors, including the Rockefeller Foundation, Gordon & Betty Moore Foundation, Calvert Impact Capital, and CSAA Insurance, fronted the restoration costs, while the Yuba Water Agency, California Department of Fire and Forestry (CalFire), and the Forest Service repaid the investors with interest. Knight explains that this model brings private capital and public benefit together, enabling forest service plans to proceed at the speed and scale needed. He notes that "stakeholders are increasingly aware that this is not a science problem, it is a finance problem."[13]

By 2024, Blue Forest had launched six FRBs, mobilizing $21.3 million in funding to support restoration projects protecting 28,312 acres in California, Oregon, and Washington state.[14] Yet, it was clear that the forest restoration problem didn't stop with project funding, leading Blue Forest to expand their work beyond structuring forest resilience bonds. At the core of this strategic pivot is Blue Forest Asset Management (BFAM), a platform making direct equity and debt investments along the entire forest restoration value chain from harvesting and hauling operations to adding processing capacity and creating new market demand for forest products. Its first fund under management, the California Wildfire Innovation Fund (CWIF), launched with a $25 million investment commitment each from CSAA Insurance Group and California's Infrastructure and Economic Development

Bank (Ibank), providing flexible funding to companies delivering scalable wildfire resilience that can yield both impact and financial return.[15]

One early investment, BurnBot, is a mechanized vegetation management innovator. BurnBot raised $20 million in Series A funding, backed by Blue Forest alongside Toyota Ventures, ReGen Ventures, and others, to scale its RV-like RX1 systems and AI-driven vegetation treatment services and has gone on to raise the next round of capital. BurnBot's RX1 transforms prescribed burns into a precision, mechanized, year-round operation that can treat fire-prone terrain 10 times faster with minimal escape risk.[16]

In addition to new investments, Blue Forest continues to work closely with the USDA Forest Service and Indigenous communities, recognizing that listening and learning from the original stewards of these lands is essential to creating a more resilient and equitable future. To date, they have helped unlock $2.91 million in funding for Indigenous-led initiatives, and in 2025 launched their first tribally-led and implemented FRB, the Colfax I FRB.

From the haze over Tahoe to smoke-clear valleys, Blue Forest is demonstrating that with the right financial structures, private investors can be powerful allies and partners to overstretched government agencies, restoring America's forests before disaster strikes.

Go Fish: How Small-Boat Fishermen Are Using Community Ownership to Stay on the Water

On a crisp spring morning in Sitka, Alaska, fisherman Tracy Sylvester readies her boat, Faithful, for another day on the water. She has been part of the Local Fish Fund, a community permit bank that helped her and over 100 local fishermen secure access to halibut and sablefish (also known as black cod) quotas they would otherwise be unable to afford. "Quota has been great because it creates accountability and safety," she explains. But "it's our parents who own this quota, and younger people just can't afford to buy in." Through this community-based loan, she found a path onto the water without taking on crushing debt.[17]

Her experience is rooted in Alaska but reflects a broader national reality. Alaska represents one of the most severe cases of fisheries loss in the country, with rural and Native communities losing much of their access to the resource. While the loss is especially visible in Southeast Alaska, fishermen across the country from New England to the Gulf of Mexico share a common concern. The cost of entering quota managed fisheries has climbed so high that entire generations are struggling to get on the water.[18]

This early morning scene captures the purpose of Catch Together: to bridge the access gap between small, locally owned fishing businesses and increasingly expensive quota markets. In many US fisheries, catch shares such as Individual Transferable Quotas give fishermen a fixed share of the total allowable catch. These systems were created to support conservation, but the high cost of securing quota makes it difficult for new or smaller operators to participate. Fishermen must pay upfront for quota, competing with established boats and large firms, including some backed by foreign investment capital, that can outbid local, American-owned businesses. Traditional banks usually will not lend on quota, viewing it as too volatile, leaving small boat operators with few financing options and vulnerable to consolidation.

Recognizing this threat to resource stewardship and the survival of local economies, Paul Parker, a veteran fisherman and community advocate, began developing an alternative in 2005. On Cape Cod, he helped pioneer one of the nation's first community permit banks, early models showing that when fishing rights are held in community structures rather than dispersed through individual leases, fishermen gain stability, young entrants gain opportunity, and coastal towns retain control over the resource that defines them.

In 2017, Parker and colleagues founded Catch Together, building on those lessons while moving toward something more ambitious: not just preserving access, but building shared ownership. Fishermen made clear that while affordable leases helped, lasting stability required having a collective stake and a collective voice.

This led to Catch Together's next chapter: supporting fishermen in building community owned cooperatives that collectively hold quota, share costs and risk, and govern their fisheries together. These cooperatives take the permit bank idea one step further, moving from shared access to shared control. Cooperative models are now emerging in Sitka,

New England, and the Gulf, where groups like the Reef Fish Shareholders Alliance have expanded access for small-scale boats while reducing bycatch and strengthening income stability.

Cooperatives recognize something fundamental: fishermen can weather uncertainty more effectively together than alone, and when communities hold quota collectively, economic and cultural value stays rooted in the places that rely on the water most. As project leader Hugh Cipparone explains, "Fishing communities from around the country face a variety of threats . . . By investing in cooperatives, we are not just preserving livelihoods, we are empowering fishermen to take control of a shared and more hopeful future."

Quota systems were created to preserve natural resources, limiting harvest to sustainable levels. But the system is only as just as the people who are able to fish under it. Without equitable financing and shared governance, consolidation accelerates, sidelining local businesses and weakening community resilience. With support from Builders Vision, the Walton Family Foundation, the Campbell Foundation, and many others, Parker and the Catch Together community have helped show that another path is possible, allowing communities to acquire fishing rights, reduce risk for small boat operators, and keep control in local hands.

As fisherman Jeff Turner of Alaska put it, "Fishing isn't just a job. It's a responsibility. We are the ones who protect the resource because we depend on it."

Catch Together offers a scalable solution. It gives small boat fishermen avenues to access quota, share risk, keep money local, and align economic incentives with conservation.[19]

Suits and Trees: The Unlikely Partnership Rewiring Capital Markets for Conservation

In the misty hollows of Appalachia, along the Tennessee–Kentucky–Virginia ridgelines, a 254,000-acre working forest is now managed for climate, wildlife, and local jobs instead of being chopped into speculative parcels. The Cumberland Forest Project is a $130 million, privately managed investment that generates financial returns from sustainable timber, carbon, and recreation while permanently protecting 121,472 ecologically critical tracts through conservation easements now managed for water quality and biodiversity.[20]

While this may sound like the natural work of a government forest management agency, it's an asset of NatureVest, a financing arm of the nonprofit The Nature Conservancy, launched in 2014 in partnership with the megabank JPMorgan Chase.

How did a decades-old nature nonprofit become a partner to a global bank? In 2014, The Nature Conservancy (TNC) and JPMorgan Chase launched NatureVest as an impact-investment platform created to attract private capital to conservation projects and scale market-based solutions for protecting land and water.[21] For TNC's then-CEO, Mark Tercek, a former Goldman Sachs banker, the partnership reflected a pragmatic evolution in how conservation could be financed at scale, combining philanthropic goals with investment discipline. Buying and managing large tracts of land for conservation often required more upfront capital than TNC could raise through donations alone, while assets such as the Cumberland Forest Project demonstrated that sustainably managed landscapes could generate financial returns capable of repaying investors. From the outset, NatureVest set out to "build private investments that use commercial capital to deliver conservation at scale."[22] A decade later, NatureVest reports a portfolio representing roughly $4 billion in committed capital, with cumulative outcomes including 7.5 million acres sustainably managed, 153,635 acres permanently protected, and major freshwater systems restored across the United States.[23]

In addition to Cumberland Forest, NatureVest is advancing water projects in the US heartland. For example, TNC's 6,000-acre Emiquon Preserve in Illinois reflects investments in reconnecting floodplain habitats and restoring wetlands to improve water quality and resilience, one of the Midwest's largest floodplain restoration efforts. In Iowa, the Cedar River restoration project protects nearly 40,000 acres of public and private lands.[24]

Crucially, NatureVest matches a range of capital sources to fit different projects. As NatureVest Managing Director Charlotte Kaiser explained in a 2021 interview, Cumberland Forest Fund investors were primarily family offices, foundation endowments, and high-net-worth individuals, while a larger vehicle like the Sustainable Water Impact Fund attracted institutional investors. Higher-risk projects sought foundation money structured as Program Related Investments. At the same time, TNC itself co-invests. By 2021, it had committed $77 million of its own money to NatureVest projects around the world.[25]

This capital structure reflects NatureVest's roots. JPMorgan Chase provided the founding capital to build the platform, an initial $5 million and multi-year support. Philanthropic foundations such as the Gordon and Betty Moore Foundation and the David and Lucile Packard Foundation funded the design phase and research, while advisors from EKO Asset Management Partners (now Encourage Capital) helped map the emerging natural capital marketplace. Since then, the model has matured into a portfolio that attracts institutional investors, sovereign partners, foundations, and families alike.

From JPMorgan Chase's vantage point, backing NatureVest was also about market design, building investable product where pent-up demand exists. The bank later noted it had provided founding support "to help spur exactly this kind of market development," with clients seeking conservation opportunities and the sector showing measurable growth.[26]

Two features make the collaboration distinctive. First, it is institution-to-institution: a top investment bank contributes structuring expertise, convening power, and multi-year funding, while a science-led nonprofit sources, diligences, and governs projects to embed conservation outcomes in term sheets, covenants, and operating plans. NatureVest's 2024 report details how each transaction includes a formal "Impact Strategy," with targets inserted into legal documents and reporting protocols, an architecture that aims to survive market cycles. Second, the partnership scales across asset classes, from timberland equity to water rights to conservation tourism, seeding a diversified, repeatable portfolio.

NatureVest has demonstrated a replicable approach: use credible conservation science to define outcomes, structure risk-adjusted returns to attract capital, and then prove that landscapes and watersheds can be protected profitably. The ridgelines of Cumberland, the floodplains of Emiquon, and the Cedar River landscapes are among the tangible proof points that creative partnerships can invest in preserving America's natural resources.

Return on Preservation: Driving Investor Returns by Stewarding Forests

On a fog-laden morning in southern West Virginia, a logging operation hums quietly on a steep Appalachian slope. A specialized winch-assist harvester, tethered to its anchor, inches forward, felling timber with mechanical precision. Inside the cab, an operator is safe from the hazards that once came with chainsaws and loose footing.

These are the Lyme Timber–managed Mountaineer Timberlands, preserved not only for their timber value but also for safer rural jobs and ecological integrity. This outcome was made possible by $20 million in New Markets Tax Credit financing in 2018. Lyme used this public–private structure to bring state-of-the-art mechanized harvesting to Appalachia, a move that protected jobs, improved safety, and ensured the long-term conservation of more than 118,000 acres of forest.[27]

The Mountaineer project exemplifies Lyme Timber's approach to managing working forests that can deliver competitive financial returns while protecting their ecological and social benefits: identify funding sources willing to pay for those benefits. Founded in 1976, The Lyme Timber Company now manages 1.3 million acres across the Northeast, Appalachia, the Lake States, and the South funded through more than $700 million of institutional investment capital.

Lyme's strategy developed when Peter Stein, a veteran of the conservation world, joined the firm in 1990. Stein had spent more than a decade at the Trust for Public Land, where he learned how to structure complex transactions that aligned conservation and economic outcomes. His arrival marked the start of Lyme's deliberate focus on partnering with government agencies and conservation nonprofits to secure permanent protections for the lands it manages.[28]

Lyme's approach seeks to identify ways to drive revenue from conservation practices in order to sustainably scale them. The firm acquires high-quality timberlands, often certified by the Forest Stewardship Council or the Sustainable Forestry Initiative, and then sells working-forest conservation easements while maintaining active, sustainable forestry operations. State natural resource agencies or conservation organizations typically purchase these easements, commitments to permanently limit development on these lands.

For Lyme's investors these proceeds help de-risk the investment and return capital early in the holding period, allowing investors to enjoy steady returns while ensuring lasting conservation. For the nonprofits and government agencies, these easements allow them to protect more land than they would be able to if buying the land directly. While government-funded easements that protect forest land typically enjoy widespread political support, they are seldomly funded at levels that would allow state agencies to do this work alone.

Institutional capital has been central to Lyme's growth. The firm has raised a series of closed-end funds, each larger than the last, scaling from one-off $1–10 million acquisitions to multi-hundred-million-dollar portfolios. Its investors include endowments, foundations, insurance companies, and pension funds, many with an explicit mandate to invest in nature conservation.

In 2019, Lyme expanded beyond traditional timberland deals, launching the $50 million Lyme Conservation Opportunities Fund to invest in mitigation banking and forest carbon projects.[29] Through this fund, Lyme purchases land that contributes ecologically important streams, wetlands, and endangered species habitat. Real estate developers, required by law to offset negative environmental impacts of projects elsewhere, purchase credits from Lyme that these lands produced once they are certified for their ecological benefit. Other corporations committed to reducing their carbon footprint similarly pay Lyme for forest restoration projects that sequester carbon. Early investments in the fund include projects to restore and preserve wetlands in Central Florida and the Fort Worth, Texas region.

Generating reliable long-term economic and environmental value also helps Lyme Timber access lower-cost investment capital. Lyme acquired the West Virginia Mountaineer Timberlands with the help of New Markets Tax Credits, a federal subsidy aimed at encouraging private investment in low-income communities (the same program that helped finance some of the affordable housing and health clinic investments described in Chapter 6). Lyme used the financing not only to sustain the forest as a working landscape but also to introduce safer, more efficient logging technologies that could be replicated elsewhere.[30] In this way, a federal tax program designed to spur economic development became a tool for advancing environmental resilience and workforce safety. In Pennsylvania and elsewhere, Lyme has also tapped into state clean water revolving funds to help finance acquisitions.[31]

Leveraging tools like conservation easements, carbon markets, and public finance programs enables Lyme to generate financial returns for investors on par with its competitors. This work does lead to inevitable controversy and criticism that Lyme's profit motive is ultimately incompatible with environmental commitment. But walking the line between profit and environmental protection has allowed Lyme Timber to tap large pools of institutional capital while also serving as steppingstone for impact investors eager to see their capital put to work to preserve American forests.

While our forests and farms and fisheries are a set of public goods Americans have always relied on, increasingly our technology platforms play a similar role: an essential part of our daily lives even if often in the background of our day-to-day decisions. As with our natural resources, this is an area where large companies are making decisions to maximize short-term profits while others muster counter-efforts to balance profit and public benefit. As with our natural resources, this is often not a level playing field when it comes to which side can access financing. The next chapter describes how investors are finding a range of ways to invest in a future where more Americans can access technology and in which our technology is as good for us and our country as it is for the companies profiting from it.

8 | Technology Should Be Accessible and Safe

Few forces are reshaping American life as quickly or as unevenly as technology. In little more than a decade, digital platforms, artificial intelligence, and data-driven systems have become central to how Americans work, learn, communicate, shop, receive healthcare, and participate in civic life.

Technology is creating sweeping consequences across nearly every domain Americans care about: wages and job security, mental health, education, access to information, and economic mobility. Decisions made today about how technologies are designed, financed, governed, and deployed will reverberate for decades.

Private investment is accelerating this transformation at an extraordinary scale. In 2024 alone, global private investment in artificial intelligence exceeded $100 billion, with US companies capturing the majority of that funding.[1] That total exceeds all grantmaking by US based foundations. Venture capital, private equity, and corporate balance sheets are pouring money into technologies that promise rapid growth and outsized returns. That capital rewards speed, scale, and engagement, often before the social consequences of new tools are fully understood.

Unsurprisingly, Americans are uneasy. Taken together, survey data from Pew Research Center, the US Surgeon General, and the American Psychological Association show that while Americans recognize technology's benefits, a majority are concerned that digital platforms and AI are undermining mental health, job security, and social cohesion.[2] Parents, educators, and health professionals increasingly associate social media use with rising rates of anxiety, depression, loneliness, and sleep disruption among children and adolescents.[3] Adults also report feeling overwhelmed, isolated, or manipulated by algorithm-driven platforms designed to maximize attention.

At the same time, artificial intelligence is introducing a new layer of economic uncertainty. While AI promises productivity gains, it also threatens to disrupt millions of jobs, including in white-collar occupations that were once considered insulated from automation. Many American workers worry about whether technology will create new opportunities fast enough to replace the ones it displaces and who will benefit from those gains.

Avoiding harm is only one side of the technology challenge. The other is uneven access. For all the talk of a digital economy, tens of millions of Americans still lack reliable, affordable high-speed internet. Rural communities, Tribal lands, and low-income urban neighborhoods are disproportionately affected.[4] Students without broadband struggle to complete homework. Small businesses cannot compete online. Patients miss out on telehealth services. In an economy where digital access increasingly determines opportunity, lack of connectivity becomes a structural barrier to participation.

Taken together, these dynamics present a twin challenge: ensuring that all Americans can access the benefits of technology, while also ensuring that technology does not undermine mental health, economic security, or democracy. Market forces are not going to drive mainstream investors to solve these challenges. Their incentives to pursue the fastest and biggest returns will continue to flow capital to technology companies optimized for advertising, engagement, and growth at all costs that have amplified polarization, exploited attention, and externalized social harms.

Against this tide, what can investors who care about long-term outcomes for Americans do differently? This chapter explores three complementary approaches investors are using to capitalize alternative business models that balance profitability with access and safety.

- How can investors help expand who has access to technology by financing the infrastructure that enables participation in the digital economy, even where conventional investors see limited upside?

  Community broadband is a prime example. Providers serving rural and low-income areas often offer stable but modest returns, too small for private equity, too risky for traditional lenders. The non-profit investor Connect Humanity is stepping into this gap, assembling blended capital stacks that combine public funding with mission-aligned investment that supports left-behind communities to develop and own high-quality internet services.
- How can investors expand who can access the start-up capital often required to turn an idea into a product or service at scale?

  Venture funding still flows disproportionately to a narrow set of founders pursuing businesses that serve relatively well-off customers, often disconnected from the challenges most Americans face. Firms like Kapor Capital have developed new investment frameworks that explicitly evaluate whether technology products address real social needs and whether founding teams reflect the full range of American communities. By changing how investment decisions are made, these investors seek to redirect innovation toward solving problems such as financial exclusion, biased algorithms, or inequitable access to education.
- How can "impact owners" buy a stake in and influence the companies building essential technologies that will shape our future?

  Sometimes, investors conclude that the only way to change a technology's trajectory is to own it. This concept of impact ownership rests on a simple premise: when platforms shape public discourse, mental health, or economic opportunity at massive scale, governance matters as much as innovation. Buying equity stakes, or even entire companies, becomes a way to embed different values directly into how technology is run.

Technology will continue to transform American life. Will this transformation support or harm America's long-term future? These investors are finding ways to invest in a technology future that brings more people access to technology that helps more Americans.

A Tale of Two Networks: Financing Community Ownership for Rural Broadband

The rural town of Enfield, North Carolina, where more than one in three families live below the federal poverty line, took a meaningful step toward digital equity in 2022. A $350,000 investment enabled local internet service provider Wave 7 Communications to begin expanding its fixed-wireless network, bringing affordable broadband to more than 400 households in a community of just over 2,300 people.[5]

Wave 7 was founded by LaShawn Williamson, who visited Enfield regularly through her husband's family and became increasingly frustrated by the area's limited and expensive internet connectivity options. Incumbent providers often charged close to $100 per month for unreliable service. With Connect Humanity's financing, Wave 7 began offering symmetrical broadband plans starting at $40 per month, with higher-speed options available and a policy of not disconnecting customers who fall behind on payments.[6]

Enfield's experience reflects a broader national challenge. While federal data now suggest that most US households technically have access to broadband meeting the FCC's 100/20 Mbps benchmark, competition remains thin. More than a third of Americans have access to only one high-speed provider or none at all, leaving many communities with little leverage over price, quality, or reliability.[7]

The social consequences of this gap are well documented. Broadband access increasingly determines access to education, healthcare, and economic opportunity. During the COVID-19 pandemic, students sat in parking lots to complete homework, rural patients struggled to access telehealth services, and small businesses faced limits on participation in the digital economy. The damage of being shut out of affordable and reliable internet is likely to get worse.[8]

Yet the economics of rural broadband remain misaligned with conventional investment models. Extending fiber or fixed-wireless infrastructure to sparsely populated areas can cost as much as or more than urban builds, but with far fewer customers per mile. A well-run, rural broadband network can generate reliable profits, but not at the level that would attract private equity investors. The mainstream debt providers, for whom the financial return prospects could work, consider these investments too risky.[9]

Public funding has helped but not solved the problem. Over the past decade, more than $100 billion in federal and state subsidies have been allocated to broadband expansion, yet progress has been uneven. Funds have often gone to incumbent providers, outdated technologies, or auction bids that ultimately proved infeasible to execute.[10]

Connect Humanity was created to address this structural financing gap. The nonprofit impact investor provides low-cost, flexible, non-dilutive loans and revenue-based financing to community-centric broadband providers such as municipal networks, electric cooperatives, Tribal ISPs, and small local operators that commit to affordability and universal service.[11]

It is built on the core insight that community broadband networks can offer reliable revenues and profits. This may not meet private equity expectations, but as Connect Humanity CIO Brian Vo explained in a 2025 interview, they generate "a type of cashflow that was utility-like with monthly recurring revenue . . . uncorrelated to market returns" that can service affordable debt.[12]

As a nonprofit investor focused on expanding affordable broadband, Connect Humanity tackles market complexity that drives other investors away. It invests alongside government grant programs such as BEAD and ReConnect, helping providers meet matching requirements and accelerate construction timelines. In Alabama's Macon County, for example, a $500,000 Connect Humanity loan helped unlock $3.9 million in total capital to extend fiber to more than 5,500 residents and businesses.

Connect Humanity embeds digital equity covenants directly into its financing agreements. These provisions require transparent pricing, prohibit digital redlining, and encourage ongoing engagement with local stakeholders, seeking to ensure that community outcomes remain central even as networks scale. Rather than trying to minimize community influence, as mainstream developers often do, Vo sees Connect Humanity's mandate to give community members a seat at the table of network design and to preserve affordability.[13] Unlike private-equity models that acquire and consolidate local ISPs, Connect Humanity avoids taking ownership stakes. Communities retain control of their infrastructure, while capital is repaid through predictable cash flows tied to service delivery rather than exits.[14]

Connect Humanity has invested an initial pilot portfolio of roughly $4 million, tracking around a 12% gross internal rate of return, with particularly strong performance reported from its revenue-based financing investments. Across grants and investments, Connect Humanity reported in 2024 that it helped partners unlock more than $112 million in broadband funding for network construction and adoption efforts.[15]

That proof of concept has allowed the organization to articulate a broader ambition: helping to build a durable capital market for community broadband. Connect Humanity has begun working with the Federal Reserve Banks of New York and Dallas on efforts to crowd in private capital and has publicly outlined plans to raise a $50–$100 million Community Broadband Fund to scale this approach nationally.[16] Raising capital is a challenge, however, when financial returns sit above what foundations typically seek in their Program-Related Investments but still below what mainstream investors expect for the risk they perceive in this approach.

The Enfield project illustrates what becomes possible when capital is structured for public good rather than short-term gain. Students can participate fully in online learning, small businesses can reach customers beyond county lines, and seniors can access telehealth without leaving home. Connect Humanity's experience suggests that rural broadband is not an intractable infrastructure challenge. It is a solvable investment problem when incentives are aligned with community outcomes.

Gap Closing Investment in Technology

When Mitch Kapor helped create Lotus 1-2-3 in the early 1980s, he helped unlock the personal computer as a tool for everyday work. Lotus' software enabled millions of people to perform complex financial and analytical tasks without specialized training for the first time. That experience left Kapor with a lasting conviction that technology can dramatically expand opportunity, but only if it is intentionally designed to do so. Decades later, that belief would become the foundation of Kapor Capital.

Kapor Capital's co-founder, Freada Kapor Klein, arrived at technology from a different direction. Trained as a social policy researcher, her career focused on workplace systems: how hiring, promotion, and organizational culture determine who thrives and who is pushed out. In 1984, she joined

Lotus to lead employee relations and organizational development, charged with building a more humane and inclusive employer long before diversity and inclusion became standard concerns in the tech sector.

Together, the Kapors translated these complementary perspectives—software as leverage and workplace systems as destiny—into Kapor Capital, an Oakland-based venture capital firm founded in 2009. The firm invests in early-stage technology companies designed to close gaps of access, opportunity, and outcome, particularly for low-income communities and communities of color.[17]

This philosophy is operationalized through Kapor Capital's gap-closing framework. The firm begins analysis of potential investee companies by identifying a specific, measurable gap the company aims to close such as unequal access to quality jobs, financial stability, or essential services. Kapor Capital then evaluates whether the company's core product or business model directly narrows that gap, whether growth reinforces that outcome, and whether the business can scale sustainably. They seek to invest in companies that embed gap-closing impact in the mechanics of how it creates value.[18]

Mitch Kapor has described this approach in simple terms: investors should ask whether technology is bringing the top and bottom of society closer together, or pushing them further apart. That question acts as a filter for capital deployment, governance expectations, and founder support.

Kapor Capital has developed a similar approach to assessing the founders of the companies seeking its capital. They focus on "distance traveled" rather than reviewing a founder's credentials out of context. Using this approach, for example, a state university graduate who is the first in her family to have attended college would likely have traveled further than an Ivy League graduate who attended her parents' alma mater. This approach seeks to assess the founder's leadership potential, not to apply affirmative action criteria.

Kapor Capital has shown that this approach can deliver strong financial performance. As of 2024, Kapor Capital had invested over $106 million into more than 170 companies. The firm publicly disclosed the results of its early funds, reporting top-quartile IRR and TVPI compared to venture benchmarks between 2011–2019.[19] And rather than holding onto proprietary investment insights, the Kapors shared their approach to investment screening in their 2023 book *Closing the Equity Gap*, encouraging other venture capitalists to copy them.[20]

Several Kapor Capital portfolio companies illustrate how gap-closing technology works in practice.

- Interviewing.io addresses bias embedded in technical hiring. Traditional recruiting processes privilege pedigree, networks, and resume signals that systematically disadvantage some capable engineers. Interviewing.io enables candidates to demonstrate skills directly, and often anonymously, through technical interviews, expanding access to high-growth technology jobs and helping employers identify overlooked talent.

- As teachers and parents worry about the sweeping disruption of AI to student learning, Newsela is instead improving K–12 student literacy by delivering tailored and engaging learning materials. Newsela reports that its platform has more than 40 million registered students and over 3 million registered teachers, operating in roughly 90% of US K–12 schools. Newsela is also a financial success so far, reaching unicorn $1 billion valuation status in 2021 with a $100 million Series D capital raise.

- Penny Finance tackles the longstanding divide in access to financial guidance. Personalized financial planning has traditionally been available only to affluent households. Penny Finance uses technology to deliver tailored financial mentoring to people without access to traditional advisors, helping users make informed decisions about budgeting, saving, and long-term financial health.

Kapor Capital is setting out to demonstrate that when investors deliberately align capital with gap-closing outcomes, technology can become a tool for shared prosperity rather than a force that deepens inequality.

A Seat at the Table: Why Foundations Bought Private Stock in an AI Giant

What can a charitable foundation do when many of the most consequential forces shaping people's lives are driven by private investment on an unprecedented scale? And what happens when the grants, policy advocacy, and research they fund seem vanishingly small compared to the hundreds of billions of private capital flowing into new technologies?

These questions are confronting many American foundations as artificial intelligence moves rapidly from research labs into workplaces, schools, healthcare systems, and government services. Massive private investment is accelerating AI's development, setting the pace and direction of change for technologies with the potential to shape economic opportunity, the quality and availability of jobs, access to information, and democratic accountability. In 2024, private venture and equity investment in AI alone exceeded total US foundation grantmaking across all issue areas.[21]

It was in this context that, in early 2024, the Omidyar Network brought together Ford Foundation and Nathan Cummings Foundation to purchase shares in the AI company Anthropic, one of the leading artificial intelligence companies behind models such as Claude.[22,i] At a moment when most capital flowing into frontier AI was focused on speed, scale, and competitive advantage, these institutions invested with a different objective: to attempt to ensure that public interest considerations help shape decisions about the development and deployment of AI.

According to Omidyar Network CEO Mike Kubzansky, the Network purchased Anthropic shares to help influence its direction. The purchase was made into a company "recognized for its commitment to transparency, accountability, and safety" as a way of "ensuring a voice on the cap table to help the company preserve and achieve its stated social impact considerations and guardrails."[23] While the foundations did not own as many shares as other investors, they believed their public standing as institutions recognized for their commitment to people and society, and their expertise in addressing social issues, would enable them to enter into meaningful dialogue with the company's leadership.

For both Ford and Omidyar, the Anthropic investment fits within longerstanding approaches to using capital to shape markets. Ford Foundation was an early pioneer of impact investing among foundations, helping to formalize Program Related Investments in the 1969 tax reform bill, and then went on

---

[i] The shares became available as part of a sale of the estate of Sam Bankman-Fried. In addition to the foundations, major investors included a sovereign wealth fund, hedge fund, and institutional investors.

to build a global PRI portfolio. Under the leadership of Darren Walker, a former Wall Street lawyer and community investor in Harlem, it extended its impact investing approaches in 2017, creating a new Mission Investing team with a mandate to invest $1 billion of Ford Foundation's endowment over 10 years in investments that could shift mainstream capital markets and business to support Ford's aim of reducing inequality.[24,ii]

Under this approach, Ford has made targeted investments intended to build missing market infrastructure or demonstrate alternative business models, including anchor investments in Novata, an impact-data platform designed to support private-market accountability, and Nine Dean, a holding company aiming to show that firms that invest more deliberately in workers can outperform peers over time.[25]

Seen in this light, Ford's decision to invest in Anthropic is consistent with its broader mission investing strategy: an effort to engage early with a company likely to shape core economic and social systems, and to influence how questions of accountability, equity, and human impact are addressed as the technology matures.

Omidyar Network's path to the Anthropic investment follows a similar logic, shaped by a different institutional history. Founded in 2004 after Pierre Omidyar's sale of eBay, Omidyar Network was built around what Amy Klement, one of its early senior leaders, described as a "problem first, tool second" philosophy, starting with the underlying social challenge and then selecting the mix of grants, investments, policy work, and ecosystem building most likely to address it.

Over time, this approach led Omidyar to work across financial inclusion, civic participation, independent media, education, and digital governance. As portfolios matured, Omidyar spun out independent entities, including Flourish Ventures (financial inclusion), Luminate (civic engagement and digital rights), Imaginable Futures (education), and Spero Ventures (early-stage emerging technology), while the Network refocused on upstream systemic change.

In recent years, the Network has increasingly focused on artificial intelligence. Omidyar has combined grants, policy engagement, and

---

[ii]The author was an advisor to Walker and the Ford Board in the development of this new program.

selective investments on the view that ownership can provide a more durable channel for influence than external advocacy alone.

By the end of 2025, the foundations' Anthropic investment was on a trajectory to pay off financially. The company's latest round of funding valued the company at almost $200 billion with the potential for a $300 billion IPO in 2026.[26] Whether the purchase can influence the way Anthropic develops and deploys its products, and how they impact people, remains to be seen. Regardless of the outcome, it is an important innovation for foundations seeking to fulfill their missions at a time when massive private investment in disruptive technology is driving so many social outcomes.

Impact Ownership: The People's Bid for TikTok

What to do when you believe a company's fundamental business model is producing widespread social harm? Regulation can set guardrails at the margins, and philanthropy can fund research, pilots, and alternatives. But, neither directly alters the incentives embedded in how a business makes money. In those cases, the most direct way to change outcomes may be the bluntest one: to buy the company and run it differently. That was the logic behind billionaire businessman Frank McCourt's "People's Bid" to acquire the US operations of video platform TikTok, to put long-standing ideas about a healthier internet into practice.

As of 2024, TikTok counted roughly 170 million users in the United States. A majority of American teenagers use TikTok, many of them daily, and a significant share report being on the app "almost constantly." The platform's influence now extends well beyond entertainment, shaping music, news consumption, political discourse, and cultural norms.

That reach has also made TikTok controversial. Researchers and pediatric health experts have raised concerns that its design contributes to addictive usage patterns and mental health issues, especially among children and adolescents. These social concerns intersect with national-security anxieties. TikTok's original parent company, ByteDance, is headquartered in China, and US lawmakers from both parties have warned that Chinese law could compel the company to provide access to user data or influence content moderation decisions. In response, Congress passed legislation in early 2024 requiring ByteDance to divest TikTok's US operations or face a nationwide ban.

That's when McCourt stepped in with the "People's Bid." At the time he explained: "We see this potential acquisition as an incredible opportunity to catalyze an alternative to the current tech model that has colonized the internet," describing the bid as a way to "give individuals and creators on the platform the value and control they deserve regarding who has access to their data and how it is used."[27]

The bid was the next phase of McCourt's commitment to reshaping the digital ecosystem. In 2021, he launched Project Liberty, committing $500 million of his own money to a long-term effort to rebuild the internet around open protocols, user data ownership, and democratic governance. Through Project Liberty, McCourt has funded academic research and policy work and backed the development of the Decentralized Social Networking Protocol, an open-source framework designed to give users control over their digital identity and data.[28] McCourt had also previously committed $200 million in donations to the Public Policy school of his alma mater, Georgetown.

Against that backdrop, the People's Bid can be understood as an effort to move from theory to practice. McCourt has argued that while research and advocacy can diagnose problems in the digital economy, they rarely change the incentives of platforms operating at global scale. Ownership, by contrast, offers the ability to embed different governance standards directly into a company's operating model. His consortium proposed acquiring TikTok's US business without retaining ByteDance's proprietary recommendation algorithm, rebuilding the platform instead on open protocols like DSNP.[29] The aim was to shift incentives away from maximizing engagement toward what he has described as an "intention economy," in which users have agency over how content is curated and how their data generates value.[30]

The People's Bid attracted a broad coalition of supporters. High-profile figures including Kevin O'Leary joined as investors, while Reddit cofounder Alexis Ohanian signed on as a strategic adviser. The bid was also publicly endorsed by Sir Tim Berners-Lee, the inventor of the World Wide Web, who supported the effort's emphasis on open protocols and user control as a corrective to today's centralized internet architecture, and by Prof. Jonathan Haidt, who has written extensively about the mental health damage that online platforms are creating in young Americans.[31]

In spirit, the bid paralleled Elon Musk's purchase of Twitter two years earlier. Musk framed the purchase as necessary to protect free speech, arguing that the platform had become a critical public square whose content moderation amounted to censorship. In his view, ownership was the only lever capable of quickly reshaping the platform's rules and norms.

In early 2026, McCourt's proposal ultimately failed. The US government instead endorsed a solution involving a different consortium of investors structured to meet national-security requirements while allowing TikTok's US operations to continue. ByteDance's reluctance to sell its recommendation algorithm further complicated the People's Bid.[32]

Despite its failure to acquire TikTok, the People's Bid illustrates an emerging strategy of "impact ownership." When socially consequential technologies operate at planetary scale, and are financed primarily through private markets, influencing outcomes may require moving beyond grants and regulation toward ownership itself.

While this and previous chapters explored how innovative investors are improving access and affordability for a range of issues most Americans care about, we now turn to a more fundamental question: How do we ensure that everyone has fair access to financing? America at its best holds out an essential promise, that our society and economic system rewards hard work, great ideas, and strong leadership, regardless of where someone comes from or how they started out in life. But turning those ideas and skills into success often requires investing capital that most people do not have themselves. To make sure your ability to secure investment is determined by your potential and not by who you are or where you come from could be the foundational act of investing in America.

9 | Who You Are and Where You Live Should Not Stop You Getting an Investment

The quality of your business idea, your discipline and skill to pull it off, your family's ability to repay a mortgage over time: those are the factors that should determine whether you get a loan or investment. That is both fair and efficient, as these are the factors that will not only offer opportunity but also allocate capital to its most productive purposes.

In practice, however, investors and lenders often ask additional questions when assessing an investment option: Who are you? And, where are you from? For millions of entrepreneurs and families, those two factors quietly determine whether the door to capital opens for them.

The evidence is stark. Black and Latino entrepreneurs are significantly less likely than White peers to receive bank loans, even after controlling for credit scores, revenue, and business characteristics. Federal Reserve surveys consistently find that Black-owned businesses are roughly half as likely to be fully approved for financing as white-owned firms and more than twice as likely to avoid applying altogether because they expect to be denied.[1] Women-owned businesses face similar barriers, receiving a disproportionately small share of small-business lending and 3% of venture capital financing despite comparable performance.[2]

Geography compounds these gaps. Rural borrowers face higher denial rates and fewer lender options than urban counterparts, while businesses located in low-income or majority-Black neighborhoods encounter tighter credit standards and higher borrowing costs.[3] Venture capital remains overwhelmingly concentrated in three coastal metropolitan areas (the Bay Area in Northern California, New York, and Boston), leaving promising founders elsewhere to compete for scraps.[4]

These disparate outcomes result from the incentives that lead capital to flow most easily to people and places where it has always flowed. Concerted efforts, most notably the 1977 Community Reinvestment Act, have sought to shift these incentives and upend these dynamics. But other trends exacerbate them. Bank consolidation has reduced the number of relationship lenders who know local markets and borrowers personally, with 5,000 banks left in America down from 18,000 in the mid-1980s.[5] Automated underwriting favors standardized profiles and penalizes borrowers with thinner credit files or unconventional income histories.

This chapter shows that the structural barriers to fair investment access are not insurmountable. With concerted effort, effective cross-sector partnerships, perseverance, and deep roots in underserved communities, banks, credit unions, venture capitalists, foundations, and investment intermediaries are building the pipes that enable investment to flow based on what investees and borrowers are building not who they are or where they are building it.

The consequences ripple outward. Businesses that access credit grow more quickly, hire more local workers, and are more resilient to shocks. Families who secure fair mortgages build more long-term wealth, creating the foundations for financial health over generations.[6] Communities with lenders gain confidence from knowing someone believes in their future. Investing in *all* of America is a powerful way to unlock the potential of our people and places and help create an economy that brings opportunities to all.

Banking on the People Banks Forget[7]

On a summer evening in Clarksdale, Mississippi, Delta Blues Alley Café quietly comes alive. Inside, owner Jecorry Miller, once a respiratory therapist, serves savory bites. To start the business took a small-business loan that had long eluded him. Financing finally came through the nonprofit lending arm of a community bank from Arkansas, Southern Bancorp. Paired with coaching and flexible terms, Miller accessed what mainstream lenders didn't offer: a fair-terms, mission-aligned loan that turned an idea into a storefront and local jobs.

Founded in 1986 in Arkadelphia, Arkansas, Southern Bancorp was launched to adapt the community banking model pioneered on Chicago's South Side to serve the rural communities of the Mississippi Delta. It galvanized support from Arkansas governor Bill Clinton, corporate leaders like Walmart Chairman Rob Walton, and local civic institutions such as the Winthrop Rockefeller Foundation, which committed \$10 million in seed capital to address rural poverty and underinvestment.[8]

Today, Southern lives out its dual-structure model: a regulated deposit-taking bank (Southern Bancorp Bank) and a nonprofit CDFI (Southern Bancorp Community Partners). Together, they hold almost \$3 billion in assets and deliver a comprehensive mix of products, including small business finance, mortgages, downpayment assistance, and financial coaching. Southern reports operating across 56 branches serving around 65,000 customers in Arkansas and the Mississippi Delta.

Southern's story of what is possible when committed leaders galvanize cross-sector support and work creatively with communities is not unique. Take Self-Help Credit Union, founded in the early 1980s by civil rights advocates Martin Eakes and Bonnie Wright through their work at the nonprofit Center for Community Self-Help in Durham, North Carolina. Self-Help was built around the core belief that ownership is essential to equality and freedom. Self-Help was chartered as a credit union in 1983 and now reports operating a network of over 80 branches in North Carolina and surrounding states, serving more than 235,000 members, and having delivered $12 billion in financing through more than 176,000 loans to families, individuals, and organizations.[9]

Self-Help is well known for its role in financing affordable homeownership, including through partnerships that helped preserve manufactured housing communities, support minority-owned small businesses, and expand access to mortgages for borrowers shut out of conventional credit markets. Self-Help also played a catalytic role in the early growth of the community development banking sector, demonstrating that disciplined underwriting and mission alignment could coexist over decades.

Another early leader is Hope Enterprise Corporation, founded in 1994 in Jackson, Mississippi, by Bill Bynum, one of Self-Help's early leaders who moved to Mississippi at the invitation of a local economic development leader to manage a grant to launch Hope Enterprises. The following year, Hope formed a Credit Union. Today, HOPE operates across Arkansas, Louisiana, Mississippi, Tennessee, and Alabama, managing more than $4.5 billion in assets and loans deployed through its family of CDFI entities. HOPE has become one of the most important providers of fair finance in majority-Black and rural communities, financing small businesses, churches, health clinics, grocery stores, and affordable housing developments.[10]

A newer example is American Pride Bank, a minority-owned bank based in Macon, Georgia, that has distinguished itself by designing credit products for borrowers who demonstrate grit, work ethic, and entrepreneurial drive but lack traditional, positive credit histories. Rather than relying solely on automated scoring models, American Pride combines relationship banking with creative underwriting, using deposits to back loans that reflect how people actually build lives and businesses.

Community banks and credit unions are not just rural focused. Some provide financing to overlooked and underserved small businesses and families in large cities. Others have been formed to serve specific communities across the country. La Raza Development Fund, for example, is a national CDFI affiliated with the nonprofit advocacy group UnidosUS, that serves Latino communities.

The work to expand who can access fair financing has historically generated strong bipartisan political support. Governor Clinton's involvement in the launch of Southern in the 1980s helped lead him to support as President the creation of the CDFI Fund at the Treasury Department in 1994. The Fund certifies CDFIs (now more than 1,300 nationwide) and has provided annual grant awards that support their lending and technical capacity. The CDFI caucus in the Senate includes 12 Republicans and 12 Democrats.

More recently, the US Treasury Department in 2021 made $9 billion of long-term investments into CDFIs and Minority Depository Institutions[i] through the Emergency Capital Investment Programs, aimed to expand lending in low- and moderate-income and minority communities. Incentives reduce interest rates and dividend payback when institutions increase lending to targeted communities, directly tying cost of capital to impact. The Fund has also set up programs to support CDFIs to raise capital through the commercial bond market.

The vision that small business owners and families are not penalized for where or who they are when they need access to credit unites these efforts. Banks and credit unions that mobilize deposits from local community members and national supporters and provide tailored investments in overlooked communities are essential to realize this vision. These examples typify what it takes to implement that mission: civic visionaries, public-private partnerships, political advocacy, and community connection. From Jecorry Miller's Clarksdale café to multi-billion-dollar financial institutions, capital paired with care can invest in all of America.

Small Checks, Big Pipes: Getting Financing Flowing to the Small Businesses Banks Leave Behind

On the outskirts of Las Vegas, Validity Construction Services had big ambitions to expand into government-sector contracts to stabilize its growth. Traditional banks continually dismissed the company's owner, Zain Burke, citing inconsistent cash flow and insufficient collateral. Then, through a referral to the CDFI Community Reinvestment Fund (CRF), Burke

---

[i] Minority Depository Institution (MDI) is a designation made by the US Treasury Department given to federally regulated banks or credit unions that are majority-owned or majority-governed by people of color and recognized by regulators for serving predominantly minority communities.

discovered the Nevada Battle Born Growth Microloan Program, part of Calvert Impact's Access Small Business Program. That loan changed the trajectory of his business and serves as a vivid example of how targeted capital and trust can unlock opportunity for small businesses left behind by mainstream finance.[11]

Small businesses like Burke's that employ fewer than 50 people are the backbone of the US economy. The country's 30 million small businesses make up 99.9% of all businesses, employ nearly 60 million Americans, almost half of private sector jobs, and generates more than 40% of US GDP. Without them, local economies, innovation pipelines, and community stability would erode.[12]

Yet small businesses, especially those that do not operate in the relatively well-off neighborhoods of major cities, struggle to access financing. The idea that a small business owner can walk into a local bank and convince the manager to back their dream is a quaint image from America's past. A modern wave of bank consolidation has left many communities without a local bank that is not accountable to regional or national bosses sitting in faraway cities. And increased regulation since the 2008 financial crisis has left banks more wary of making tailored loans to local small business.

The government has long recognized the need to support small business lending through programs like the Small Business Administration. Now private investment innovators are stepping in to extend the reach of government programs and mobilize private capital to fill the financing gap.

Calvert Impact was founded in 1988 as the nonprofit affiliate of a socially responsible asset management pioneer, with a mission to democratize capital markets. As a nonprofit intermediary, based in Maryland, it opened pathways for individual investors to deploy dollars into impact-driven opportunities that traditional finance overlooked. A keystone Calvert Impact offering since 1995 is the Community Investment Note, a loan pool that anyone can invest in with a minimum of $20. That infrastructure enabled small-scale investors to fund impact initiatives with the same sophistication as institutional players.[13]

Building on that platform, Calvert Impact now operates the Access Small Business Program, a national initiative marrying public and private capital to serve underbanked entrepreneurs. The program provides capital to community lenders such as CDFIs, credit unions, and minority depository institutions by pooling funds from the federal State Small Business Credit Initiative (SSBCI) program with private investment, bolstered by a $140 million warehouse credit facility led by Goldman Sachs' Urban Investment Group. The program harnesses the capacity of these community-based investors to originate and service loans to small businesses who lack access to conventional financing.[14] Through this model, Calvert enables lenders to extend five times the lending capacity for every dollar of their own capital by leveraging pooled public–private infrastructure, standardized underwriting, and shared reporting platforms.

Calvert has also co-created place-based investment initiatives that build connections between local asset owners and the local businesses they want to see thrive. With the Ours to Own campaign launched in 2015, it created an online investment portal that allowed investors to target their Community Note purchase to investments in specific places (initially in Denver and Minneapolis). And it helped organize Benefit Chicago, an initiative to channel local foundation and Donor Advised Fund investments into local small businesses and nonprofits, working in partnership with the Chicago-based MacArthur Foundation and the Chicago Community Trust.

These types of creative approaches to extending credit beyond where it comfortably flows have proven especially crucial in times of crisis. During the Covid crisis, community banks were essential in many places to ensure small businesses could access emergency government loan support. For Calvert's part, it reports that its pandemic-era recovery funds, working through 40 community lenders, helped ~6,000 small businesses, more than 80% of which were owned by or serving historically overlooked people, while 90% were very small, the kinds of business least likely to have access to reasonably priced bank loans.[15]

Calvert Impact Capital has now mobilized more than $5 billion through its Community Investment Notes and related products, funding community organizations, small business engines, and environmentally sustainable initiatives globally. It serves as a crucial pipe that connects retail investors with community-based lenders who can bring capital to small business owners otherwise shut out from access to investment.[16] It also demonstrates the intentionality, perseverance, creativity, and investment savvy required to pull this off.

Investing in the Rest of America

When Crystal McDonald launched Acrew, a recruiting-software start-up in New Orleans, she knew the odds were stacked against her. Talented founders in her city simply didn't have the venture capital networks their peers on the coasts could tap. Winning a pitch competition on the Rise of the Rest bus tour changed that. The $100,000 investment from the fund's seed portfolio came with direct mentorship from Steve Case, Jean Case, and multiple members of the team from Revolution investments, support she says was critical to Acrew's growth. For McDonald, the money mattered, but the network mattered even more, opening doors that had been closed to founders from places like New Orleans.[17]

Rise of the Rest was born in 2014 out of Steve Case's belief that talent is evenly distributed, but opportunity is not. Case had spent two decades building America Online from an early online service in 1985 into the world's largest internet company, taking it public, and leading its high-profile merger with Time Warner. After leaving AOL in 2003, he and his wife Jean, a former AOL marketing executive who became an influential voice in impact investing and chair of the National Geographic Society, founded Revolution LLC in Washington, D.C. in 2005. Their goal was to back "built-to-last" businesses across the country, especially in places ignored by the venture capital clusters of Silicon Valley, New York, and Boston.

From Revolution's early years investing in companies like Zipcar, LivingSocial, and Sweetgreen, the Cases saw firsthand the constraints facing entrepreneurs outside these investment centers. Data confirmed the imbalance: for decades, roughly 75% of US venture capital flowed to just three states, California, New York, and Massachusetts.[18] Start-ups in the rest of the country, no matter how promising, often struggled to raise capital without relocating, draining jobs and potential from their home regions. The Cases believed making occasional investments in other regions would not be enough to close this gap. There needed to be a dedicated platform to channel early-stage capital and mentoring into these overlooked markets.

Rise of the Rest began as a series of bus tours through places like Pittsburgh, Detroit, Cincinnati, Nashville, and Puerto Rico, where Case and his team hosted pitch competitions and met with local founders, investors, and civic leaders. By late 2017, the effort had become its own dedicated seed fund. The Rise of the Rest Seed Fund launched with $150 million in commitments from a high-profile roster of investors including Jeff Bezos, Eric Schmidt, Meg Whitman, Ray Dalio, and members of the Walton and Koch families. The fund was co-led by Case and J.D. Vance, at the time best known as the author of *Hillbilly Elegy,* his autobiography of growing up in the kind of places overlooked by investors.

From its headquarters in Washington, D.C., Rise of the Rest has built a portfolio that now includes more than 200 companies in more than 100 cities. Investments range from Acrew in New Orleans to BenchPrep, an education-technology company in Chicago, and Catalyte, a Baltimore-based firm using AI to identify and train overlooked talent for software development. According to Revolution, nearly a dozen of its investees have reached valuations above $100 million, and the initiative has tracked the launch of more than 1,400 new regional venture capital firms over the past decade. The fund's impact shows up not just in valuations but in more mature business ecosystems that now retain their high-growth start-ups rather than exporting them to the coasts.[19]

Financially, Rise of the Rest is a market-rate investment vehicle. While it has not publicly disclosed target IRRs or overall realized returns, it operates alongside Revolution's other funds, which have produced high-profile exits, and its backers expect both returns and regional economic impact. The model's early traction allowed the team to raise a second $150 million fund in 2019, bringing total committed capital to $300 million across two seed funds.[20]

The rationale for such a fund remains strong. While the share of early-stage venture capital going to non-coastal states has more than doubled in the past decade, from $7.5 billion in 2013 to $16.8 billion in 2024, three states still capture the lion's share of total venture capital. Case notes that even modest shifts in allocation can have outsized effects in rising cities, where a single growth-stage employer can transform a downtown economy. In his view, investing in overlooked places isn't charity; it's a structural necessity.

For the Cases, Rise of the Rest is as much about narrative change as it is about capital deployment. By showing up in cities from Des Moines to Birmingham, riding a branded bus, and shining a national spotlight on local founders, they aim to challenge the assumption that all serious start-ups must be based within a few zip codes. The fund's early-stage investments are designed to anchor high-potential companies in their home communities, letting wealth and jobs compound locally rather than concentrate elsewhere.

Other investors are pursuing a similar approach, targeting investments in founders who are overlooked or serving neglected markets, rather than operating from underserved places. Kapor Capital, described in the technology chapter, invests in "gap closing" opportunities with founders who typically lack the educational credentials that attract mainstream venture capital. Impact America Fund, founded by Kesha Cash, is built on the conviction that the venture market systematically overlooks some of the most promising founders and that this bias leaves significant value on the table. Having now raised more than $175 million, Cash has made investing in underrepresented founders, particularly Black entrepreneurs and others building for underserved markets, the core of both her investment strategy and impact thesis. That approach is reflected in portfolio companies like CareAcademy, which built a leading workforce training and credentialing platform for home-care agencies and exited in 2025 through an acquisition by Activated Insights, and Esusu, a fintech company that helps renters build credit by reporting on-time rent payments and has grown into a unicorn valued at over $1 billion. Together, these investments underscore Cash's central bet: that founders the market ignores are often the ones best positioned to build scalable businesses, deliver strong financial returns, and expand economic opportunity at the same time.

Crystal McDonald's story captures the essence of the mission to close the investment/opportunity gap. Without Rise of the Rest, Acrew might have joined the long list of promising regional start-ups that never scale for lack of capital. With it, she gained not just a check, but a network of mentors and a validation that told other investors she was worth betting on. Multiply that by 200, and you start to see why Steve and Jean Case and their partners are determined to keep showing up in unlikely places until access to investment is as evenly distributed as talent.

From Burial Insurance to Urban Rebirth: How Prudential's 150-Year Journey in Newark Shows the Potential of Investing in a Local Community

With bright sun shining through a massive skylight and surrounded by caringly restored wrought-iron steelwork, the lobby of the Hahne building in Newark, New Jersey, is a welcoming place to meet, take a break, or shop. For residents who remembered the decades the building sat as a shuttered eyesore and symbol of the city's challenges, the multi-use building is also an invigorating symbol of resilience and resurgence. It is a powerful manifestation of what can happen when a company brings all its assets, including its investment capital and expertise, to help uplift the city it operates in.

Insurance giant Prudential traces its roots to Newark in 1875, established as the Widows and Orphans Friendly Society to offer affordable burial insurance to working families. That mission to serve mainstream America has defined its corporate ethos. As former CEO John Strangfeld remarked: "Prudential was founded to serve working families . . . our higher purpose is to pursue inclusive growth that benefits shareholders, customers and society."[21]

This broad mission has long been intertwined with the complex history of its corporate hometown of Newark. In the summer of 1967, amid a wave of national protests for racial justice, an uprising in Newark led to the burning of the Central Ward. Faced with a choice of retreating to another city or the suburbs, Prudential decided to stay in Newark and not only work to rebuild the city but also use its products and services to advance pathways to economic opportunity. It pursued programs to promote more equitable access to financial solutions and launched a corporate foundation in 1976 with a strong emphasis on supporting Newark. Decades before the term "impact investing" was coined, it also began making for-profit investments in Newark to support the city's emerging community development corporations and affordable housing developers.

Prudential recommitted to the grantmaking and impact investing work in 2014, organizing its efforts around the concept of "shared value"—that the company could use grants, impact investments, and the core expertise of its business to help more people become financially secure and to use investment as a tool for social and economic progress in Newark and globally. Prudential committed at a White House event the following year to grow its impact investing portfolio to $1 billion.

Rather than running this work in silos, the foundation and impact investing team worked together under the leadership of Lata Reddy, a former civil rights attorney and long-time Prudential leader. As the Senior Vice President of Inclusive Solutions, Reddy has a mandate to harness Prudential's full business capabilities and standing in the local community to promote inclusive economic opportunity and sustainable growth.[22]

Downtown Newark now shows the results of this approach. Working alongside community leaders and political officials, and able to galvanize other investors and developers, Prudential has been instrumental in the creation of the Teachers Village, a $150 million mixed-use development project that spans five blocks, offering 204 moderately priced apartments, three charter schools, public open space, and 65,000 sq ft of retail. It led the restoration of the Hahne Building, a former flagship department store, now restored into a multi-use commercial building with 160 apartments, commercial space including for a local university, and Newark's first Whole Foods store.

While they ultimately attracted commercial investors, these developments could not have sourced purely commercial capital from the start. Mainstream lenders lacked Prudential's confidence in Newark's future and were skittish to lend for the development of rental housing in downtown Newark where they did not see recent evidence of demand. They also lacked the broader context about assets in the city and how Prudential and others were leveraging them to make the area more vibrant.

In the area around the Hahne Building, Prudential spent $400 million to build a new headquarters when some people suggested it was time to leave. They also used grants to help fund the restoration of a city park across the street. Collectively, this work has catalyzed a cycle of renewal and investment in downtown Newark and beyond.

Beyond the blocks surrounding Prudential's Newark headquarters, Newark has revived its economic and social engines of progress. Its population grew 12% from 2010–2020, the fastest population growth rate in a century.[23] Like other American cities, it continues to face social and economic challenges, especially in some particularly isolated neighborhoods.

But the success of the development work downtown has created the foundation for a more optimistic future.

And within Prudential, the impact investing work similarly evolves. In 2022, Prudential shifted this $1 billion portfolio out of Inclusive Solutions and into its Global Investment Management business. This move brings the experts who developed a high-impact investment approach into a business with more than $1 trillion in assets and positions them to meet growing client demand for impact investing products and services.

Investing in Main Street: Local Foundation Stepping in to Support Rural Economic Vitality

Near the headwaters of the Mississippi River in Minnesota's historic "Wood Basket," Grand Rapids is in many ways a typical rural American town. Built up in the early 20th century around a paper mill, Grand Rapids has faced the challenge of sustaining jobs as the company's local operations shrank. The paper mill now accounts for approximately 8% of local economic production, down from an estimated 45% in the late 1990s.

Against this backdrop, small businesses and local community organizations are essential to the community's ongoing vitality.[24] Yet, as in other rural areas, access to affordable financing has eroded over decades. Bank consolidation has sharply reduced the presence of local lenders nationwide: since the mid-1980s, the number of US commercial banks has fallen by more than 70%, from over 18,000 institutions to fewer than 5,000 today.[25] Rural counties have been hit hardest. Between 2012 and 2022 alone, the United States lost more than 2,700 bank branches, with rural areas experiencing closures at nearly twice the rate of urban communities.[26]

The seat of 45,000-person Itasca County, Grand Rapids is better off than many similar towns in that it does have bank branches. But the bankers who work there are hard-pressed to make the type of small and affordable loans that some local businesses need. Rural lending becomes structurally unattractive for loans below $10,000. Smaller loan sizes, higher servicing costs, long travel distances, and thin margins make it difficult to sustain relationship-based lending in remote communities, especially under post-2008 regulations that make non-standardized business loans more expensive. Government programs like the Small Business Administration and the

Farm Credit System play an essential role in filling this gap, together supporting hundreds of billions of dollars in lending. Yet even these large programs leave many rural entrepreneurs, cooperatives, and community-based organizations without access to flexible, locally informed capital.

But Grand Rapids has one major advantage: a local investor committed to working alongside the community to make the kind of small, patient loans that will advance the economic vitality and beauty of the town and its rural surroundings. The Blandin Foundation has played this role since the late 1980s, when its leaders recognized that fulfilling the mission of its founder required more than just giving grants.[27]

Founded in 1941, Blandin Foundation was created through the vision of Charles K. Blandin, a schoolteacher, newspaperman, entrepreneur, and owner of the Blandin Paper Company, and has been funded primarily through his estate.[28] With its assets growing substantially after the sale of the company in 1977, Blandin Foundation has become the largest rural-based, rural-serving foundation in Minnesota, committed to supporting the Grand Rapids Area, and rural livelihoods throughout the state.

The Foundation began using Program-Related Investments in the late 1980s to complement its grantmaking as a practical response to the imperative to support local nonprofits and businesses that could create jobs as the mill economy receded. It invested in funds focused on capitalizing rural businesses, including in partnership with the University of Minnesota, and made loans to nonprofit social enterprises such as Minnesota Diversified Industries, whose Grand Rapids manufacturing center provides employment to people with disabilities.

To undertake its investing work efficiently, Blandin Foundation often partners with the Grand Rapids Economic Development Authority, one of ~300 similar state-mandated organizations across Minnesota tasked with promoting local economic development. Loan capital from Blandin helps GREDA to expand its capacity to lend to local small businesses and economic development projects aligned with the town and region's broader economic development plans. Blandin also works with the Itasca County Economic Development Corporation to identify similarly aligned investment opportunities. In addition, Blandin uses loan guarantees and fund investments.

What does this look like in practice?

- Local small business owners in Grand Rapids can access low-interest, long-term loans for as little as $3,000 for improvements like new paint or signage, the type of investment that can go a long way to preserving an attractive downtown, but that business owners are often hard-pressed to finance on their own or through the bank.
- During the Covid shutdowns, the Foundation supported GREDA, IEDC, and Cohasset Economic Development Authority to set up an emergency loan program for local small businesses that enabled them to keep their lights on and people paid while waiting for the federal aid that arrived later.
- New apartments are being built by a private developer on a lot downtown in support of the local land use plan after Blandin provided GREDA with a $100,000 loan to remediate environmental damage on the land that had kept it from being developed for years.

Blandin's approach mirrors a growing group of foundations that are using program-related and mission-related investments to strengthen local economies outside of major Coastal Cities. Community foundations such as those in Omaha, Vermont, Maine, and Greater Green Bay have followed the early example of peers in Greater Cincinnati and Cleveland to launch locally focused impact investing programs, often working with local community lenders to originate and manage small business, housing, and nonprofit loans.

Minneapolis-based impact investing advisor Susan Hammel, working with Chicago's Impact Engine, mapped impact investing initiatives in the 12 states of the Midwest. They found 416 funds making impact investments locally in 2014.[29] Framing is important. For many of these foundations, impact investing resonates when described as a way to support local communities and build local wealth rather than to address national or global issues.

Like Prudential in Newark, Blandin Foundation shows how an institution can use investment to complement grantmaking to secure the long-term vibrancy of its neighborhood. It also serves as a challenge to other similar foundations: If the Blandin Foundation can find ways to invest its assets to support its aspirations in the Wood Basket of Northern Minnesota, what more could your investment assets be doing to serve rural communities?

Many of the investors, in this and previous chapters, have worked with government to invest in ways that help address the challenges facing too many American families and communities. Their example highlights how mutually beneficial partnerships can be forged between investors and government. Investors get the financial support they need to be able to compete to help address social challenges not just to profit from them. And government gets private capital necessary to scale up solutions. The next chapter describes five ways government can invest in America, not to replace private investors, but to work alongside them effectively and efficiently.

10 | How Government Can Invest in America

The US capital markets have played a singular role in creating the world's most dynamic and richest economy. US investors are historically unrivalled in allocating investments to opportunities that generate the greatest financial returns. But what happens when those opportunities for return are not the opportunities where investment capital could matter most to drive long-term prosperity for more Americans?

Historically, when private capital failed to flow to places the nation needed it to most, policymakers have set rules, built institutions, shared risk, and created incentives that made it rational for private capital to invest in national priorities. As economic historian Chris Hughes notes in his recent book, *Marketcrafters*, many of the capital markets Americans now treat as permanent features of the economy were deliberately constructed through government action.[1] Most notably, before the government stepped in to revive the homebuilding and lending industry during the Great Depression, housing loans only covered half the purchase price and had to be repaid in five years. Farms, small businesses, highways projects: all have access to loans because of government interventions that have bolstered the limited lending private markets would otherwise make in these areas.

Over the past century, the US government has developed four basic tools to steer investment into national priorities. These tools can now be used to steer more lending to scale the solutions this book has described and to expand financing to solve the national challenges most Americans agree need solving. And momentum is gathering for a fifth approach that could accelerate and expand this agenda. Government:

- *invests directly*, using loans or equity when private capital collapses or strategic industries are at stake;
- *shares risk* through guarantees and commitments to purchase assets, turning "too risky" markets into financeable ones;
- *uses tax incentives* to change the math of investment, expanding availability and lowering the cost of capital in priority sectors;
- *mobilizes investment capital*, such as that in public pensions and State Treasuries, to make targeted investments aimed at spurring local, long-term economic growth; and
- could *set up new standing investment vehicles*, like a sovereign or industrial fund, to finance long-term national priorities.

Across decades and administrations, especially in the first half of the 20th century, government used these tools to steer capital to invest in America. Political space is opening again for these approaches. After decades of advocating for unregulated markets as the most efficient allocators of capital, many Republicans have come to recognize the need to manage markets to reduce the human cost of that efficiency. And after decades of focusing on constraining investors from doing harm, many Democrats now recognize they cannot achieve their priorities without leveraging private investment to finance them.

Advocating for efficient ways to mobilize investment capital is a winning political move for most elected officials. By choosing from and adapting these approaches, lawmakers can help solve the challenges that unite us.

Don't Call It a Bailout: How Government Can Steer Private Capital to Finance National Priorities

At moments of crisis, the US government has often invested in America directly, making loans and equity investments in sectors and companies deemed crucial to the national interest.

During the Great Depression, the federal government created the Reconstruction Finance Corporation to lend directly to banks, railroads, and industrial companies when private credit collapsed. In the aftermath of the 2008 financial crisis, Congress and multiple federal agencies stabilized the banking system and rescued the domestic auto industry through direct loans and equity investments. The same instinct underlies the Small Business Administration's Disaster Loan Program, which provides direct loans to households and small businesses after hurricanes, wildfires, and floods.

These interventions are widely accepted because they occur during emergencies. Doing nothing could be far worse. But what if government did not wait for a crisis to invest in America?

In a few important areas, it already does not. One of the clearest examples is the Department of Energy's Loan Programs Office (now housed within DOE's Office of Energy Dominance Financing). In 2010, the office made a $465 million loan to a little-known electric vehicle company called Tesla. The loan allowed Tesla to build its first US manufacturing facility and scale production. Tesla repaid the loan in full, with interest, years ahead of schedule.[2] Today, the company has mobilized billions of dollars of private capital issuing stocks and bonds and anchored a domestic advanced transportation supply chain.

The Department of Transportation has taken a similar approach through the Transportation Infrastructure Finance and Innovation Act (TIFIA) program, created in 1998 to provide long-term, low-cost federal credit for major surface transportation projects.[3] Rather than taking ownership stakes, TIFIA uses direct loans, loan guarantees, and standby lines of credit to absorb early risk and improve project economics, catalyzing tens of billions of dollars in lending and well over $100 billion in total public and private infrastructure investment.

Similar logic animates the Department of Defense's long-standing role in early-stage technology development. Since the Cold War, agencies like the Defense Advanced Research Projects Agency (DARPA) have partnered with private companies to advance semiconductors, aerospace, networking, and other foundational technologies. More recently, the Department of Defense created the Office of Strategic Capital to expand the use of loans and other financial tools to support companies working in areas deemed critical to national security.[4]

Direct lending can also be a powerful tool. But, outside wartime mobilization and economic emergencies, the American people have historically been wary of letting government act as a direct investor, especially to highly visible, national companies (as compared to small or rural businesses). As with many investment tools, investment decisions can be perceived to be politically motivated. Capital can flow to those who are best connected or most aligned with the priorities of the people in power not the best able to use it to create impact and profits.

There is, however, another more characteristically American way to steer investment capital toward public priorities. Instead of government picking companies, it can shape incentives so that independent, for-profit investors find it attractive to invest in socially valuable parts of the economy. One way is to provide concessionally priced capital to professional fund managers who agree to invest in priority areas.

The clearest example of the first approach is the Small Business Investment Company program. Created in 1958, the SBIC program licenses private investment funds, enabling them to borrow long-term, fixed-rate, relatively low-cost debt from the federal government. Today, roughly 300 SBICs are active across the country, managing more than $50 billion.[5]

Under the program, licensed fund managers can borrow up to $175 million (per license and $350 million total) in 10-year debt from the US Treasury at rates typically about one percentage point above the 10-year Treasury yield. When the fund manager invests at higher rates than it pays on this debt, it can share the profits with its other investors, helping managers attract institutional capital that is seeking the highest risk-adjusted financial return.

The Department of Defense has sought to adopt this approach. In 2023, it announced a partnership with the SBA to channel defense funding through the SBIC program to support investments in companies critical to national security.[6]

This structure is now being adapted to other national priorities. In 2025, a bipartisan bill, the American Ownership and Resilience Act, proposed the creation of Employee Ownership Investment Companies. Modeled on the SBIC program, the legislation proposes $5 billion of low-cost loans be made available to fund managers like Apis and Heritage who finance companies converting to worker ownership.[7]

Even without new programs, small tweaks to the SBIC program can steer capital to new areas. Regulations that remove targeted loans (such as employee ownership transition financing) from the $350 million leverage cap or that fast-track applications from aspiring licensees would attract more private investors in these markets.

This approach could be extended further. Many Community Development Financial Institutions (CDFIs) have more opportunities to make productive investments than capital to meet them. During the pandemic, policymakers explored creating a 7(a)-style guarantee program for CDFIs, enabling them to sell loans and dramatically expand lending capacity, an idea that continues to gain attention.

Crucially, the SBA programs, and proposals like the American Ownership and Resilience Act, are structured to be self-sustaining. Fees cover losses so they do not require additional taxpayer funding. The SBA's Small Business Investment Company has in fact returned $1.5 billion to the US Treasury in the last 24 years.[8] That zero-subsidy characteristic transforms their political potential in our time of large federal deficits and divided government.

Risk Happens: Government Guarantees to Catalyze Private Investment in America

For all the sophistication of modern finance, much of private investment still comes down to one core activity: managing risk. Capital flows readily to markets where outcomes are predictable and data is abundant. Unfortunately, many of the investments America needs most do not fit that profile. First-of-a-kind energy production technologies carry technical and scale-based risk. First-time homebuyers in underinvested communities often lack credit histories. Students without parents able to co-sign loans look risky on paper, even with strong long-term earning prospects. These real and perceived risks often translate into chronic underinvestment.

Government can change this dynamic through guarantees and commitments to purchase investments. Once an investment model is proven and scaled, risk often declines and the need for public support can fade. But to get there, government often must help bridge the gap.

Loan guarantees draw on one of the federal government's most powerful assets: the market's trust that the United States will repay its obligations. When government offers a guarantee, private capital becomes available to borrowers who would otherwise be shut out, and the cost of that capital falls. Importantly, government does not need to pick every borrower or underwrite every loan. Instead, it can work alongside banks, investors, and specialized lenders who already know how to source and manage deals.

This approach has been instrumental in forging the modern US economy. The 30-year fixed-rate mortgage famously began when the Federal government in the 1930s guaranteed housing loans and committed to buy mortgages that banks originated.[9] Two decades earlier, Congress created what became the Farm Credit System to provide a dependable source of rural credit through a network of borrower-owned, privately run cooperative lenders. Farm Credit has long benefited from the implicit guarantee found in investors' belief that the US government would bail out a failing System lender. Today, the Farm Credit System has grown into a major source of rural finance, with more than $500 billion in total assets supporting farmers, agribusinesses, and rural infrastructure.[10]

Beyond its support for housing finance generally, government has targeted guarantees to specific groups. To support veterans returning from service during the Second World War, Congress created a loan guarantee program in what is now the Department of Veterans Affairs that guaranteed 50% of the loan of a mortgage originated for veterans. Nearly 3 million veterans used the benefit, in some markets representing a substantial share of new home purchases (though infamously largely inaccessible to African American veterans).

In more recent times, for small business finance, the SBA's 7(a) program guarantees up to 75–85% of qualifying loans. Lenders can sell the guaranteed portion into a secondary market, freeing capital for additional lending. Recent experience shows the promise of extending this approach into other areas. The Department of Energy's Loan Programs Office has transformed access to investment for many new energy technologies. By September 2025 it reports having issued $94 billion in loans and loan guarantees.[11]

On a smaller scale, similar risk-sharing tools quietly underpin essential community infrastructure. The Health Resources and Services Administration's Health Center Facility Loan Guarantee Program is designed to lower financing costs for community health centers by guaranteeing up to 80% of eligible project financing (construction, expansion, renovation, and modernization).[12] Congressional appropriations in 2018 supported guarantees for almost $900 million in new loans, small by Wall Street standards but attractive for CDFIs that expanded health clinic lending.[13]

In K–12 education, the Department of Education's Credit Enhancement for Charter School Facilities Program took a different route, making grants to intermediaries that then leverage private lending and bond markets for charter facilities. Program tracking compiled by the National Charter School Resource Center shows that as of 2020, credit enhancement awards had helped leverage approximately $7.4 billion in financing across 813 charter school transactions.[14]

Beyond Farm Credit, rural business finance has long relied on guarantees as well. USDA's Business & Industry (B&I) Guaranteed Loan Program exists to make lenders more willing to extend credit in rural communities by reducing risk through a federal guarantee.[15] A 2025 economic assessment submitted to Congress reports that from 2005–2024, B&I leveraged an additional $12.4 billion in other capital and estimates the program supported more than 750,000 jobs from 2012–2022.[16]

Yet the politics of these loan programs rarely reward portfolio outcomes. Many people associate government guarantee programs more readily with the collapse of the Department of Energy-supported solar company Solyndra than with the creation of the mortgage market or farm lending. While the Solyndra bankruptcy cost the US government ~$500 million, that represented less than 4% of the total loan program that supported Solyndra. And few people likely know that the Energy Department loan guarantee program has recently reported earning six times more in interest payments ($6.2 billion of revenue) than paying out in losses.

Whether the goal is scaling new climate technologies, expanding access to homeownership, financing education and workforce pathways, or strengthening essential community services, loan guarantees are one proven way government can close the financing gap, turning temporary public support into durable private markets.

Give Them a Tax Break: Making the Math Work for Investing in America

Investors don't typically pass on opportunities to invest in America because they are willfully unpatriotic. They pass because they pursue investments with more reliable risk-adjusted returns than many investments that could create opportunities for more Americans offer. Providing tax breaks on the profits of these investments could change investor calculation and unlock substantial capital flows.

Tax incentives for investors are not a new or partisan idea. For more than a century, these programs have helped channel capital into oil and gas exploration, electricity generation, agriculture, and domestic manufacturing, lowering the cost of capital in sectors widely viewed as essential to growth, security, and competitiveness.[17] Against that history, today's opportunities to use tax policy to expand housing, strengthen supply chains, or rebuild industrial capacity are not a break from the past, but an update to a familiar American playbook.

For nearly four decades, the Low-Income Housing Tax Credit (LIHTC) has been the federal government's primary engine for producing and preserving affordable rental housing. LIHTC works by offering investors a dollar-for-dollar credit against federal tax liability in exchange for providing equity to income-restricted housing developments, reducing project debt and making rents affordable while allowing investors to earn competitive, predictable returns.[18] Since its creation in 1986, LIHTC has financed roughly 4 million affordable homes, serving more than 9 million households nationwide.[19] Recognizing its central role, Congress made key LIHTC enhancements permanent in the 2025 tax legislation.

Opportunity Zones apply similar logic to investments in under-resourced neighborhoods. Created with bipartisan support as part of the 2017 Tax Cuts and Jobs Act, the program allows investors to defer and partially or fully exclude capital gains taxes if those gains are reinvested in designated low-income communities. The incentive mobilized more than $100 billion in investment, but outcomes have been uneven.[20] With the Opportunity Zones tax break made permanent in 2025, there is an opportunity to strengthen guardrails so tax benefits translate into real community outcomes.[21]

The CHIPS and Science Act shows how tax incentives can reshape industrial investment. Passed in 2022 with rare bipartisan support, the law includes a 25% advanced manufacturing investment tax credit that lowers the after-tax cost of building semiconductor fabrication facilities in the United States.[22] Combined with grants, CHIPS has unlocked hundreds of billions of dollars in announced private investment.[23]

Looking ahead, similar thinking is emerging in the field of homeownership finance. The 2026 proposed SHARE Act would offer federal tax relief to investors who finance shared appreciation mortgages that meet rules for fairness and consumer protection. Shared appreciation mortgages have the potential to garner widespread support as they offer elected officials a way to support making homeownership more affordable without needing home prices to fall.

Working From Home: Harnessing Public Capital to Build Broader Local Prosperity

Imagine you are an elected State Treasurer. On your desk are two sets of numbers. One shows the scale of the capital you are responsible for investing: tens of billions of dollars in state Treasury funds and the pension assets for state workers. The other shows the unmet need for investment in your state: communities short on affordable housing, small businesses struggling to access credit, manufacturers unable to secure working capital loans to expand, and students and workers facing rising costs for college and job training programs.

You know that private markets are allocating capital to what they perceive as opportunities for generating the highest risk-adjusted returns. This process, left on its own, is not delivering enough investment in the places and sectors that matter most to your state's long-term prosperity. In this context, those assets create both a responsibility and opportunity: the responsibility to protect retirement security for teachers, firefighters, police officers, and other public servants; and the opportunity to ensure that this capital also improve the long-term prospects of the state and its residents.

State and local public pension systems now hold more than $6.5 trillion in assets, roughly twice the size of the entire US private equity industry.[24] In addition, the national Thrift Savings Plan (TSP), the retirement savings plan for US federal employees and members of the uniformed services, holds more than $1 trillion in assets across more than 7.2 million participants and beneficiaries.[25]

The idea that some of that capital could be explicitly aimed at addressing social challenges is not new. Since the 1970s, some state pension plans have experimented with Economically Targeted Investments (ETIs) that seek to steer state pension funds to investments in that improve economic conditions in the state, typically through investments that drive job growth and affordable housing.

California's $500 billion pension fund, CalPERS, was among the earliest and most visible adopters, launching ETI programs in the late 1980s and early 1990s that ultimately committed several billion dollars to affordable housing, urban redevelopment, and later in-state private equity through initiatives such as the California Initiative. This work helped establish that place-based investing could be pursued within a large public pension system while remaining consistent with fiduciary standards.[26] Similarly, in Texas in 1988, voters approved a state constitutional amendment authorizing public investment systems to allocate up to 1% of assets to investments intended to promote job creation and economic growth in the state, embedding economic development directly into the state constitution.[27]

New York City has operated one of the country's longest-running ETI programs through its public pension systems, which by 2023 had invested more than $1.6 billion in support of 45,000 affordable housing units and community development projects over several decades.[28] In New York City's 2025 campaign for Comptroller, the elected official who oversees New York City's $300 billion in public pension assets, the ultimate victor Mark Levine committed that if elected he would mandate the City pension funds to invest $4 billion in New York City affordable housing.[29]

Beyond pensions, state treasuries have emerged as an even more politically tractable place to experiment. Unlike pension funds, treasury-managed assets are not tied directly to retiree benefits, giving treasurers more flexibility to deploy capital in ways that can face less political scrutiny.

Under Treasurer Michael Frerichs, Illinois has led in recent experimentation, enacting the Sustainable Investing Act of 2019 that authorized the Treasurer to consider the social impact in Illinois of the assets their office manages.[30] The law passed with bipartisan support and provided a durable foundation for programs that link state deposits to small business lending, agricultural finance, affordable housing, community development, and the example discussed in the education chapter of guaranteeing college loans to Illinois residents.

Vermont Treasurer Mike Pieciak partnered with the Vermont Housing Finance Agency in 2024 to relaunch "10% for Vermont initiative" with a $50 million commitment to support the development or preservation of more than 1,065 affordable homes statewide.[31] Similarly, the Colorado legislature in 2025 authorized the State Treasurer to invest up to $50 million of state funds in bonds and other instruments designed to expand affordable housing financing across the state.[32]

Some states have gone further still by building permanent funds that resemble sovereign wealth funds. New Mexico has established a State Investment Council to manage a suite of funds, primarily from royalty payments and taxes from oil and mineral rights that manage more than $50 billion, providing annual income to the state general fund. Earnings from the fund support public education and other state priorities, converting finite resources into a lasting financial asset for future generations. While primarily invested with out-of-state managers, the Council has committed more than $500 million to invest in private equity managers that create jobs in New Mexico, and has set up a $20 million fund to co-invest alongside venture capital funds directly in New Mexico companies.[33]

In every state, there are companies, fund managers, and entrepreneurs ready to put capital to work building what communities say they need. And in every state, there are public assets already invested in the markets. Imagine what would be possible if more of these assets were harnessed to address pressing community needs, recognizing that long-term economic health and long-term financial returns are deeply intertwined.

If You Don't Build It, the Capital Won't Come: Why Bipartisan Interest Is Growing in a Sovereign Wealth Fund for Critical Investments

Imagine a rare earth refinery in Louisiana ready to expand the production of materials critical to advanced manufacturing and national defense. It could be profitable in the long term, but banks and bond markets consider it too risky, and private equity investors are unwilling to finance a company that requires large capital investment that will not pay off for years.

What if the US government could step in with the growth financing it needs from an investment fund mandated to invest precisely in this type of critical industry? That is the promise of a sovereign wealth fund: a government-owned investment vehicle that deploys public capital strategically in sectors that generate broad national benefits but remain under-funded by private markets.

The idea of a sovereign wealth fund that could directly invest in under-capitalized, critical markets builds on precedent established with the Reconstruction Finance Corporation during the Great Depression. A precursor to the Small Business Administration that was created 20 years later, RFC made direct loans to businesses and financed military industrial expansion.

Political interest in reviving this approach has gained momentum in recent years. The Industrial Finance Corporation Act of 2021 proposed to create an Industrial Finance Corporation of the United States (IFCUS). IFCUS would deploy up to $50 billion to support domestic manufacturing, supply-chain resilience, and advanced technologies.[34] This is modeled on development finance institutions such as the International Finance Corporation, that the US helped create in 1956, and the US government's Development Finance Corporation that operates outside the country. Only this time, the focus would be on using investment to spur economic growth at home. The Biden administration also explored the idea, led by Daleep Singh, then Deputy National Security Advisor for International Economics.

The concept has attracted bipartisan interest. During the 2024 Presidential election campaign, Donald Trump endorsed creating a US sovereign wealth fund to compete with China's state-directed investment model. Prominent business leaders echoed the case. Pat Gelsinger, former

CEO of Intel, publicly supported the idea, arguing that rebuilding US semiconductor capacity would require strategic public capital alongside private investment.[35]

President Trump signed an executive order in February 2025, directing the Departments of Treasury and Commerce to develop a plan for such a fund within 90 days.[36] Treasury and Commerce reportedly submitted proposed plans to the White House in mid-2025, but they were not immediately implemented amid disagreement over structure and execution details.[37] One political challenge is identifying how to capitalize the fund, given the persistent deficits the US federal government runs, in contrast to the surplus from natural resources sales that typically capitalize sovereign wealth funds elsewhere.

Despite this complexity, pressure is likely to grow for tools that can mobilize gap-filling investment at scale as geopolitical competition intensifies and supply-chain vulnerabilities become harder to ignore. Whether under the name of a sovereign wealth fund or another industrial finance vehicle, this is an idea that could gain bipartisan momentum in the coming years.

These examples demonstrate that government interventions in private capital markets are necessary and feasible but also difficult to design well and politically fraught. Government can positively shape how capital flows in America, but only if it does so with discipline, humility, and a clear-eyed understanding of what influences market behavior. Direct lending can catalyze entire industries. Guarantees can quietly build foundational markets, from mortgages to farm credit to small business finance. Concessional capital programs like SBIC can attract private fund managers to places and people that capital would otherwise ignore. Tax incentives can make investments work for investors as well as they work for society. And public balance sheets, from state treasuries to permanent funds, can be mobilized to invest in local prosperity without sacrificing fiduciary duty.

Outside crises, however, Americans have long been wary of government "socializing the economy" by making decisions about where investment should flow, a role many Americans believe should be left to private sector investors. They know investment incentives can easily lead to corruption and power grabs. And even well-intentioned government programs are often exploited or ignored. Investors are voracious in exploiting loopholes that allow them to profit from government programs without taking on the extra risk or steering investment where it would not have gone anyway. Investors will also be unsentimental about ignoring programs designed to attract their capital into more socially useful investments if the programs do not create tangible and reliable incentives.

For many Americans, our economy is in crisis. The cost of poorly constructed government intervention is real. But the cost of not trying is increasingly untenable: an economy that fails too many of the people who depend on it.

The tools described here are not substitutes for private capital markets. They extend markets into places they are failing to reach in ways that will be good for the people they serve. Used carefully, they allow government to steer capital without owning companies, to absorb risk without socializing losses, and to invest in America without bailouts. In a moment of deep economic anxiety and political mistrust, that may be the most American approach available.

11 | How You Can Invest in America

One risk of reading a book like this is that it can feel like a spectator sport. You read about venture capitalists, pension funds, federal agencies, and billion-dollar initiatives shaping the economy and may reasonably conclude that investing in America is something other people do.

I hope you can see yourself in one of these examples. Even if you do not, everyone reading this book has the power to invest in America. As this chapter describes, you can invest in America yourself, through your religious institution, your charitable assets, the company you work for, and even how you vote.

Before getting specific about the many ways many of us can get involved, I want to remind you that nothing in this chapter is investment advice. I am not telling you what to buy, sell, or hold, and I am not your financial advisor. What follows is a menu of possibilities, examples of the work others are doing to make it easier for those with different levels of wealth and influence to put your money to work in ways that strengthen American communities and expand opportunities while still respecting financial realities. My goal is to broaden your sense of what is possible and, if necessary, embolden you to demand that your employer, banks, brokers, and the other financial professionals who may advise you do a better job in helping you to invest in America.

Put Your Money Where the Impact Is: Deposit with Community Banks That Invest in America

If you are one of the roughly 95% of American households with a bank account, you already participate in the financial system every day. Where you place your deposits matters.

Banks do not simply store money. They lend it. Deposits are the raw material that banks use to lend to families to buy homes, to businesses to meet payroll, to developers to build, and to the government. When deposits flow to the largest national banks, they tend to be deployed wherever returns are easiest to generate, and into larger deals, often far from the communities where the deposits originated and loans are most needed.

But there is an alternative. When you deposit with a community bank or credit union, your deposits are far more likely to be reinvested locally. And many of these institutions have strong track records of working hard and creatively to prudently invest that money in ways that expand opportunity and fair finance for people and communities that may be overlooked and underserved. Their work to extend credit is especially important as traditional banks have reduced their lending to small businesses in many markets after a wave of bank consolidation. (There are now fewer than 5,000 banks in the United States, down from more than 14,000 in 1984.) Many banks have also become more reluctant to lend to small businesses in the wake of regulations following the Great Financial Crisis 20 years ago.

Pioneering community banks and credit unions like Southern, Self-Help, Hope, and American Pride Bank help close the finance access gap for aspiring homeowners and business owners who live and work outside major investment hubs, as we saw earlier. There is likely a community bank or credit union near where you live. And if you prefer to focus more on issues than places, you can also deposit with a range of banks focused on making loans that address specific issues, such as financing companies that provide loans for clean energy production.

Unfortunately, bank consolidation, regular financial upheaval, and savvy marketing campaigns have created a sense that only banking with the largest banks is prudent. When you tell your family or financial advisors you want to move your cash deposits to a community bank, you will likely hear three objections.

The first is about deposit insurance. Deposits up to $250,000 in any one bank are insured by the federal government. If the bank fails, the government has committed to make sure you get your deposit back. But what happens if you have more than $250,000? Through the IntraFi Network, a single bank can get more than $100 million insured through access to a program that spreads funds across many banks while you maintain a single banking relationship. IntraFi's ACT program, launched in partnership with the Community Development Bankers Association, also allows deposits to be placed with one community bank and distributed across others while preserving insurance coverage.

The second pushback you may receive is that community banks do not really need deposits because they are constrained by a lack of equity. This is the notion that even if you place your deposits with one of them, they will not be able to lend that out because they do not have enough of their own money to cover potential losses on new loans. While that has been true for many and remains true for some, it is less true today. The federal government's Emergency Capital Investment Program (ECIP), created in 2021, provided more than $8.5 billion of long-term, low-cost equity-like capital to 175 community development banks and credit unions serving low-income communities.[1] For many of these institutions, the binding constraint today is not equity but deposits. Community banks often have potential borrowers they are eager to lend to but they cannot make these loans without your deposits.

The third pushback is that community banks offer poorer service or are simply inconvenient because they are smaller institutions. Financial technology has dramatically narrowed the gap between what small and large banks can offer. Many community banks now provide online banking, mobile apps, remote deposit, bill pay, wire services, and cash-management tools that meet the needs of most customers. Banking locally may also come with more personal service.

This does not mean every community bank will meet every need. Just like with any bank, you still need to do your own research and check services, rates, liquidity, and digital capabilities. But for many people, switching to a community bank is no longer a choice between impact and convenience. In many cases, you can have both. You may be able to access current technology, similar products, and comparable rates, while also investing in local communities.

No Accredited Investor Required: New Pathways for Retail Investors to Invest in America

Once your cash is squared away, you may have some money invested through a brokerage account. Your brokerage holdings can also invest in America. Historically, most of the opportunities described in this book such as venture funds, private credit vehicles, and direct deals were available only to qualified investors who meet relatively high thresholds of wealth, income, or financial knowledge. That remains true in many cases. But innovators have worked creatively over the last 20 years to build new pathways through which all investors can invest in America.

One of the longest-standing examples is the Calvert Community Note. What is now Calvert Impact Capital, a nonprofit that invests money to create positive social and environmental change alongside financial profit, launched the Community Note in 1995. It became one of the first products to allow everyday people, not just big institutional investors, to invest through their regular brokerage accounts in portfolios supporting areas such as affordable housing, small businesses, and community projects. The minimum for an online purchase is now $20.

Over time, the Calvert Community Note has financed many of the innovators featured in this book. The Community Note offers retail investors a direct way to support the same ecosystem-building strategies typically reserved for institutions by investing in funds, Community Development Finance Institutions (CDFIs), and social enterprises that prioritize broader ownership, access to services, and resilience.

Other organizations have followed Calvert's example to raise retail funds through institutional brokerage channels with a proliferation of experimentation in this area in the mid-2010s, spurred in part by a US Treasury bond guarantee program. Virginia-based nonprofit CDFI Capital Impact Partners (now part of Momentus Capital) opened up new capital for CDFIs when it changed its model in 2017 from relying solely on bank loans and foundations to selling bonds directly to individual investors. Because Capital Impact's track record of very high repayment gave these bonds solid credit ratings, investors have rushed to buy them, and they have since raised more than $500 million through multiple offerings.[2]

Other CDFIs followed suit. The CDFI arm of the affordable housing developer Enterprise issued its first retail note in 2017, expanding access to impact investing while financing affordable housing on a larger scale. Since then, Enterprise has raised hundreds of millions of dollars through its note program, engaging everyday investors eager to support housing stability while earning predictable returns. Philadelphia-based Reinvestment Fund, Chicago's Low-Income Investment Fund, and North Carolina's Self-Help Credit Union also replicated this approach.

Another option, C-Note, was launched in 2016 to make it easy for investors to deposit cash with CDFIs and other mission-focused lenders. Its online Flagship Fund is available to anyone with a bank account and has a $1 investment minimum. For larger portfolios, C-Note offers customized, targeted investments to CDFIs that allow investors to support specific regions or social issues.

Municipal bonds offer another underappreciated pathway for retail investors to invest in America. Firms like Florida's Community Capital Management have built impact-oriented municipal bond strategies with minimum investments typically around $250,000, helping move billions of dollars into underserved communities, climate-resilient infrastructure, and essential public services. Investors can select municipal bond offerings that advance solutions to specific issues such as racial equity, climate adaptation, or economic inclusion rather than settling for a generic approach.

Impact investors like Blue Haven Initiative have helped elevate this strategy. In interviews and public writing, Blue Haven's co-founder Liesel Pritzker has described how municipal markets often charge higher borrowing costs to Black and historically marginalized communities, not because of fundamentals, but because of neglect and bias. Focusing the municipal bonds in your portfolio on those that will support these communities or finance projects that expand opportunity or reduce inequality (such as transportation infrastructure or school construction) can be an effective way to invest in America.[3] Advocacy organization Activest has also identified opportunities for investors to advance opportunity through municipal bond investing. By allocating capital intentionally, investors can earn competitive returns while lowering the cost of capital for communities long forced to pay a premium.

Following the Great Depression, regulations restricted private, early-stage investing to wealthy individuals, based on the idea that they were sophisticated enough to avoid scams and had safety nets to handle losses. These laws created barriers that left regular investors with few options to invest in early start-ups and entrepreneurs with few options to raise capital from the general public. This also meant that most investors were prevented from investing in start-ups.

The 2012 Jumpstart Our Business Startups (JOBS) Act changed the game for everyday investors. Championed by Jean and Steve Case, the founder of AOL, and advocates for democratizing venture investing, the Act enabled crowdfunding platforms to flourish. Now, anyone can invest in mission-driven, early-stage companies or lend to nonprofits and individuals directly, often with low minimums and small fees. There is likely a platform to help you make an impact, whether you want to support education, local businesses, or green energy.

Working for Impact Twice: Investing Donor Advised Fund Assets in America

Donor-advised funds (DAFs) are among the fastest-growing vehicles in American philanthropy. More than a million people have DAF accounts that collectively hold more than $250 billion. Once money enters a DAF, it has already received its charitable tax deduction, making the contribution irrevocable. Think of a DAF like a one-way charitable bridge: funds move from your personal possession to a qualified non-profit, with no return trip allowed.

While it waits, it is invested. But typically it is invested in ways that do not aim to create positive social impact.

This raises a question: If the capital is destined for public benefit anyway, why not invest it for impact in the meantime?

In her December annual 2024 letter, philanthropist MacKenzie Scott wrote that she had asked her investment managers to invest her assets in funds and companies "focused on for-profit solutions" to the challenges she targets in her philanthropy. That way, she wrote, "the money can help address these issues twice," once while it is invested, and again when it is given away.[4]

DAFs are an obvious place for anyone who does not have billions to invest or donate to set up this double-impact engine. ImpactAssets spun out of Calvert Foundation (the precursor to Calvert Impact) in 2010 precisely to meet this demand. Today, it supports more than $4 billion through its DAF and advisory services. ImpactAssets has enabled donors to invest directly in many of the same strategies featured throughout this book, including energy production, affordable housing, and inclusive ownership. In addition to supporting its clients to invest in deals and funds individually, ImpactAssets facilitates the creation of collaborative investment pools, channeling capital into place-based housing strategies, funds supporting diverse fund managers, and enterprises expanding access to essential services.

Newer platforms like CataCap, co-founded by one of ImpactAssets' founders, are lowering barriers further, enabling DAF holders to deploy capital into impact investments with minimums as low as $250. By pooling these relatively small investments, CataCap can help donors invest in private impact strategies that are not set up to take small checks.

Community foundations, the original DAF providers, are joining in. The Greater Cincinnati Community Foundation helped lead the way in the early 2010s with a strategy focused on impact investing within the regional community. Larger Community Foundations, such as the Boston Foundation and Silicon Valley Community Foundation, have followed with dedicated impact investing teams sourcing and managing investments in affordable housing and other local priorities. So have smaller foundations in places like Nebraska and Maine.

The largest DAF account managers are affiliated to mainstream asset managers (e.g., Vanguard, Fidelity, and Schwab). Individuals in these organizations are pushing to support impact investing options, but face the inertia of large bureaucracies organized around mainstream asset management, not impact. They will invest in America when their clients push them to do so or take their accounts to providers who do. If you are one of their clients, you can help make that happen.

Full Faith and Credit: Investing Religious Assets in America

Religious communities played a crucial role in catalyzing the impact investing movement before it had a name. They can be a powerful force now in broadening the work of investing in America.

In many ways, the modern socially responsible investing movement began when communities of Catholic women religious demanded that the institutions managing their investments align them with their religious convictions. This followed Vatican II (1962–1965), which called religious orders to live their faith more fully through engagement with the modern world. Pioneering Sisters moved to take greater control of the investment assets they held in endowments aimed at supporting their Order's ongoing work and funding their retirement.

In the 1970s and 1980s, these orders became early leaders in socially responsible investing, most visibly through divestment from apartheid South Africa. They also seeded some of the nation's earliest community development financial institutions. This "Nun money" provided patient capital, early loan guarantees, and foundational deposits to fledgling CDFIs that would later become pillars of community finance, such as Hope and Self-Help. Their willingness to invest before models were proven helped establish the infrastructure that today channels billions of dollars into underserved communities.

Today, that legacy carries new urgency. As the Sisters in many orders age and begin planning for the stewardship of their assets beyond their lifetimes, there is growing determination to ensure those assets are permanently aligned with mission. Elizabeth Garlow has helped lead this effort through Charism, an initiative designed to support religious orders in deploying their capital for lasting impact while honoring their spiritual and fiduciary responsibilities.

Other faith traditions are similarly using their assets to invest in ways consistent with their faith that also bring investment capital to address broader opportunities for communities.

Trinity Wall Street, the historic Episcopal church in lower Manhattan, owned large tracts of land on which New York's Financial District was built. With profits from the development of this land, they have built a charitable foundation with a $6 billion endowment of diversified investments, now committed in part to impact strategies focused on affordable housing, homelessness, and racial equity, particularly in New York City. These investments complement Trinity's substantial grantmaking in the same areas, reflecting an integrated approach of deploying capital both philanthropically and financially to address systemic challenges in the communities it serves.

In the African Methodist Episcopal Church, leaders increasingly recognize that church property can play a galvanizing role in the development of historically Black communities. Through Crossing Capital, Rev. Sidney Williams, a former Wall Street banker turned New Jersey AME pastor, has helped structure transactions that mobilize church-owned land for mixed-use affordable housing, commercial space, and community facilities, particularly in neighborhoods where long-term residents face displacement from gentrification. Through a process he describes as "Fishing Differently," he helps church leaders and congregations reassess how they can harness their real estate and financial assets to serve the mission of the church beyond just creating a place for worship. By blending philanthropic, congregational, and private capital, the platform demonstrates how congregations can unlock underutilized assets by attracting investors and developers to the community who can support them realize their vision, rather than exploiting their lack of investment experience.

In the Jewish community, Brooklyn-based FJC has pioneered approaches to enabling donors to provide working capital loans to nonprofits. Through its Agency Loan Fund, FJC has provided loans that enable nonprofits to bridge delayed government payments and expand services without resorting to expensive credit. These loans exemplify a long-standing Jewish philanthropic tradition, also present in other faith groups, of using capital to strengthen institutions, not just fund programs. The Muslim community has also held long-established approaches to lending that include ethical considerations and commitment to transparency and fairness.

It's unlikely your church has the good fortune of literally owning Wall Street. But if you are part of a faith community, especially if you serve your religious institution on a finance or stewardship committee, these examples hopefully prompt a simple question: How could your religious institution harness its assets to live its values by investing in America?

Show Me the Impact: TFW When Your Wealth Advisor Is Excited You Want to Invest in America

If you work with a financial advisor, private bank, or a family office investment team, ask yourself a simple question: Would they treat my interest in investing in America as an exciting opportunity to help me align my capital with my values?

While the advisor community has not yet explicitly organized around the term "Invest in America," the best do increasingly provide impact investing options. At the large brokerage firms, internal teams now support wealth advisors to respond to client impact investing interest. At Morgan Stanley, the Investing with Impact Platform, launched in 2012, has grown into one of the largest wealth-management impact offerings. Goldman Sachs bought the impact investing advisor Imprint Capital in 2015. The Imprint Capital team now serves Goldman clients, developing impact-aligned investment strategies. For their part, JPMorgan launched a $150 million Global Impact Fund in 2021 and continues to advise clients with an interest in other impact investments.

Independent wealth advisory firms and outside investment advisors are also increasingly set up to support clients to identify, assess, and make impact investments. Some have hired professionals with track records working in CDFIs, in private foundation impact investing programs, or in nonprofits to support their existing advisors. Other wealth advisors have launched as "impact native" firms, specifically serving clients to implement impact investing strategies.

Despite this momentum, the established wealth advising industry tends to be a force of inertia, instinctually wary of investment mandates that go beyond maximizing financial return or minimizing taxes for clients. Many wealth advisors, focused on conventional portfolios, view impact investing and the specific opportunities to invest in America described here with skepticism. They believe that one of the important parts of their job is to stop their clients getting excited about risky investments they have not researched sufficiently. These advisors often do not distinguish between investments that are unreasonably risky and those that are focused on driving impact in a financially responsible way.

In the end, this is your money. There are many ways to invest in America that meet a wide range of risk and return needs. If your advisor is not excited to help you invest in America, it could be time to get one who is.

Making Capital Work Three Times for Foundations and Family Offices

If you have any influence over private foundation assets, there are many opportunities for you to advance an agenda to invest in America. Large private foundations like Ford and MacArthur helped create the modern impact investing movement in the 1970s and 1980s, after working with Congress to create the formal Program-Related Investment (PRI) designation in 1969. Now foundations are accelerating their innovative use of PRIs, expanding to deploy their endowment assets in market-rate impact investments, and creatively using loan guarantees, purchase commitments, and other tools to catalyze private investments that can help fuel solutions.

If the Blandin Community Foundation in the Minnesota Wood Basket has figured out how to invest in its community as we saw in Chapter 9, what excuse do foundations working in other communities have?

While MacKenzie Scott writes about having her capital work for impact twice, how about three times? A foundation can deposit their cash in a local community bank, helping that money support local families buying homes and small businesses driving economic vibrancy. It could pledge that cash as a guarantee for loans its grantees are taking out, lowering the rate on their financing. (If your grantee has a $10 million real estate project and your loan guarantee reduces the interest rate they pay for it by three percentage points, that guarantee would produce the functional equivalent of an additional $300,000 grant to the organization, creating a new way for you to support their work.) Organizations like Mission Investors Exchange and Confluence Philanthropy are helping foundations across the country to innovate and learn from each other in this work.

Beyond innovating specific deal structures, foundations are increasingly integrating their investing and grants practices. The Sobrato Organization, headquartered in Silicon Valley, focuses on affordable housing, education, and economic mobility. It integrates grants, impact investments, and real estate development to preserve housing affordability in one of the country's most expensive regions. Philadelphia-based Spring Point Partners blends philanthropy and impact investing to support education, worker ownership, and community resilience, often using grants to derisk early investments. In Utah, a group of organizations support the integrated investing and impact work of Jim Sorenson, including a foundation, impact investing advisory firm, and a University institute.

This playbook has options for large and small foundation alike. If you work at or take part in the governance of a foundation, you can push to align grants and investments, use guarantees creatively, and recognize that all the foundation's assets can be a tool to invest in advancing the foundation's mission.

Made in America, Reinvested at Home: Harnessing Corporate Capital

For much of the 20th century, many large American corporations understood themselves as stewards of the places they called home, such as Johnson & Johnson in New Brunswick, New Jersey, Ford in the Detroit area, and Eastman Kodak in Rochester, New York. They supported local housing, schools, and civic institutions not out of charity alone, but because their manufacturing, workforce, and headquarters were co-located. The prosperity of the company and the prosperity of the people living in the company towns were intertwined.

As supply chains globalized and headquarters became disconnected from production, many companies lost that sense of place-based responsibility. But the spirit has not disappeared. Companies like Prudential are modern examples of corporations reinvesting in the local communities that sustain their long-term success.

For many companies, the social challenges this book describes will also challenge their bottom line. These companies need consumers to thrive to buy their products and services. They also need the healthcare and education systems to help support a productive workforce. They need reliable energy production and abundant natural resources.

What can they do to help solve these challenges with the more than $30 trillion in financial assets they control?[5] They can deposit their cash with local community banks and credit unions if they have a commitment to a specific place, or deposit with targeted community banks nationally. They can also use venture funds to invest in companies that are both making money and solving national challenges. As one example, in 2020 PayPal committed more than $500 million in deposits to banks and credit unions serving people of color and investments in companies that could drive racial equity. Building on this and similar examples, the nonprofit Economic Opportunity Coalition was launched in 2022 to support companies partnering with government to make investments and use other corporate assets to advance more broadly shared American prosperity.

Beyond encouraging your company to use their treasury assets to invest in America, you could potentially go further by considering how its core business could support this work. Allivate Impact Capital, launched in 2022, channels client assets into investments that expand access to housing and employee ownership. The Allivate team spun out of Woodforest Bank, originally a small community bank in Texas that expanded significantly when it became Walmart's in-house banking partner. Both serving Walmart customers across the country and being employee-owned gave the Woodforest community investing team a differentiated understanding of the imperative and opportunity in its community investing work. Instead of just making community investments to fulfill its own regulatory obligation, Woodforest saw an opportunity to create a new business doing this work for others. Allivate is an example of what is possible when a company sees investing in America not just as a way to meet regulatory obligations or customer expectations, but as a business opportunity.

If you work at a large company, ask: Where does the treasurer keep corporate cash? Are deposits placed with community banks? Is the company investing in housing affordability, health, education, and economic development in the places where employees live? How can it manage its workers' pension fund to set them up for a comfortable retirement in a country with abundant opportunities for the next generation? How could we use our core business to advance broader American prosperity? What can I do from where I sit in the company to help my company invest in America?

Your Ballot as Balance Sheet

In the end, you don't need any money to help invest in America. You just have to show up to vote.

State Treasurers and City Comptrollers are among the most powerful and least discussed financial actors in America. Together, state public pension funds manage more than $5 trillion, while city and local systems control hundreds of billions more. Treasurers and governors also control trillions in government treasury assets. At the federal level, the Thrift Savings Plan holds over $1 trillion in retirement assets for federal workers and members of the uniformed services, with its investment policies determined by a five-member Board whose members are nominated by the President and include members approved by the House and Senate.

These pools of capital increasingly sit at the center of political controversy, pulling pension investing into broader ideological debates. But investing in America is not about ideology. It is about whether we use investment capital to expand opportunity, strengthen communities, and support the American dream for more people.

As voters, you can ask candidates how they plan to steward public assets. Will they follow examples like New York City and Illinois, using their pension and treasury assets to channel finance to affordable housing developers and companies extending fair loans to college students otherwise shut out of affordable loan options? Will they support credit programs, guarantees, and proposals for an American-style development finance institution or sovereign wealth fund?

Asset managers who charge billions of dollars each year to manage these assets work hard to influence where these assets are invested. Imagine if voters stood up a similar effort to ensure treasurers and comptrollers invest these assets for America.

Choosing What Your Money Makes Possible

Investing in America is not reserved for the leaders of large institutions, billionaires, or policymakers. It is something that millions of people can do by making everyday financial choices with intention.

The question is not whether capital shapes our economy. It always does. The real question is how we can intentionally shift where it flows. Every deposit, investment, grant, and vote conveys who matters, who counts, and which futures are worth financing. Choosing differently does not require purity or heroics. It requires intention and attention.

Throughout this book, we have seen that markets are powerful but incomplete. Left on their own, they tend to overinvest in what is familiar, scalable, and immediately profitable and underinvest in what is new, local, requires patience, and often essential to long-term prosperity for our country.

America faces great challenges. Fortunately, there are many tools available to finance the solutions to them. Community banks, retail notes, donor-advised funds, faith-based investing, public balance sheets, and corporate capital all offer ways to put our money to work building the kind of country we want to live in.

None of this guarantees success. Investing always involves risk. But choosing not to engage carries its own risk: an economy that works too well for too few, and not well enough for the rest.

Why I Invest in America

My American journey has been made possible by people and institutions that invested in me at pivotal moments, giving me the chance to seize opportunity and build a better future for my family. I choose to invest in America so I can help others have a similar chance.

I also invest in America because of how deeply rewarding it is to learn from, know, and support the people who show up every day to build products and services that extend fair access to financing and opportunity. And I invest in America because it is one small contribution I can make to the 250-year effort to help this country more fully live up to its founding ideals.

Investing in America is an act of optimism. It is a vote of confidence in the people and places around us and a belief that we can create an economy that shares prosperity more broadly. America has built one of the most dynamic economies in the world; it is time we put the full power of our vast investments to work to renew faith in an American dream that works for everyone.

Notes

Chapter 1

1. Jenn Pryce and Beth Bafford of Calvert Impact developed this description of capital markets as water flowing like a river that requires civil engineers to find new ways to channel to new places. See Pryce, J. (2025). *Calvert Impact's market-shaping strategy for the future of impact.* ImpactAlpha (14 May). Available at: https://impactalpha.com/calvertn-impacts-market-shaping-strategy-for-the-future-of-impact/ (accessed 28 January 2026).
2. Bugg-Levine, A. and Emerson, J. (2011). *Impact investing: Transforming how we make money while making a difference.* Hoboken, NJ: John Wiley & Sons.

Chapter 2

1. Unsung History. (2022, 18 July). Unsung history: The unusual codicil in Benjamin Franklin's Will [video]. Available at: https://www.unsunghistory podcast.com/videos/unsung-history-the-unusual-codicil-in-benjamin-franklins-will/ (accessed 20 January 2026).
2. Liberty Fund. (n.d.). *The works of Benjamin Franklin, Vol. XII: Letters and Misc. Writings 1788–1790, Supplement, Indexes.* Online Library of Liberty. Available at: https://oll.libertyfund.org/titles/franklin-the-works-of-benjamin-franklin-vol-xii-letters-and-misc-writings-1788-1790-supplement-indexes (accessed 20 January 2026).

3. City of Boston Archives. (n.d.). *Guide to the Franklin Fund records* (PDF). Available at: https://www.cityofboston.gov/images_documents/Guide%20to%20the%20Franklin%20Fund%20records_tcm3-20691.pdf (accessed 20 January 2026); Yenawine, B.H. (n.d.). *The Franklin trusts of Boston and Philadelphia: A historical analysis.* Syracuse University. https://surface.syr.edu/hst_etd/30/ (accessed 20 January 2026).

4. Hartle, T. (2022). Benjamin Franklin bankrolled 200 years of small business loans. *Christian Science Monitor*, 2 June. Available at: https://www.csmonitor.com/Books/Book-Reviews/2022/0602/Benjamin-Franklin-bankrolled-200-years-of-small-business-loans (accessed 20 January 2026).

5. Economic Policy Institute. (n.d.). *The productivity–pay gap.* https://www.epi.org/productivity-pay-gap/ (accessed 20 January 2026).

6. Board of Governors of the Federal Reserve System. (n.d.). *Report on the economic well-being of U.S. households.* https://www.federalreserve.gov/consumerscommunities/shed.htm (accessed 20 January 2026).

7. Bankrate. (n.d.). *Emergency savings report.* https://www.bankrate.com/banking/savings/emergency-savings-report/ (accessed 20 January 2026).

8. LendingClub. (2023, 28 February). *60% of Americans now living paycheck to paycheck, down from 64% a month ago.* https://ir.lendingclub.com/news/news-details/2023/60-of-Americans-Now-Living-Paycheck-to-Paycheck-Down-from-64-a-Month-Ago/ (accessed 20 January 2026).

9. Federal Reserve Board. (n.d.). *Survey of consumer finances.* https://www.federalreserve.gov/econres/scfindex.htm (accessed 20 January 2026).

10. Federal Reserve Board. (2020). *Disparities in wealth by race and ethnicity in the 2019 Survey of Consumer Finances.* https://www.federalreserve.gov/econres/notes/feds-notes/disparities-in-wealth-by-race-and-ethnicity-in-the-2019-survey-of-consumer-finances-20200928.html (accessed 20 January 2026).

11. Gale, W.G., Hall, O., and Sabelhaus, J. (2025, 24 July). *Taxing the Great Wealth Transfer. Milken Institute Review.* https://www.milkenreview.org/articles/taxing-the-great-wealth-transfer?IssueID=58 (accessed 24 January 2026).

12. Hacker, J.S. (2006). *The great risk shift: The new economic insecurity and the decline of the American Dream.* Oxford: Oxford University Press.

13. Autor, D., Levy, F., and Murnane, R. (2003). Why are there still so many jobs? *Journal of Economic Perspectives* 17(3): 3–30.

14. Employee ownership is one of three planks of a new "ownership econ-omy," built on the foundation of more people being able to own the company they work for, the house they live in, and the capital markets themselves. Ida Rademacher has promoted this work through a range of initiatives with the Aspen Institute. Keeley, T. and Sorenson, J. (2025). Democratizing American prosperity. *National Review* (3 March).

15. Aspen Institute Financial Security Program. (n.d.). *Financial insecurity in America*. https://www.aspeninstitute.org/programs/financial-security-program/ (accessed 20 January 2026).

16. Abello, O. (2022). Can a private equity model build wealth for workers of color? *Next City*, August 2. https://nextcity.org/features/can-a-private-equity-model-build-wealth-for-workers-of-color (accessed 20 January 2026).

17. National Center for Employee Ownership. (n.d.). *Employee ownership by the numbers*. https://www.nceo.org/research/employee-ownership-by-the-numbers (accessed 20 January 2026).

18. Rutgers Institute for the Study of Employee Ownership. (n.d.). *Employee ownership & ESOPs: What we know from recent research* (Research brief, Apr. 2025). Available at: https://cleo.rutgers.edu/articles/employee-ownership-esops-what-we-know-from-recent-research/ (accessed 20 January 2026).

19. Federal Reserve Board. (2023). Changes in U.S. family finances from 2019 to 2022. *Board of Governors of the Federal Reserve System*, October 18. https://www.federalreserve.gov/publications/changes-in-us-family-finances-from-2019-to-2022.htm (accessed 20 January 2026).

20. Project Equity. (n.d.). *2.3 million small businesses nationwide owned by aging boomers preparing to retire*. https://project-equity.org/press-releases/2-3-million-small-businesses-nationwide-owned-by-aging-boomers-preparing-to-retire-puts-1-in-6-employees-jobs-at-risk-based-on-a-project-equity-study/ (accessed 20 January 2026).

21. Mosaic Capital Partners. (n.d.). *Employee ownership buyout model*. https://www.mosaic-cp.com/employee-ownership-buyout/ (accessed 20 January 2026).

22. Common Trust. (n.d.). https://www.common-trust.com/ (accessed 20 January 2026).

23. Common Trust. (2025). Consumer Direct Care Network transitions to employee ownership, benefitting 135,000 caregivers. *Common Trust Blog* (26 August). https://www.common-trust.com/blog/consumer-direct-care-network-employee-ownership-trust (accessed 20 January 2026).

24. Dubner, S.J. (2024). Should companies be owned by their workers? *Freakonomics Radio* (Episode 587, 8 May). https://freakonomics.com/podcast/should-companies-be-owned-by-their-workers/ (accessed 20 January 2026).

25. PR Newswire. (2021). Veteran investor Damien Dwin launches Lafayette Square with $100 million financing from Morgan Stanley. https://www.prnewswire.com/news-releases/veteran-investor-damien-dwin-launches-lafayette-square-with-100-million-financing-from-morgan-stanley-301206081.html (accessed 20 January 2026).

26. Lafayette Square. (2025). *Form 10-K for fiscal year 2024*. U.S. Securities and Exchange Commission. https://www.sec.gov/ix?doc=/Archives/edgar/data/1849089/000184908925000005/ls-20241231.htm (accessed 20 January 2026).

27. Ford Foundation. (2025). New holding company Nine Dean to invest in quality jobs that drive business growth. *Ford Foundation News and Press*, 3 June 2025. https://www.fordfoundation.org/news-and-stories/news-and-press/news/new-holding-company-nine-dean-to-invest-in-quality-jobs-that-drive-business-growth/ (accessed 20 January 2026).

28. Lafayette Square. (2025). *Form 10-K for fiscal year 2024*. U.S. Securities and Exchange Commission. https://www.sec.gov/ix?doc=/Archives/edgar/data/1849089/000184908925000005/ls-20241231.htm (accessed 20 January 2026).

29. Jobs for the Future. (n.d.). Honest Jobs: A tech startup driving fair-chance hiring. https://www.jff.org/blog/honest-jobs-tech-startup-driving-fair-chance-hiring/ (accessed 20 January 2026).

30. Jobs for the Future. (n.d.). *JFF Ventures overview*. https://www.jff.org/work/jff-ventures/ (accessed 20 January 2026); PR Newswire (2022). Jobs for the Future launches new venture arm to invest in workforce and employment tech. Press release (22 October). https://www.prnewswire.com/news-releases/jobs-for-the-future-launches-new-venture-arm-to-invest-in-workforce-and-employment-tech-301653760.html (accessed 20 January 2026).

31. World Education Services. (n.d.). *Mariam Assefa Fund*. https://www.wes .org/social-impact/wes-mariam-assefa-fund/ (accessed 20 January 2026).

32. Benjamin, E.T. (2024). Interview with Phenix Capital: Esther T. Benjamin, Chief Executive Officer, World Education Services (4 March 2024). *Phenix Capital Faces of Impact*. https://phenixcapitalgroup.com/ thought-leaders-interviews/esther-t-benjamin-world-education- services (accessed 20 January 2026).

33. Mission Driven Finance. (2023). WES lead commitment announce- ment. *Mission Driven Finance News and Insights*, 23 May 2023. https:// www.missiondrivenfinance.com/news/wes-lead-commitment-mdf- capital-partners/ (accessed 20 January 2026).

Chapter 3

1. *Improved dwellings for the poor.* (1885). *The Jewish Chronicle* (London), 13 March. Cited in Tarn, J.N. (1973). *Five per cent philanthropy*. Cambridge: Cambridge University Press.

2. Harvard Joint Center for Housing Studies. (2023). *America's rental housing 2023*. Cambridge, MA: Harvard University. Full report PDF available at: https://www.jchs.harvard.edu/sites/default/files/media/imp/rh06_ americas_rental_housing.pdf (accessed 20 January 2026).

3. National Low Income Housing Coalition. (n.d.). *The gap: A shortage of affordable homes*. https://nlihc.org/gap (accessed 20 January 2026).

4. Joint Center for Housing Studies of Harvard University. (2025). *The state of the nation's housing 2025*. Cambridge, MA: Harvard University, esp. pp. 6–8, 30–35. https://www.jchs.harvard.edu/state-nations-housing- 2025 (accessed 20 January 2026).

5. Conroy, E. and Graetz, N. (2025). *Ousted from opportunity: Eviction's adverse impact on parenting college students*. New America, 26 June. Available at: https://newamerica.org/education-policy/briefs/what-happens-student- parents-threatened-with-eviction/ (accessed 20 January 2026).

6. U.S. Department of Housing and Urban Development. (2024). *The 2024 annual homelessness assessment report (AHAR) to Congress. Part 1: Point-in-time estimates of homelessness*. Washington, DC: HUD. Available at: https://www.huduser.gov/portal/publications/2024-ahar-part-1-pit- estimates-of-homelessness.html (accessed 20 January 2026).

7. Adamczyk, A. (2025). Typical mortgage payment has more than doubled in five years. *Investopedia*. 31 January. https://www.investopedia.com/new-zillow-data-shows-typical-mortgage-payment-has-more-than-doubled-in-just-5-years-8784090 (accessed 20 January 2026).

8. Joint Center for Housing Studies of Harvard University. (2025). Home prices surge to five times median income, nearing historic highs. *JCHS Blog*. https://www.jchs.harvard.edu/blog/home-prices-surge-five-times-median-income-nearing-historic-highs (accessed 20 January 2026).

9. Urban Institute. (n.d.). *Reducing the racial homeownership gap.* https://www.urban.org/policy-centers/housing-finance-policy-center/projects/reducing-racial-homeownership-gap (accessed 20 January 2026).

10. National Association of Realtors. (2025). *Profile of home buyers and sellers: First-time buyer share falls to historic low.* https://www.nar.realtor/newsroom/first-time-home-buyer-share-falls-to-historic-low-of-21-median-age-rises-to-40 (accessed 20 January 2026).

11. Up for Growth. (2023). *2023 housing underproduction report.* https://upforgrowth.org/apply-the-vision/2023-housing-underproduction/ (accessed 20 January 2026); Brookings Institution (2024). *Make it count: Measuring our housing supply shortage* (26 November). https://www.brookings.edu/articles/make-it-count-measuring-our-housing-supply-shortage/ (accessed 20 January 2026).

12. Harvard Joint Center for Housing Studies. (2025). *The state of the nation's housing 2025* (cited via media summaries). Cambridge, MA: Harvard University. Available at: https://www.jchs.harvard.edu/state-nations-housing-2025 (accessed 20 January 2026).

13. Martin, M. and Mercein, T. (2025). Correspondence with author, October (unpublished).

14. CalMatters. (2025). *California's homebuyer lotto was hardly a "Dream for All".* 2 May. Available at: https://calmatters.org/commentary/2025/05/dream-for-all-down-payment/ (accessed 28 January 2026).

15. Ibid.

16. Keeley, T. and Sorenson, J. (2025). Free markets and capitalism can reduce income inequality. *National Review* (3 March).

17. Homium. (n.d.). Senate's housing bill needs to enable fair shared appreciation. https://www.homium.io/blog/senates-housing-bill-needs-to-enable-fair-shared-appreciation (accessed 20 January 2026).

18. ROC USA. (n.d.). Liberty Landing Cooperative residents purchase community to become first ROC in Missouri. https://rocusa.org/blog/liberty-landing-cooperative-residents-purchase-community-to-become-first-roc-in-missouri/ (accessed 20 January 2026).

19. MHInsider. (n.d.). Manufactured housing industry trends and statistics. https://mhinsider.com/manufactured-housing-industry-trends-statistics/ (accessed 20 January 2026).

20. Regional Housing Legal Services. (2024). *Preserving homeownership in manufactured home communities* (full report PDF). Available at: https://rhls.org/wp-content/uploads/2025/09/Preserving-Homeownership-in-Manufactured-Home-Communities-1.pdf (accessed 20 January 2026).

21. Private Equity Stakeholder Project. (n.d.). *Private equity manufactured housing tracker.* https://pestakeholder.org/pesp-private-equity-manufactured-housing-tracker/ (accessed 20 January 2026).

22. Ibid.

23. The Guardian. (2024). Slash and burn: Is private equity out of control? *The Guardian* (10 October). https://www.theguardian.com/business/2024/oct/10/slash-and-burn-is-private-equity-out-of-control (accessed 20 January 2026).

24. ROC USA. (n.d.). My story: Paul Bradley. https://rocusa.org/blog/my-story/ (accessed 20 January 2026).

25. Freddie Mac Multifamily. (n.d.). *Resident-owned communities podcast transcript.* https://mf.freddiemac.com/docs/MFPodcast_ROC_USA_Transcript.pdf (accessed 20 January 2026).

26. Calvert Impact. (n.d.). *Resident ownership capital partner profile.* https://calvertimpact.org/investing/partner/resident-ownership-capital (accessed 20 January 2026).

27. ROC USA. (2024). *Our impact — how ROC USA supports resident owned communities.* Available at: https://rocusa.org/our-impact/ (accessed 20 January 2026).

28. Community Vision Capital & Consulting. (2025). *Community Vision finances $3.4 million loan for Integrity Community Solutions' acquisition and revitalization of manufactured home and RV community in Columbia, CA* (13 February 2025). https://communityvisionca.org/community-vision-finances-3-4-million-loan-for-integrity-community-solutions-acquisition-and-revitalization-of-manufactured-home-and-rv-community-in-columbia-ca/ (accessed 20 January 2026).

29. Ibid.

30. Peralta Soloff, K. (2021). How Camp North End evolved from a missile assembly plant to a neighborhood hotspot. *Axios Charlotte* (28 April). https://www.axios.com/local/charlotte/2021/04/28/how-camp-north-end-evolved-from-a-missile-assembly-plant-to-a-neighborhood-hotspot-256063 (accessed 20 January 2026).

31. Camp North End. (n.d.). About us: History. https://camp.nc/about/history/ (accessed 20 January 2026).

32. Baird, R. (2025). Email correspondence with author. 11 November.

33. Scott, T. (2017). Senator Scott introduces the bipartisan Investing in Opportunity Act. Press release (5 October). https://www.scott.senate.gov/media-center/press-releases/senator-scott-introduces-the-bipartisan-investing-in-opportunity-act/ (accessed 20 January 2026).

34. Baird, R. (2025). Interview with author. 9 June.

35. Economic Innovation Group. (2023). *Print-friendly OZ fact sheet* (Opportunity Zones facts and figures). Available at: https://eig.org/wp-content/uploads/2023/06/Print-Friendly-OZ-Fact-Sheet.pdf (accessed 20 January 2026).

36. Economic Innovation Group. (2025). *The impact of Opportunity Zones on housing supply* (working paper summary). Available at: https://eig.org/opportunity-zones-housing-supply/ (accessed 20 January 2026).

37. Theodos, B. and Meixell, B. (2025). Opportunity Zones need to be retooled to achieve impact. *Urban Institute* (12 May). https://www.urban.org/urban-wire/opportunity-zones-need-be-retooled-achieve-impact (accessed 20 January 2026).

38. U.S. Department of Housing and Urban Development. (n.d.). *Section 4 program impact: Jubilee Housing, Washington, DC* case study. Available at: https://www.hudexchange.info/news/section-4-program-impact-jubilee-housing-washington-dc/ (accessed 20 January 2026).

39. Recovery Café Network. (n.d.). Jubilee's beginnings. https://www.recoverycafenetwork.org/jubilee-housing-dc/ (accessed 20 January 2026).

40. Enterprise. (n.d). How It All Started. How It All Started | Enterprise Community Partners (accessed March 1 2026).

41. CDFI Fund. (2025). *Snap stat: A view of the certified CDFI universe.* https://www.cdfifund.gov/system/files/2025-04/SNAPSTAT_2025_031225.pdf (accessed 22 January 2026).

42. Rothstein, R. (2018). *The color of law*. New York: Liveright Publishing.

43. Federal Reserve Bank of St. Louis. (2018). The Community Reinvestment Act's history and future. *On the Economy* (24 January). https://www.stlouisfed.org/on-the-economy/2018/january/community-reinvestment-act-history-future (accessed 20 January 2026).

44. U.S. Department of Housing and Urban Development. (n.d.). *LIHTC Property-level data*. Available at: https://www.huduser.gov/portal/datasets/lihtc/property.html (accessed 20 January 2026).

45. Office of the Comptroller of the Currency. (2014). *Low-income housing tax credits. Community Developments Insights* (March). https://www.occ.gov/publications-and-resources/publications/community-affairs/community-developments-insights/pub-insights-mar-2014.pdf (accessed 20 January 2026).

46. Enterprise Community Loan Fund. (n.d.). *Impact Note*. https://www.enterprisecommunity.org/capabilities/community-development-financial-institution-cdfi/impact-note (accessed 20 January 2026).

47. Enterprise Community Partners. (n.d.). *Green Communities* (program overview). Available at: https://www.enterprisecommunity.org/impact-areas/resilience/green-communities (accessed 20 January 2026).

48. Rocky Mountain PBS. (2025). Berg, A. (19 April). 'One solution to Denver's housing shortfall? Living with 18 roommates'. Available at: https://www.rmpbs.org/blogs/housing-transportation/peoples-mansion-denver-co-op (accessed 20 January 2026).

49. Colorado Housing Accelerator Initiative (CHAI). (2025). *2024 impact report*. Denver, CO: CHAI. https://chaifunds.com/wp-content/uploads/2025/02/CHAI-2024-Impact-Report-Final.pdf (accessed 20 January 2026).

50. Gary Community Ventures. (n.d.). *History*. Available at: https://garycommunity.org/about-us/history/ (accessed 20 January 2026).

51. Gary Community Ventures. (n.d.). Who is Gary Community Ventures? https://garycommunity.org/frequently-asked-questions/ (accessed 20 January 2026).

52. Toner, C. (2025). Interview with author. 3 November.

53. National Low Income Housing Coalition. (2025). *State housing profile: Colorado*. https://nlihc.org/sites/default/files/SHP_CO.pdf (accessed 20 January 2026).

54. Common Sense Institute. (n.d.). *Denver housing affordability report.* https://www.commonsenseinstituteus.org/colorado/research/housing-and-our-community/denver-housing-affordability-report (accessed 20 January 2026).

55. Colorado Housing Accelerator Initiative. (2024). *CHAI 2023 impact report.* Available at: https://chaifunds.com/wp-content/uploads/2024/07/CHAI-2023-Impact-Report-Final.pdf (accessed 20 January 2026). *(This is the full impact report rather than the generic homepage.)*

56. Colorado Department of Local Affairs, Demography Office. (n.d.). *Research briefs.* https://demography.dola.colorado.gov/assets/html/researchbriefs.html (accessed 20 January 2026).

57. Community Solutions. (2025). *About built for zero.* Community Solutions. Available at: https://community.solutions/built-for-zero (accessed 30 January 2026).

58. U.S. Department of Housing and Urban Development. (2023). *2023 Annual Homelessness Assessment Report to Congress: Part 1.* HUD User. Available at: https://www.huduser.gov/portal/sites/default/files/pdf/2023-AHAR-Part-1.pdf (accessed 30 January 2026).

59. Community Solutions. (2025). *Community solutions raises $135 million from impact investors focused on housing and homelessness.* Community Solutions Press. Available at: https://community.solutions/press/community.solutions-raises-135-million-from-impact-investors-focused-on-housing-and-homelessness (accessed 30 January 2026).

60. Community Solutions. (2023). *Community solutions acquires third property in Jacksonville dedicated to solving veteran homelessness, preserving existing affordable housing.* Press release, March 4, 2023. Available at: https://community.solutions/press/press-release-community-solutions-acquires-third-property-in-jacksonville-dedicated-to-solving-veteran-homelessness-preserving-existing-affordable-housing (accessed January 30 2026).

Chapter 4

1. U.S. Energy Information Administration. (2025). U.S. electricity prices have increased faster than inflation. *Today in Energy*, 14 May 2025. https://www.eia.gov/todayinenergy/detail.php?id=65284 (accessed 22 January 2026).

2. American Council for an Energy-Efficient Economy. (2024). *Data update: City energy burdens.* Policy brief with information on U.S. household energy burden showing distribution of energy costs relative to income. https://www.aceee.org/policy-brief/2024/09/data-update-city-energy-burdens (accessed 22 January 2026).

3. U.S. Census Bureau. (2024). How do power outages affect households? *American Housing Survey Stories,* 2 October 2024. https://www.census.gov/library/stories/2024/10/power-outages.html (accessed 22 January 2026).

4. U.S. Department of Energy. (2024). DOE releases new report evaluating increase in electricity demand from data centers. Lawrence Berkeley National Laboratory data summary. https://www.energy.gov/articles/doe-releases-new-report-evaluating-increase-electricity-demand-data-centers (accessed 22 January 2026).

5. Fervo Energy. (2025). *Fervo energy secures $206 million in new financing to accelerate Cape Station development.* Press Release, 11 June 2025 https://fervoenergy.com/fervo-secures-new-financing-to-accelerate-development/ (accessed 22 January 2026).

6. U.S. Energy Information Administration. (n.d.). How much electricity does an American home use? EIA FAQs. https://www.eia.gov/tools/faqs/faq.php?id=97&t=3 (accessed 22 January 2026).

7. ThinkGeoEnergy. (2021). Fervo energy raises $28M Series B led by Capricorn. https://www.thinkgeoenergy.com/fervo-energy-raises-28m-to-scale-next-gen-geothermal-tech/ (accessed 22 January 2026).

8. Fervo Energy. (2024). Fervo energy secures additional $255 million funding. Press release. https://www.fervoenergy.com/fervo-energy-secures-additional-255-million-funding/ (accessed 22 January 2026).

9. Business Wire. (2025). Fervo energy raises $462M Series E. https://www.businesswire.com/news/home/20251210925924/en/Fervo-Energy-Raises-462-Million-Series-E (accessed 22 January 2026).

10. Capricorn Investment Group. (n.d.). Cleaning up live: Ion Yadigaroglu, pioneering impact investor. https://capricornllc.com/news/cleaning-up-live-ion-yadigaroglu-pioneering-impact-investor/ (accessed 22 January 2026).

11. Fervo Energy. (2024). Fervo energy raises $244 million to accelerate deployment of next-generation geothermal. Press release, 29 February 2024. https://fervoenergy.com/fervo-energy-raises-244-million-to-accelerate-deployment-of-next-generation-geothermal/ (accessed 22 January 2026).

12. World Economic Forum. (n.d.). Capricorn Investment Group. https://www.weforum.org/organizations/capricorn-investment-group/ (accessed 22 January 2026).

13. MCJ Collective. (n.d.). Ion Yadigaroglu. *Inevitable Podcast.* https://mcj.vc/inevitable-podcast/ion-yadigaroglu (accessed 22 January 2026).

14. Aalo Atomics. (2024). Aalo Atomics raises $27M Series A to deploy factory-built nuclear plants. Press release. https://www.aalo.com/post/aalo-atomics-raises-27m-series-a (accessed 22 January 2026).

15. Aalo Atomics. (2025). *Aalo Atomics secures $100 million Series B to build modular nuclear plants.* Press release, August 2025. Available at: https://www.aalo.com/post/aalo.closes-100m-series-b (accessed 22 January 2026).

16. Nuclear Energy Institute. (2024). Fissionary episode 7: Charles Oppenheimer. Podcast episode. https://www.nei.org/news/2024/fissionary-episode-7-charles-oppenheimer (accessed 22 January 2026).

17. Oppenheimer, C. (2024). The World Bank should fund nuclear energy. *Context News.* https://www.context.news/just-transition/opinion/charles-oppenheimer-the-world-bank-should-fund-nuclear-energy (accessed 22 January 2026).

18. Business North Carolina. (2018). Dave Kirkpatrick's SJF makes green by investing in sustainable projects. 2 July 2018. https://businessnc.com/dave-kirkpatricks-sjf-makes-green-by-investing-in-sustainable-projects/ (accessed 22 January 2026).

19. PR Newswire. (2021). AES acquires U.S. renewables developer Community Energy. Press release, 20 December 2021. https://www.prnewswire.com/news-releases/aes-acquires-us-renewables-developer-community-energy-adding-10-gw-of-renewable-projects-to-growth-pipeline-301448495.html (accessed 22 January 2026).

20. PR Newswire. (2021). SJF ventures closes fifth fund at $175 million. Press release, 4 February 2021. https://www.prnewswire.com/news-releases/sjf-ventures-closes-fifth-fund-at-175-million-301222568.html (accessed 22 January 2026).

21. Solar Power World. (2017). ConnectDER receives funding to expand utility meter collar adapter. 15 February 2017. https://www.solarpowerworldonline.com/2017/02/connectder-receives-funding/ (accessed 22 January 2026).

22. Prime Coalition. (n.d.). Catalytic Investing. https://www.primecoalition.org/catalytic-investing (accessed 24 January 2026).

23. Prime Coalition. (n.d.). Our impact. https://www.primecoalition.org/investments (accessed 22 January 2026).

24. Entrepreneurs for Impact. (n.d.). Dawn Lippert: CEO of Elemental Excelerator. https://www.entrepreneursforimpact.com/dawn-lippert-ceo-elemental-excelerator (accessed 22 January 2026).

25. Price, D. (2021). *Elemental Excelerator's climate-tech unicorns develop locally, deploy globally. ImpactAlpha*, 30 September 2021. Available at: https://impactalpha.com/elemental-excelerators-climate-tech-unicorns-develop-locally-deploy-solutions-globally/ (accessed 22 January 2026).

26. PR Newswire. (2024). Elemental Excelerator and Wilson Sonsini create new funding mechanism to fast-track development funding for climate technologies. Press release, 17 July 2024. https://www.prnewswire.com/news-releases/elemental-excelerator--wilson-sonsini-create-new-funding-mechanism-to-fast-track-development-funding-for-climate-technologies-302175074.html (accessed 22 January 2026).

27. Elemental Impact. (2025). *2024 Annual report: Investing in entrepreneurs. Deepening Local Impact.* https://elementalimpact.com/2024-annual-report/ (accessed 22 January 2026).

Chapter 5

1. National Center for Education Statistics. (n.d.). *Public education expenditures.* https://educationdata.org/public-education-spending-statistics (accessed 23 January 2026).

2. OECD. (n.d.). *Programme for International Student Assessment (PISA).* https://www.oecd.org/pisa (accessed 23 January 2026).

3. Education Data Initiative. (n.d.). *Average cost of college.* https://educationdata.org/average-cost-of-college (accessed 23 January 2026).

4. National Center for Education Statistics. (n.d.). *The Nation's Report Card (NAEP).* https://nationsreportcard.gov (accessed 23 January 2026).

5. Stanford University. (n.d.). *Education recovery scorecard.* https://educationrecoveryscorecard.org (accessed 23 January 2026).

6. Education Data Initiative, "Student Loan Debt Statistics," https://educationdata.org/student-loan-debt-statistics (accessed 23 January 2026).

7. Texas Education Agency. (2023). *House Bill 2 summary.* https://tea.texas.gov/about-tea/government-relations-and-legal/government-relations/house-bill-2 (accessed 23 January 2026).

8. Texas Education Agency. (n.d.). *College, career, and military readiness (CCMR) achievement updates.* PDF. https://tea.texas.gov/sites/default/files/taa-2024-09-19-college-career-or-military-readiness-outcomes-bonus-reports-updates.pdf (accessed 23 January 2026).

9. The Commit Partnership. (2025). *Maycomb Capital invests in Education Is Freedom to expand postsecondary readiness across Dallas County.* https://www.commitpartnership.org/insights/latest-learnings/maycomb-capital-invests-in-education-is-freedom-to-expand-postsecondary-readiness-across-dallas-county (accessed 23 January 2026).

10. AtoZ Impact News. (2025). *Why we invested in Maycomb.* AtoZ Impact News, 4 April 2025. https://news.atozimpact.org/why-we-invested-in-maycomb-122653622583 (accessed 23 January 2026).

11. Phillips, A. (2025). Author interview with Andi Philip, 14 November 2025.

12. ImpactAssets. (2025). *ImpactAssets 50 profile: Maycomb Capital.* ImpactAssets 50: A global database of impact investment fund managers. https://impactassets.org/ia50/fund.php?id=a01RQ00000O8FgpYAF (accessed 23 January 2026).

13. Maycomb Capital. (2025). *Maycomb Capital Fund II fact sheet.* https://assets.marincf.org/pdfs/MCF-Maycomb-Fact-Sheet-01.02.25.pdf (accessed 23 January 2026).

14. Mission Investors Exchange. (2018). *Prudential, Kresge and Steve Ballmer back Maycomb Capital's pay-for-success fund.* Mission Investors Exchange, 14 May 2018. https://missioninvestors.org/news/prudential-kresge-and-steve-ballmer-back-maycomb-capital-s-pay-success-fund (accessed 24 January 2026).

15. Maycomb Capital. (n.d.). *Hello Family, a continuum of prenatal and early childhood services in Spartanburg, SC.* Maycomb Capital. https://www.maycombcapital.com/the-community-outcomes-fund/hello-family-a-continuum-of-prenatal-and-early-childhood-services-in-spartanburg-sc/ (accessed 23 January 2026).

16. Phillips, A. (2025). Author interview with Andi Philip, 14 November 2025.

17. Philanthropy Roundtable. (2025). *Building charter schools for the future with Equitable Facilities Fund.* https://www.philanthropyroundtable.org/building-charter-schools-for-the-future-with-equitable-facilities-fund/ (accessed 23 January 2026).

18. Walton Family Foundation. (n.d.). *Building equity initiative.* https://www.waltonfamilyfoundation.org/building-equity-initiative (accessed 23 January 2026).

19. RealClearEducation. (2020). *Tapping Wall Street to fund charter schools.* https://www.realcleareducation.com/articles/2020/01/31/tapping_wall_street_to_fund_charter_schools_110390.html (accessed 23 January 2026).

20. Education Pioneers. (n.d.). *Anand Kesavan – alum profile.* https://educationpioneers.org/alum/anand-kesavan/ (accessed 23 January 2026).

21. U.S. Department of Education. (2019). *Equitable Facilities Fund project narrative.* https://www.ed.gov/sites/ed/files/2020/12/EFF-USED-CE-grant-Project-Narrative-2019-F-redacted.pdf (accessed 23 January 2026).

22. Equitable Facilities Fund. (2025). *EFF 2024–2025 impact report.* Equitable Facilities Fund. https://eqfund.org/about/in-the-news (accessed 24 January 2026).

23. PR Newswire. (2024). *Equitable Facilities Fund announces most successful bond issuance to date to support educational equity.* https://www.prnewswire.com/news-releases/equitable-facilities-fund-announces-most-successful-bond-issuance-to-date-to-support-educational-equity-302293234.html (accessed 23 January 2026).

24. Equitable Facilities Fund. (n.d.). *Equitable Facilities Fund overview.* https://eqfund.org (accessed 23 January 2026).

25. Social Finance. (n.d.). *ADTC Career Impact Bond case study.* https://socialfinance.org/work/career-impact-bond/adtc/ (accessed 23 January 2026).

26. Social Finance. (n.d.) American Diesel Training Centers Career Impact Bond. https://socialfinance.org/work/adtc/ (accessed 1 March 2026).

27. Student Freedom Initiative. (n.d.). *Student Freedom Initiative — Programs at a glance.* https://studentfreedominitiative.org/programs-at-a-glance/ (accessed 23 January 2026).

28. U.S. Department of Education. (n.d.). *Federal Student Aid portfolio summary.* https://studentaid.gov/data-center/student/portfolio (accessed 23 January 2026).

29. Brookings Institution. (n.d.). *Student loans, the racial wealth divide, and why we need full student debt cancellation.* Brookings Institution. https://www.brookings.edu/articles/student-loans-the-racial-wealth-divide-and-why-we-need-full-student-debt-cancellation/ (accessed 23 January 2026).

30. State Higher Education Executive Officers Association. (n.d.). *State Higher Education Finance (SHEF) report.* SHEEO. https://shef.sheeo.org/report/ (accessed 23 January 2026).

31. College Board. (n.d.). *Trends in college pricing and student aid.* College Board Research. https://research.collegeboard.org/trends/college-pricing (accessed 23 January 2026).

32. The Institute for College Access & Success. (n.d.). *Student debt and the racial wealth gap.* TICAS. https://ticas.org/affordability-2/a-supplemental-wealth-based-pell-grant-how-to-meet-unaddressed-need-and-close-racial-gaps-in-student-loan-borrowing/ (accessed 23 January 2026).

33. Consumer Financial Protection Bureau. (n.d.). *Private student loans report.* https://www.consumerfinance.gov/data-research/research-reports/private-student-loans-report/ (accessed 23 January 2026); Consumer Financial Protection Bureau. (n.d.). *Credit invisibles report.* https://www.consumerfinance.gov/data-research/research-reports/data-point-credit-invisibles/ (accessed 23 January 2026).

34. Scott, M. (2024). *Investing. Yield Giving Essays*, 18 December 2024. https://yieldgiving.com/essays/investing/ (accessed 23 January 2026).

35. Pollard, J. (November 26, 2025). *MacKenzie Scott's college roommate once loaned her $1K. Now it's the billionaire's turn to invest.* AP News. https://apnews.com/article/ce25dd95df46653c13d0701c49c98c51 (accessed 23 January 2026).

36. Illinois State Treasurer. (n.d.). *Student Empowerment Fund.* https://www.il-sef.com/about-student-empowerment-fund (accessed 23 January 2026).

37. Reach Capital. (n.d.). *Getting actionable insights into an invisible crisis: student mental health.* https://medium.com/reach-capital/getting-actionable-insights-into-an-invisible-crisis-student-mental-health-dcb8bb581df (accessed 23 January 2026).

38. Renbarger, M. (2023). *How Shauntel Garvey went from being a chemical engineer to building one of the largest edtech-focused venture funds in the world.* Business Insider, 24 May 2023. https://www.businessinsider.com/investor-shauntel-garvey-edtech-venture-capital-reach-capital-2023-5 (accessed 23 January 2026).

39. EdTechReview. (n.d.). *Reach Capital raises $215M to invest in education startups.* https://www.edtechreview.in/news/san-francisco-based-reach-apital-raises-215m-to-invest-in-education-startups/ (accessed 23 January 2026).

40. Herrera, J. (February 7, 2022). *Beep Beep! Expanding the Family With the Reach Roadrunners.* Reach Capital. https://www.reachcapital.com/resources/news/beep-beep-expanding-the-family-with-the-reach-roadrunners/ (accessed 23 January 2026).

41. Reach Capital. (2022). *Reflecting on our impact on K-12 since 2015: K-12 impact report.* Reach Capital. https://www.reachcapital.com/resources/thought-leadership/reflecting-on-our-impact-on-k-12-since-2015/ (accessed 23 January 2026).

42. Koenig, R. (2020). *An app for student emergency aid finds new urgency during pandemic.* EdSurge, 23 December. Available at: https://www.edsurge.com/news/2020-12-23-an-app-for-student-emergency-aid-finds-new-urgency-during-pandemic (accessed 29 January 2026).

43. Beam. (2024). *2024 impact report.* Available at: https://www.bybeam.co/2024-impact-report (accessed 29 January 2026).

44. Beam. (2021). *Beam raises oversubscribed $2.4MM seed round to bring cash assistance to people when they need it most.* Available at: https://www.bybeam.co/newsroom-post/beam-raises-2-4-m (accessed 29 January 2026); PR Newswire (2022). *Beam announces $6.4M Series A to create the next generation of the social safety net.* Available at: https://www.prnewswire.com/news-releases/beam-announces-6-4m-series-a-to-create-the-next-generation-of-the-social-safety-net-301682238.html (accessed 29 January 2026).

45. Lumina Foundation. (n.d.). *Goal 2025.* https://www.luminafoundation.org/news-and-views/a-bold-vision-for-a-prosperous-future/ (accessed 23 January 2026).

46. Lumina Foundation. (n.d.). *Stronger Nation attainment data.* https://strongernation.luminafoundation.org (accessed 23 January 2026).

47. Lumina Foundation. (n.d.). *Attainment goals and strategy.* https://www.luminafoundation.org/stronger-nation (accessed 23 January 2026).

48. Kresge Foundation & Lumina Foundation. (2017). *Driving postsecondary success with impact investing.* https://www.luminafoundation.org/resource/driving-postsecondary-success-with-impact-investing/ (accessed 23 January 2026).

49. Lumina Foundation. (n.d.). *Impact investing strategy.* https://www.luminafoundation.org/our-work/impact-investing/ (accessed 23 January 2026).

50. Lumina Foundation. (2025). *Multi-state higher education initiative announcement.* https://www.luminafoundation.org/news-and-views/lumina-initiates-multi-state-effort-using-higher-ed-to-drive-economic-prosperity/ (accessed 23 January 2026).

51. ECMC Group. (n.d.). *Education Impact Fund.* https://www.ecmcgroup.org/what-we-do/education-impact-fund (accessed 23 January 2026).

52. ECMC Foundation. (n.d.). *Education Innovation Ventures.* https://www.ecmcfoundation.org/what-we-do/education-innovation-ventures (accessed 23 January 2026).

53. ECMC Group. (n.d.). *How learning and evaluation drive our grantmaking and investing strategies.* https://www.ecmc.org/news/ecmc/how-learning-and-evaluation-drive-our-grantmaking-and-investing-strategies (accessed 22 January 2026).

54. ECMC Foundation. (n.d.). *Education Innovation Ventures.* https://www.ecmcfoundation.org/what-we-do/education-innovation-ventures (accessed 22 January 2026).

Chapter 6

1. Kaiser Family Foundation (KFF). (n.d.). *The burden of medical debt in the United States.* KFF. https://www.kff.org/health-costs/the-burden-of-medical-debt-in-the-united-states/ (accessed 23 January 2026).

2. Kaiser Family Foundation (KFF). (2022). *Health care debt in the U.S.: The broad consequences of medical and dental bills.* KFF. https://www.kff.org/health-costs/kff-health-care-debt-survey/ (accessed 23 January 2026).

3. Peterson–KFF Health System Tracker. (n.d.). *U.S. health spending.* Peterson Center on Healthcare and KFF. https://www.healthsystemtracker.org/chart-collection/u-s-spending-healthcare-changed-time/ (accessed 23 January 2026).

4. Centers for Disease Control and Prevention (CDC). (n.d.). *Life expectancy in the United States.* National Center for Health Statistics. https://www.cdc.gov/nchs/data-visualization/life-expectancy/ (accessed 23 January 2026).

5. Centers for Disease Control and Prevention (CDC). (2019). *Racial/ethnic disparities in pregnancy-related deaths—United States, 2007–2016. Morbidity and Mortality Weekly Report* (MMWR). https://www.cdc.gov/mmwr/volumes/68/wr/mm6835a3.htm (accessed 23 January 2026).

6. University of North Carolina Cecil G. Sheps Center for Health Services Research. (n.d.). *Rural hospital closures.* https://www.shepscenter.unc.edu/programs-projects/rural-health/rural-hospital-closures/ (accessed 23 January 2026).

7. March of Dimes. (n.d.) *Maternity care deserts report.* March of Dimes. https://www.marchofdimes.org/research/maternity-care-deserts-report.aspx (accessed 23 January 2026).

8. Kaiser Family Foundation (KFF). (2022). *Health care debt in the U.S.: The broad consequences of medical and dental bills.* KFF. https://www.kff.org/health-costs/kff-health-care-debt-survey/ (accessed 23 January 2026).

9. Primary Care Development Corporation (PCDC). (n.d.). *Financing CrescentCare's new facility in New Orleans.* PCDC. https://www.pcdc.org/press-release/crescentcare-announcement/ (accessed 23 January 2026).

10. Health Resources and Services Administration (HRSA). (n.d.) *New data on health center patients.* HRSA. https://www.hrsa.gov/about/news/press-releases/new-data-health-center-patients (accessed 23 January 2026).

11. Health Resources and Services Administration (HRSA). (n.d.). *Health center program: Number of FQHCs and service sites.* HRSA. https://bphc.hrsa.gov/about-health-center-program (accessed 23 January 2026).

12. Primary Care Development Corporation (PCDC). (n.d.). *Capital financing programs for primary care.* PCDC. https://www.pcdc.org/capital-financing/ (accessed 23 January 2026).

13. Primary Care Development Corporation (PCDC). (n.d.). *New Markets Tax Credits (NMTC) program overview.* PCDC. https://www.pcdc.org/capital-financing/nmtc/ (accessed 23 January 2026).

14. Capital Impact Partners. (2025). *Capital Impact Partners awarded $85 million in New Markets Tax Credits.* Capital Impact Partners. https://www.capitalimpact.org/blog/capital-impact-partners-awarded-85-million-in-new-markets-tax-credits/ (accessed 23 January 2026).

15. Capital Impact Partners. (n.d.). *Health care focus area.* Capital Impact Partners. https://www.capitalimpact.org/focus/health-care/ (accessed 23 January 2026).

16. HOPE Credit Union. (n.d.). *HOPE joins USDA to announce major investment in the Mid-South.* HOPE Credit Union. https://www.hopecu .org/inthenews/press-releases/hope-joins-usda-to-announce-major-investment-in-the-mid-south (accessed 23 January 2026).

17. BlueHub Capital. (n.d.). *Lowell Community Health Center expansion financing.* BlueHub Capital. https://bluehubcapital.org/impact/impact-stories/lowell-community-health-center (accessed 23 January 2026).

18. Indigenous Economic Development Community of Practice. (2025). Health and Community Center Advances Native Hawaiian Health on Kealakehe Hawaiian Home Land (La'i Pua Community Health Center). *Indigenous Economic Development Community of Practice.* August 13. https://www.indigenouscop.org/healthcare/lai-pua-community-health-center (accessed 23 January 2026).

19. Flagship Pioneering. (n.d.). *Process.* Flagship Pioneering. https://www .flagshippioneering.com/process (accessed 23 January 2026).

20. *MIT Technology Review.* (2020). *How Moderna's COVID-19 vaccine works.* December 15, 2020. https://www.technologyreview.com/2020/12/15/1013358/moderna-covid-vaccine-biotech-flagship-pioneering/ (accessed 23 January 2026).

21. U.S. Department of Health and Human Services. (n.d.). *Center for the Biomedical Advanced Research and Development Authority (BARDA).* ASPR. https://aspr.hhs.gov/AboutASPR/ProgramOffices/BARDA/Pages/default.aspx (accessed 23 January 2026).

22. Centers for Disease Control and Prevention (CDC). (n.d.). *Maternal mortality prevention.* CDC. https://www.cdc.gov/maternal-mortality/index.html (accessed 23 January 2026).

23. Centers for Disease Control and Prevention (CDC). (n.d.). *Maternal mortality.* CDC. https://www.cdc.gov/reproductivehealth/maternal-mortality (accessed 23 January 2026).

24. *Roots Community Health Center Metrics.* Available at: https://roots communityhealth.org/impact/metrics/ (accessed 6 February 2026); *Roots Community Health Locations.* Available at: https://rootscommunityhealth .org/our-work/health-wellness-services/medical-services/locations/ (accessed 6 February 2026).

25. Commonfund Institute. (2025). *Health conversion foundations: Preserving community health in a changing landscape.* Commonfund, October 7, 2025. https://www.commonfund.org/blog/health-conversion-foundations-preserving-community-health-in-a-changing-landscape (accessed 23 January 2026).

26. The California Endowment. (2024). *The California Endowment to align $4 billion in investments with mission. Philanthropy News Digest,* February 26, 2024. https://philanthropynewsdigest.org/news/california-endowment-to-align-4-billion-in-investments-with-mission (accessed 23 January 2026).

27. The California Endowment. (n.d.). *Building trust & equity: The California Endowment's impact investing and mission-related investments.* The California Endowment. https://www.calendow.org/app/uploads/2024/02/TCE_Racial-Equity-Report_FINAL-110223.pdf (accessed 23 January 2026).

28. McElhaney, A. (2024). The California endowment will plow its entire $4 billion into mission investments. *Institutional Investor,* February 21. https://www.institutionalinvestor.com/article/2cvmgqddlhtwe5fe6wem8/portfolio/the-california-endowment-will-plow-its-entire-4-billion-into-mission-investments (accessed 23 January 2026).

29. The Colorado Health Foundation. (n.d.). *Financials.* https://coloradohealth.org/about-us/financials (accessed 23 January 2026).

30. The Colorado Health Foundation. (2025). *Rewiring capital: How The Colorado Health Foundation is reimagining impact investment.* Available at: https://coloradohealth.org/news/blog/rewiring-capital-how-colorado-health-foundation-reimagining-impact-investment (accessed 5 February 2026).

31. Radding, D. (2023). *Improving health, investing in social good.* Kaiser Permanente, Look Inside KP Northern California, December 19. https://lookinside.kaiserpermanente.org/improving-health-investing-in-social-good/ (accessed 23 January 2026).

32. Taylor, L. A. (2018). *Housing and health: An overview of the literature. Health Affairs* (Health Policy Brief), June 7, 2018. https://www.healthaffairs.org/do/10.1377/hpb20180313.396577/ (accessed 23 January 2026).

33. Healthcare Anchor Network. (2021). *Kaiser Permanente Thriving Communities Fund*. Healthcare Anchor Network, July 28, 2021. https://healthcareanchor.network/2021/07/kaiser-permanente-thriving-communities-fund/ (accessed 23 January 2026).

34. CommonSpirit Health. (n.d.). *Community investment program*. CommonSpirit Health. https://www.commonspirit.org/impact/community-health-initiatives/community-investment-program (accessed 23 January 2026).

35. Boston Medical Center. (n.d.). *BMC invests $6.5 million to help combat homelessness*. Boston Medical Center. https://www.bmc.org/about-us/stories/bmc-invests-65-million-help-combat-homelessness (accessed 23 January 2026).

36. Local Initiatives Support Corporation (LISC). (2018). *A bold new $45 million partnership takes aim at the health gap*. LISC, March 13, 2018. https://www.lisc.org/our-stories/story/bold-new-45-million-partnership-takes-aim-health-gap/ (accessed 23 January 2026).

37. Rush University Medical Center. (2020). *Investing with impact*. Rush, February 25, 2020. https://www.rush.edu/news/investing-impact (accessed 23 January 2026).

38. Optum Ventures. (n.d.). *Portfolio*. Optum Ventures. https://www.optumventures.com/portfolio (accessed 23 January 2026).

39. Lavine, R. (2023). *CVS Health ups its investment firepower as it moves into primary care. Global Corporate Venturing*, February 22, 2023. https://globalventuring.com/corporate/vijay-patel-cvs-health-ventures/ (accessed 23 January 2026).

40. JPMorgan Chase. (2022). *JPMorgan Chase makes new investment in Centivo*. JPMorgan Chase. https://www.jpmorganchase.com/newsroom/press-releases/2022/new-investment-in-centivo (accessed 23 January 2026).

41. Erickson, D. (2023). *The fifth freedom: Guaranteeing an opportunity-rich childhood for all*. Washington, DC: Brookings Institution Press.

42. Quantified Ventures. (2020). *Announcing a new outcomes fund to support mothers and families affected by substance use disorder*. Quantified Ventures, October 22, 2020. https://www.quantifiedventures.com/blog/new-health-outcomes-fund (accessed 23 January 2026).

43. Institute for Child Success. (n.d.). *About us*. Institute for Child Success. https://www.instituteforchildsuccess.org/about-us/ (accessed 23 January 2026).

44. PR Newswire. (2022). *First-of-its-kind project to use private-sector funding to reduce asthma for NYC Medicaid recipients*. January 12, 2022. https://www.prnewswire.com/news-releases/first-of-its-kind-project-to-use-private-sector-funding-to-reduce-asthma-for-nyc-medicaid-recipients-301459634.html (accessed 23 January 2026).

45. Modify Health. "ModifyHealth Raises $13.5M in Funding to Expand Food-as-Medicine Solutions." December 4 2024. https://www.prnewswire.com/news-releases/modifyhealth-raises-13-5m-in-funding-to-expand-food-as-medicine-solutions-302314267.html (accessed 1 March 2026).

46. Investing in Flourishing Communities. (n.d.). *Investing in flourishing communities*. https://www.investinginflourishing.org (accessed 23 January 2026).

47. Aylward, D. (2025). *Author email exchange with Antony Bugg-Levine*, 29 December 2025.

Chapter 7

1. Joselow, M. (2025). *A conservative's plan to sell public land faces MAGA pushback. New York Times*, June 27. https://www.nytimes.com/2025/06/27/climate/public-lands-sell-off-maga.html (accessed 23 January 2026).

2. Rockefeller Foundation. 2023. *A new generation cultivates tomorrow with sustainable farming*. Rockefeller Foundation. https://www.rockefellerfoundation.org/grantee-impact-stories/a-new-generation-cultivates-tomorrow-with-sustainable-farming/ (accessed 23 January 2026).

3. Woodcock Foundation. (n.d.). *Perennial Fund I investment profile*. Woodcock Foundation. https://woodcockfdn.org/investment/perennial-fund/ (accessed 23 January 2026).

4. Global AgInvesting. (2024). *Mad Capital secures $78M for Fund II amid robust demand for U.S. regenerative ag*. Global AgInvesting, June 2024. https://globalaginvesting.com/mad-capital-secures-78m-for-fund-ii-amid-robust-demand-for-us-regenerative-ag/ (accessed 23 January 2026)

5. Toniic. (n.d.). *Why Toniic members invested in Mad Capital's Perennial Fund II. Medium.* https://medium.com/why-toniic-members-invested/why-toniic-members-invested-in-mad-capitals-perennial-fund-ii-1ee0d600985e (accessed 23 January 2026).

6. National Center for Family Philanthropy. (n.d.). *Effective family philanthropy: The Woodcock Foundation.* NCFP. National Center for Family Philanthropy. *Effective Family Philanthropy: The Woodcock Foundation.* 2023. https://www.ncfp.org/resources-tools/effective-family-philanthropy-woodcock-foundation (accessed 24 January 2026).

7. Woodcock Foundation. (2023). *Investment policy statement with focus on shareholder engagement.* National Center for Family Philanthropy. https://www.ncfp.org/wp-content/uploads/2023/10/Investment-Policy-with-Focus-on-Shareholder-Engagement-Woodcock-Foundation-2023.pdf (accessed 23 January 2026).

8. Iowa Soybean Association. (n.d.). *The first mile of success: Engaging farmers to build supply chain commitments.* Iowa Soybean Association. https://www.iasoybeans.com/newsroom/article/the-first-mile-of-success-engaging-farmers-to-build-supply-chain-commitments (accessed 23 January 2026).

9. Quantified Ventures. (n.d.). *Soil and water outcomes fund.* Quantified Ventures.https://www.quantifiedventures.com/soil-and-water-outcomes-fund (accessed 23 January 2026).

10. Green Finance Institute (GFI Hive). (n.d.). *Soil and Water Outcomes Fund case study.* Green Finance Institute. https://hive.greenfinanceinstitute.com/gfihive/revenues-for-nature/case-studies/soil-and-water-outcomes-fund/ (accessed 23 January 2026).

11. Soil and Water Outcomes Fund. (2024). *Soil and Water Outcomes Fund surpasses 300,000 enrolled acres, pays farmers $10.5 million in 2023.* February 16. https://theoutcomesfund.com/swof-pays-farmers-105-million-in-2023.

12. Iowa Soybean Association. *The first mile of success: Engaging farmers to build supply chain commitments* (includes the $120M Walmart–PepsiCo investment detail). March 14, 2024. (accessed 24 January 2026). https://www.iasoybeans.com/newsroom/article/the-first-mile-of-success-engaging-farmers-to-build-supply-chain-commitments

13. Green Finance Institute. (n.d.). *Forest resilience bond case study*. Green Finance Institute. https://www.greenfinanceinstitute.com/hive/revenues-for-nature/case-studies/forest-resilience-bond/ (accessed 23 January 2026).

14. Knight, Z. (2025). *Author discussion with Zack Knight*, 14 November 2025.

15. Blue Forest Conservation. (n.d.). *California Wildfire Innovation Fund*. Blue Forest Conservation. https://www.blueforest.org/finance/blue-forest-asset-management/california-wildfire-innovation-fund/ (accessed 23 January 2026).

16. Blue Forest Conservation. (n.d.). *BurnBot partner profile*. Blue Forest Conservation. https://www.blueforest.org/our-impact/insights-news-resources/partner-profile-burnbot/ (accessed 23 January 2026).

17. Walton Family Foundation. (n.d.). *A community bank that's helping fishermen stay on the water*. Walton Family Foundation. https://www.waltonfamilyfoundation.org/stories/environment/a-community-bank-thats-helping-fishermen-stay-on-the-water (accessed 23 January 2026).

18. International Collective in Support of Fishworkers. (n.d.). *Tenure rights/ USA: By, and from, the sea*. ICSF. https://icsf.net/samudra/tenure-rights-usa-by-and-from-the-sea/ (accessed 23 January 2026).

19. Kern, R. (2025). Fishermen quotes and additional contex provided through emails and discussions with author, November 2025.

20. The Nature Conservancy. (2024). *NatureVest impact report 2024*. Arlington, VA: The Nature Conservancy. https://www.nature.org/en-us/about-us/who-we-are/how-we-work/finance-investing/naturevest/ (accessed 23 January 2026).

21. CSRwire. (2014). *The Nature Conservancy and JPMorgan Chase collaborate to create a landmark conservation finance initiative*. CSRwire, April 29, 2014. https://www.csrwire.com/press_releases/37000-the-nature-conservancy-and-jpmorgan-chase-collaborate-to-create-a-landmark-conservation-finance-initiative (accessed 23 January 2026).

22. The Nature Conservancy. (n.d.). *About NatureVest*. The Nature Conservancy. https://www.nature.org/en-us/about-us/who-we-are/how-we-work/finance-investing/naturevest/ (accessed 23 January 2026).

23. The Nature Conservancy. (2024). *NatureVest impact report 2024: Portfolio and outcomes summary*. The Nature Conservancy. https://www.nature.org/en-us/about-us/who-we-are/how-we-work/finance-investing/naturevest/impact-report/ (accessed 23 January 2026).

24. The Nature Conservancy (2023). *Freshwater Network: Notable floodplain restoration projects.* Freshwater Network. https://freshwaternetwork.org/additional-resources/ (accessed 23 January 2026).

25. Kaiser, C. (2021). *What does it take to create financial products that can save the planet? Yale Insights,* Yale School of Management, June 2021. https://insights.som.yale.edu/insights/what-does-it-take-to-create-financial-products-that-can-save-the-planet (accessed 23 January 2026).

26. Petno, D. (2014). *Foreword.* In *Investing in Conservation: A Landscape Assessment of an Emerging Market,* EKO Asset Management Partners, The Nature Conservancy, and JPMorgan Chase & Co. https://www.nature.org/content/dam/tnc/nature/en/documents/InvestingIn Conservation_Report.pdf (accessed 23 January 2026).

27. CEI Capital Management. (2018). *CCML financing of the Lyme Timber Company introduces new safe logging technology.* CEI Capital Management, August 2018. https://www.ceimaine.org/news-and-events/news/2018/08/ccml-financing-of-the-lyme-timber-company-introduces-new-safe-logging-technology/ (accessed 23 January 2026).

28. Yale Center for Business and the Environment. *Peter Stein.* (n.d.). https://cbey.yale.edu/our-community/peter-stein (accessed 23 January 2026).

29. Lyme Timber Company. (n.d.). *Lyme Conservation Opportunities Fund.* Lyme Timber Company. https://www.lymetimber.com/portfolio/ (accessed 23 January 2026).

30. Green Finance Institute (GFI). (n.d.). *Lyme Timber Company LLC (TIMO and conservation easements) case study.* GFI Hive — Revenues for Nature. https://www.greenfinanceinstitute.com/hive/revenues-for-nature/case-studies/lyme-timber-company-llc-timo-and-conservation-easements/?highlight=lyme%20timber (accessed 23 January 2026).

31. Lyme Timber Company. (2018). Lyme closes on $50 million in financing from PENNVEST, providing clean water benefits to local communities. *Lyme Timber Company,* July 31. https://www.lymetimber.com/2018/07/31/lyme-closes-on-50-million-in-financing-from-pennvest-providing-clean-water-benefits-to-local-communities/ (accessed 24 January 2026).

Chapter 8

1. Crunchbase News. (2025). *Global AI funding surpassed $100B in 2024.* January. https://news.crunchbase.com/venture/global-funding-data-analysis-ai-eoy-2024/ (accessed 18 January 2026).

2. Pew Research Center. (2023). *Public awareness of artificial intelligence in everyday activities.* https://www.pewresearch.org/science/2023/02/15/public-awareness-of-artificial-intelligence-in-everyday-activities/ (accessed 18 January 2026); Pew Research Center (2022). *AI and human enhancement: Americans' openness is tempered by a range of concerns.* March 17. https://www.pewresearch.org/internet/2022/03/17/ai-and-human-enhancement-americans-openness-is-tempered-by-a-range-of-concerns/ (accessed 18 January 2026); American Psychological Association (2025). *Stress in America™ 2025: A crisis of connection.* https://www.apa.org/pubs/reports/stress-in-america/2025 (accessed 18 January 2026).

3. U.S. Surgeon General. (2023). *Social media and youth mental health: The U.S. Surgeon General's advisory.* May. https://www.hhs.gov/surgeongeneral/priorities/youth-mental-health/social-media/index.html (accessed 18 January 2026).

4. Federal Communications Commission. (2024). *2024 broadband progress report.* Released March. https://www.fcc.gov/reports-research/reports/broadband-progress-reports (accessed 18 January 2026).

5. Connect Humanity. (n.d.-a). *"Our success is tied to the success of the community": LaShawn Williamson on building a network to connect Enfield, NC.* https://connecthumanity.fund/our-success-is-tied-to-the-success-of-the-community-lashawn-williamson-on-building-a-network-to-connect-enfield-nc/ (accessed 18 January 2026).

6. Institute for Local Self-Reliance. (n.d.). *A wave of wireless connectivity crests in Enfield, North Carolina.* https://ilsr.org/articles/wave-of-wireless-connectivity-crests-in-enfield-north-carolina/ (accessed 18 January 2026).

7. Federal Communications Commission. (2024b). *2024 communications marketplace report.* https://docs.fcc.gov/public/attachments/FCC-24-136A1_Rcd.pdf (accessed 18 January 2026).

8. Pew Research Center. (n.d.). *Internet/broadband fact sheet.* https://www.pewresearch.org/internet/fact-sheet/internet-broadband/ (accessed 18 January 2026).

9. Brookings Institution. (2024). *The unique challenge of bringing broadband to rural America*. https://www.brookings.edu/articles/the-unique-challenge-of-bringing-broadband-to-rural-america/ (accessed 18 January 2026).

10. Vo, B. and Miller, C. (2025). Financing broadband in hard-to-reach communities. *Stanford Social Innovation Review*, April 16. https://ssir.org/articles/entry/financing-broadband-digital-divide (accessed 18 January 2026).

11. Connect Humanity. (n.d.–b). *How we invest*. https://connecthumanity.fund/investments/ (accessed 18 January 2026).

12. Community Broadband Bits Podcast. (2025). *Capital is power: Financing broadband for the long haul*. Episode 654. Interview with Brian Vo and Clara Miller by J. Pittman, June 25. https://muninetworks.org/content/capital-power-financing-broadband-long-haul (accessed 18 January 2026).

13. Ibid.

14. Connect Humanity. (n.d.–c). *Our work*. https://connecthumanity.fund/our-work/ (accessed 18 January 2026).

15. Connect Humanity. (2025a). *Community Broadband Fund* (two-pager). https://connecthumanity.fund/wp-content/uploads/2025/06/Connect-Humanity_Community-Broadband-Fund_2-pager.pdf (accessed 18 January 2026).

16. Connect Humanity. (2025b). *2024 in 10 highlights*. https://connecthumanity.fund/story/connect-humanity-2024-highlights/ (accessed 18 January 2026).

17. Kapor Capital. (n.d.). *Kapor Capital*. https://www.kaporcapital.com (accessed 24 January 2026).

18. Kapor Capital. (n.d.–a). *How we invest*. https://www.kaporcapital.com/how-we-invest/ (accessed 18 January 2026).

19. Kapor Capital. (2019). *Kapor Capital annual report*. https://www.kaporcapital.com/impact-reports/ (accessed 18 January 2026).

20. Kapor, M. and Kapor Klein, F. (2023). *Closing the equity gap*. New York: Harper Business.

21. Crunchbase News. (2025). *Global AI funding surpassed $100B in 2024*. January. https://news.crunchbase.com/venture/global-funding-data-analysis-ai-eoy-2024/ (accessed 18 January 2026).

22. Bank, D. (2024). With stakes in Anthropic, impact investors seek a seat at the AI table. *ImpactAlpha*, April 23. https://impactalpha.com/with-stakes-in-anthropic-impact-investors-seek-a-seat-at-the-ai-table/ (accessed 18 January 2026).

23. Omidyar Network. (2024). *Omidyar Network purchases shares of Anthropic*. Press release, April 1. https://omidyar.com/news/omidyar-network-purchases-shares-of-anthropic/ (accessed 18 January 2026).

24. Lim, D. (2017). *Ford Foundation carves out $1 billion to invest in civic mission. The Wall Street Journal*, April 5. https://www.wsj.com/articles/ford-foundation-carves-out-1-billion-to-invest-in-civic-mission-1491364861 (accessed 24 January 2026).

25. Ford Foundation. "New Holding Company Nine Dean to Invest in Quality Jobs that Drive Business Growth". June 3, 2025. https://www.fordfoundation.org/news-and-stories/news-and-press/news/new-holding-company-nine-dean-to-invest-in-quality-jobs-that-drive-business-growth/ (accessed 1 March 2026).

26. Anthropic. (2025). *Anthropic raises $13B Series F at $183B post-money valuation*. Press release, September 2.

27. McCourt, F. (2024). *Frank McCourt organizing a people's bid to acquire TikTok*. McCourt Global, May 15. https://www.mccourt.com/frank-mccourt-organizing-a-peoples-bid-to-acquire-tiktok/ (accessed 18 January 2026).

28. Project Liberty. (2025). *Decentralized social networking protocol (DSNP)*. https://www.projectliberty.io/dsnp/ (accessed 18 January 2026).

29. Madrigal, A.C. (2024). Is the TikTok ban a chance to rethink the whole internet? *The New Yorker*, May 28. https://www.newyorker.com/news/annals-of-communications/is-the-tiktok-ban-a-chance-to-rethink-the-whole-internet (accessed 18 January 2026).

30. Finan, E. (2024). Why this billionaire says his bid to buy TikTok will make social media safer for kids. *People*, August 2. https://people.com/why-this-billionaire-says-his-bid-to-buy-tiktok-will-make-social-media-safer-for-kids-8687127 (accessed 18 January 2026).

31. Reuters. (2025). Reddit co-founder Alexis Ohanian joins Frank McCourt's TikTok bid. March 3. https://www.reuters.com/technology/reddit-co-founder-alexis-ohanian-joins-frank-mccourts-bid-tiktok-2025-03-03/ (accessed 18 January 2026).

32. NPR. (2025). Supreme Court upholds TikTok law forcing ByteDance to sell or face ban. January 17. https://www.npr.org/2025/01/17/tiktok-supreme-court-decision (accessed 18 January 2026).

Chapter 9

1. Federal Reserve Banks. (2023). *2023 Small Business Credit Survey: Employer firms.* December. Figures 6 ("Share of firms fully approved for financing") and 8 ("Discouraged borrowers by owner race/ethnicity"). https://www.fedsmallbusiness.org/-/media/project/smallbizcredittenant/ fedsmallbusinesssite/fedsmallbusiness/files/2023/2023_sbcs-employer-firms.pdf (accessed 24 January 2026).

2. U.S. Small Business Administration, Office of Advocacy. (2023). *2023 small business economic profile: United States.* November. https://advocacy .sba.gov/wp-content/uploads/2023/11/2023-Small-Business-Economic-Profile-US.pdf (accessed 18 January 2026); PitchBook (2024). *2024 U.S. All In: Female founders in the VC ecosystem.* https://files .pitchbook.com/website/files.pdf/2024_US_All_In_Female_ Founders_in_the_VC_Ecosystem.pdf (accessed 18 January 2026).

3. Board of Governors of the Federal Reserve System. (2019). *Perspectives from Main Street: Bank branch access in rural communities.* November. https://www.federalreserve.gov/publications/files/bank-branch-access-in-rural-communities.pdf (accessed 18 January 2026).

4. Strebulaev, I. (2024). *Most U.S. venture capitalists remain concentrated in a few major cities: San Francisco Bay Area, New York City, and Boston* [LinkedIn post]. LinkedIn. Retrieved January 18, 2026, from https://www .linkedin.com/posts/ilyavcandpe_most-us-venture-capitalists-remain-concentrated-activity-7355644185313513472-aJBE

5. Board of Governors of the Federal Reserve System. (2019). *Perspectives from Main Street: Bank branch access in rural communities.* November. https://www.federalreserve.gov/publications/files/bank-branch-access-in-rural-communities.pdf (accessed 18 January 2026).

6. Board of Governors of the Federal Reserve System. (2022). *Survey of Consumer Finances: Net worth by race and ethnicity.* Data tables. https://www .federalreserve.gov/econres/scfindex.htm (accessed 18 January 2026).

7. Abello, O.P. (2025). *The banks we deserve.* Washington, DC: Island Press.

8. Gillette, B. (2017). Southern Bancorp helping people climb economic security ladder. *Delta Business Journal,* August 10. https://deltabusiness journal.com/southern-bancorp-helping-people-climb-economic-security-ladder/ (accessed 18 January 2026).

9. Self-Help Credit Union. (n.d.). *Our story.* https://www.self-help.org/who-we-are/about-us/our-story (accessed 18 January 2026).

10. HOPE Enterprises. (2024). *"Prosperity begins with HOPE" 2024 Impact Report.* https://www.hopecu.org/impact-reports/2024-hope-impact-report/ (accessed 18 January 2026)

11. Calvert Impact Capital. (n.d.-a). *Access Small Business Program: Zain Burke case study.* https://calvertimpact.org/investing/access-small-business-program (accessed 18 January 2026).

12. U.S. Small Business Administration. (2024). *Frequently asked questions about small business.* July 23. https://advocacy.sba.gov/2024/07/23/frequently-asked-questions-about-small-business-2024/ (accessed 18 January 2026); Bizstim. (n.d.). *Number of businesses in the U.S. with fewer than 50 employees.* https://www.bizstim.com/news/article/number-of-businesses-in-the-us-with-less-than-50-employees (accessed 18 January 2026).

13. Calvert Impact Capital. (n.d.-b). *Community Investment Note.* https://calvertimpact.org/investing/community-investment-note (accessed 18 January 2026).

14. Calvert Impact Capital. (n.d.-c). *Access Small Business Program: Structure and warehouse support.* https://calvertimpact.org/investing/access-small-business-program (accessed 18 January 2026).

15. Calvert Impact Capital. (2024). *Calvert Impact and partners launch Nevada Battle Born Growth Microloan.* Press release, July 12. https://calvertimpact.org/about/press/calvert-impact-and-partners-launch-nevada-battle-born-growth-microloan (accessed 18 January 2026).

16. Calvert Impact Capital. (2025). *Small businesses, big impact: Our commitment to the engines of economic growth.* May 5. https://calvertimpact.org/resources/small-businesses-big-impact (accessed 18 January 2026).

17. Feloni, R. (2018). High-profile investors like Jeff Bezos, Ray Dalio, and Meg Whitman are flocking to a $150 million fund nurturing startups in overlooked American cities. *Business Insider,* February 6. https://www.businessinsider.com/rise-of-the-rest-steve-case-jd-vance-2018-1 (accessed 18 January 2026).

18. Wired. (2018). Techies pitch Obama on building startups outside the Valley. *Wired,* 1 March. https://www.wired.com/story/techies-pitch-obama-on-building-startups-outside-the-valley (accessed 18 January 2026).

19. Revolution. (2024). *Rising from the Reset: 2024 Annual Report (Rise of the Rest)*. December 2024. https://www.linkedin.com/posts/revolution-llc_rise-of-the-rest-2024-annual-report-activity-7273072510374481920-854R (accessed 18 January 2026).

20. Revolution. (n.d.). Revolution's Rise of the Rest announces second $150 million fund to invest in startups based outside of Silicon Valley. Press release. https://revolution.com/press-release/revolutions-rise-of-the-rest-announces-second-150-million-fund-to-invest-in-startups-based-outside-of-silicon-valley-following-faster-than-expected-deployment-of-first-fund/ (accessed 18 January 2026).

21. Prudential Financial. (2018). Prudential Financial announces leadership succession; remarks by John Strangfeld on purpose and inclusive growth. Press release, September 12. https://investor.prudential.com/news/news-details/2018/Prudential-Financial-announces-leadership-succession/default.aspx (accessed 18 January 2026).

22. Behrman, G. (2023). ESG Next: An interview with Prudential's Lata Reddy. *NationSwell*, 10 February. https://nationswell.com/esg-next-an-interview-with-prudentials-lata-reddy/ (accessed 18 January 2026).

23. U.S. Census Bureau. (2024). *QuickFacts: Newark city, New Jersey*. https://www.census.gov/quickfacts/newarkcitynewjersey (accessed 24 January 2026).

24. Federal Reserve Bank of San Francisco. (2021). *Why small business lending matters for local economies*. https://www.frbsf.org/research-and-insights/blog/community-development/2024/10/24/small-business-credit-survey-2024/ (accessed 24 January 2026).

25. USAFacts. (2023). *What's behind the decline in U.S. banks?* https://usafacts.org/articles/whats-behind-the-decline-in-us-banks/ (accessed 24 January 2026).

26. Banking Exchange. (2024). *U.S. could lose all bank branches by 2041*. September 16. https://www.bankingexchange.com/news-feed/item/10106-us-could-lose-all-bank-branches (accessed 24 January 2026); Board of Governors of the Federal Reserve System (2019). *Perspectives from Main Street: Bank branch access in rural communities*. https://www.federalreserve.gov/publications/november-2019-bank-branch-access-in-rural-communities.htm (accessed 24 January 2026).

27. Lemm, D. Personal communication. 8 January 2025.

28. Blandin Foundation. (n.d.). *Our history*. https://blandinfoundation.org/about/our-story/our-history/ (accessed 18 January 2026).

29. Impact Engine and Cogent Consulting. (2024). *Investing for positive impact across the Midwest: Midwest impact investing landscape report*. https://www.cogentconsulting.net/wp-content/uploads/2024/09/MidWestLandscapeReport.pdf (accessed 18 January 2026).

Chapter 10

1. Hughes, C. (2024). Marketcrafters: The 100-year struggle to shape the American economy. New York: Simon & Schuster.

2. U.S. Department of Energy, Loan Programs Office. (2010). *Tesla Advanced Technology Vehicles Manufacturing (ATVM) loan*. https://www.energy.gov/lpo/tesla (accessed 24 January 2026).

3. U.S. Department of Transportation, Build America Bureau. (n.d.). Transportation Infrastructure Finance and Innovation Act (TIFIA): Program overview. https://www.transportation.gov/buildamerica/financing/tifia (accessed 24 January 2026).

4. Office of the Chief Technology Officer, U.S. Department of Defense. (n.d.). *Office of strategic capital*. https://www.cto.mil/osc (accessed 24 January 2026).

5. U.S. Small Business Administration. (n.d.-a). *SBIC directory*. https://www.sba.gov/sbic/directory (accessed 30 January 2026); U.S. Small Business Administration. (n.d.-b). *Small Business Investment Company (SBIC) program: Overview and guidance*. https://www.sba.gov/partners/sbics (accessed 24 January 2026).

6. U.S. Small Business Administration. (2025). *Investment policy statement: Small Business Investment Company Critical Technology Initiative*. January 10. https://www.sba.gov/document/policy-guidance-investment-policy-statement-small-business-investment-company-critical-technology-initiative (accessed 24 January 2026); U.S. Small Business Administration and U.S. Department of Defense. (2024). *SBA and DoD announce first licensed SBIC Critical Technologies funds*. Press release, October 22. https://www.sba.gov/article/2024/10/22/us-small-business-administration-department-defense-celebrate-successful-first-year-small-business (accessed 24 January 2026).

7. Johnson, D. (2025). *Johnson, Moore legislation aims to prevent foreign takeovers and closures of U.S. businesses.* Press release, May 7. https://dustyjohnson.house.gov/media/press-releases/johnson-moore-legislation-aims-prevent-foreign-takeovers-and-closures-us (accessed 24 January 2026).

8. RSM US LLP. (2025). *SBIC program surplus transferred to U.S. Treasury: net returns over 24 years.* March 18. https://rsmus.com/insights/industries/financial-services/recapping-a-significant-year-for-the-sbic-program-and-what-s-ahe.html (accessed 24 January 2026).

9. Federal Housing Finance Agency. (n.d.). *About Fannie Mae & Freddie Mac.* https://www.fhfa.gov/about/fannie-mae-freddie-mac (accessed 24 January 2026).

10. Farm Credit Administration. (2024). *2024 annual report.* https://www.fca.gov/template-fca/about/2024AnnualReport.pdf (accessed 30 January 2026).

11. U.S. Department of Energy, Office of Energy Dominance Financing. (2025). *EDF portfolio performance.* https://www.energy.gov/edf/edf-portfolio-performance (accessed 24 January 2026).

12. Health Resources and Services Administration, Bureau of Primary Health Care. (n.d.). *Health Center Loan Guarantee Program.* https://bphc.hrsa.gov/initiatives/health-center-loan-guarantee-program (accessed 24 January 2026).

13. Capital Link. (2024). *HRSA Loan Guarantee Program overview.* https://www.caplink.org/images/HRSA_Loan_Guarantee_Program_Overview_Webinar_9-9-2024.pdf (accessed 24 January 2026); Health Resources and Services Administration. (n.d.). Health Center Loan Guarantee Program: Loan recipients. https://bphc.hrsa.gov/initiatives/health-center-loan-guarantee-program/loan-recipients (accessed 24 January 2026).

14. National Charter School Resource Center. (2020). *CSP credit enhancement transactions dashboard.* https://charterschoolcenter.ed.gov/csp-credit-enhancement-transactions-dashboard (accessed 30 January 2026).

15. U.S. Department of Agriculture, Rural Development. (n.d.). *Business and Industry Guaranteed Loan Program.* https://www.rd.usda.gov/programs-services/business-programs/business-and-industry-guaranteed-loan (accessed 24 January 2026).

16. Summit, LLC. (2025). *USDA B&I Guaranteed Loan Program: Economic assessment.* Congressional submission. https://www.congress.gov/119/meeting/house/118602/witnesses/HHRG-119-AG22-Wstate-BrandB-20250918-SD001.pdf (accessed 24 January 2026).

17. Congressional Research Service. (2023). *Federal financial support for the U.S. energy sector.* https://crsreports.congress.gov/product/pdf/R/R44852 (accessed 24 January 2026).

18. U.S. Department of Housing and Urban Development. (n.d.). *Low-Income Housing Tax Credit overview.* https://www.huduser.gov/portal/datasets/lihtc.html (accessed 24 January 2026).

19. National Council of State Housing Agencies. (2021). *LIHTC turns 35.* https://www.ncsha.org/resource/lihtc-turns-35/ (accessed 24 January 2026).

20. U.S. Department of the Treasury. (2020). *The impact of Opportunity Zones.* https://trumpwhitehouse.archives.gov/wp-content/uploads/2020/08/The-Impact-of-Opportunity-Zones-An-Initial-Assessment.pdf (accessed 24 January 2026).

21. Theodos, B. (2021). *Opportunity Zones: Current status and options for reform.* Testimony before the Oversight Subcommittee, Ways and Means Committee, U.S. House of Representatives, November 16. Urban Institute. https://www.urban.org/sites/default/files/publication/105094/opportunity-zones-current-status-and-options-for-reform.pdf (accessed 24 January 2026).

22. Internal Revenue Service. (n.d.). *Advanced Manufacturing Investment Credit (Section 48D).* https://www.irs.gov/credits-deductions/advanced-manufacturing-investment-credit (accessed 24 January 2026).

23. Semiconductor Industry Association via CSIS. (2025). *Tracking CHIPS Act incentives: private semiconductor investments.* Center for Strategic and International Studies. https://www.csis.org/analysis/innovation-lightbulb-tracking-chips-act-incentives (accessed 24 January 2026).

24. S&P Global Market Intelligence. (2025). *US private equity AUM hits $3.128 trillion in 2024.* 2 April. www.spglobal.com/market-intelligence/en/news-insights/articles/2025/4/us-private-equity-aum-hits-3128-trillion-in-2024-88099590 (accessed 24 January 2026).

25. Federal News Network. (2025). *TSP closes out June with just over $1 trillion in assets.* 28 July. www.federalnewsnetwork.com/federal-newscast/2025/07/tsp-closes-out-june-with-just-over-1-trillion-in-assets/ (accessed 24 January 2026).

26. Munnell, A.H. and Sundén, A. (2001). *Investment practices of state and local pension funds*. Center for Retirement Research at Boston College. https://www.academia.edu/97064349/Investment_Practices_of_State_and_Local_Pension_Funds_Implications_for_Social_Security_Reform (accessed 24 January 2026).

27. Texas Constitution. (1988). *Article XVI, Section 70 (Texas Growth Fund)*. www.law.justia.com/constitution/texas/sections/cn001600-007000.html (accessed 24 January 2026).

28. New York City Comptroller. (n.d.). *Economically targeted investments (ETI) program*. www.comptroller.nyc.gov/services/financial-matters/economically-targeted-investments/ (accessed 24 January 2026).

29. Webb, D. (2026). *NYC Comptroller Levine calls affordable housing investments 'top priority,' shares details on CIO search*. Pensions & Investments (9 January). www.pionline.com/institutional-investors/pension-funds/pi-mark-levine-nyc-affordable-housing-cio-search/ (accessed 24 January 2026).

30. Illinois General Assembly. (2019). *Illinois Sustainable Investing Act* (Public Act 101-0473; HB2460). www.ilga.gov/Legislation/publicacts/view/101-0473 (accessed 24 January 2026).

31. Vermont Housing Finance Agency and Vermont State Treasurer's Office. (n.d.). *10% for Vermont (LIAC) program*. www.vhfa.org/developers/programs/liac (accessed 24 January 2026).

32. Colorado General Assembly. (2025). *Colorado Senate Bill 25-006*. www.leg.colorado.gov/bills/sb25-006 (accessed 24 January 2026).

33. New Mexico Legislature. (2023). *New Mexico Private Equity Investment Program handout*. 18 August. www.nmlegis.gov/handouts/IPOC%20081823%20Item%201%20NMSIC%20New%20Mexico%20Private%20Equity%20Investment%20Program.pdf (accessed 24 January 2026).

34. U.S. Senate. (2021). *Summary of the Industrial Finance Corporation Act (IFCUS)*. www.coons.senate.gov/wp-content/uploads/media/doc/SUMMARY%20IFCUS%20117%20v.2.pdf (accessed 24 January 2026).

35. Gelsinger, P. (2025). *A sovereign-wealth fund to keep America's technological edge*. The Wall Street Journal (15 July). www.wsj.com/opinion/a-sovereign-wealth-fund-to-keep-americas-technological-edge-ai-china-4760dc09 (accessed 24 January 2026).

36. White House. (2025). *A plan for establishing a United States sovereign wealth fund.* Executive Order (3 February). www.whitehouse.gov/presidential-actions/2025/02/a-plan-for-establishing-a-united-states-sovereign-wealth-fund/ (accessed 24 January 2026).

37. Jacobs, J. (2025). *Bessent and Lutnick sent plan for U.S. sovereign wealth fund—but White House has pushed back.* CBS News (7 May). www.cbsnews.com/news/sovereign-wealth-fund-trump-administration-white-house-pushes-back/ (accessed 24 January 2026).

Chapter 11

1. U.S. Department of the Treasury. *Emergency Capital Investment Program (ECIP).* U.S. Department of the Treasury. https://home.treasury.gov/policy-issues/coronavirus/assistance-for-small-businesses/emergency-capital-investment-program (accessed 24 January 2026).

2. Capital Impact Partners. (2024). *Capital Impact surpasses $500 million issued through its rated investment notes program.* 3 October. https://www.capitalimpact.org/blog/capital-impact-investment-notes-500-million-2024/ (accessed 31 January 2026).

3. Pritzker Simmons, L. and Simmons, I. (2018). *Liesel Pritzker Simmons and Ian Simmons: Candid conversations.* SOCAP Global, 11 October. https://socapglobal.com/2018/10/2018-10-11-liesel-pritzker-simmons-and-ian-simmons-gcp-candid-series/ (accessed 31 January 2026).

4. Scott, M. "Investing," *Yield Giving,* December 18, 2024. https://yieldgiving.com/essays/investing/ (accessed 24 January 2026).

5. Board of Governors of the Federal Reserve System (US). *Nonfinancial Corporate Business; Total Financial Assets, Level (TFAABSNNCB).* FRED, Federal Reserve Bank of St. Louis. https://fred.stlouisfed.org/series/TFAABSNNCB (accessed 24 January 2026).

Acknowledgments

A great blessing and honor in my career has been to work with a global community of insightful, generous, and committed people focused on harnessing private capital for the public good. The ideas in the book reflect what I have learned alongside many of them over the last 30 years. Recognizing that any list like this will inevitably be incomplete . . .

I am grateful for my colleagues over the years: Fred Ogana, Erastus Kibugu, Bruce McNamer, and our team and clients at TechnoServe in Kenya and Uganda who helped me appreciate what a difference even a $100 loan can make; Maria Blair, Rick Duke, David Lessing, Paul McMahon, Harsha Misra, Tom Rippin, Ashok Subramanian, and my other McKinsey colleagues and clients who helped me understand the vast power of private companies and markets and what it takes to move them; my Rockefeller Foundation colleagues including Darren Walker who gave me the space to create our impact investing work, and Margot Brandenburg, Brinda Ganguly, Justina Lai, Andrea Porter, and Terrence Strong; the team and Board members of the Global Impact Investing Network who have given me a front-row seat to the evolving impact investing industry; the Nonprofit Finance Fund team and Board and its founder Clara Miller who helped me hone my finance wonk to English translation skills; Damien Dwin and the Lafayette Square team for their tireless work to make impact investing scale with integrity; Jack Moriarty, David Williams, and Katic Deal from Lafayette Square Institute who helped me recognize we can still find bipartisan support for the right ideas expressed in an inclusive way; Don Baylor, Jr. and Anne Havard of Worker Solutions who are doing the hard work to support companies improve the financial security of American workers; Edwin Macharia and Robin Miller and the team at Axum; Caleb Ballou and Trace Welsh of Trimtab for their relentless focus on putting the impact in impact investing; Shannie Lotan and Jeremy Hockenstein for challenging me to get clear and stay focused; Sandra Navalli who first brought me into the classroom at Columbia Business School, Kelly Ifill who collaborated in teaching a version of this book there in 2025, Kate Lee and the Columbia Caseworks team for helping us make case studies about two of the inspiring stories in this book, and my CBS teaching assistants and students over the years; Tom Kalil and the Renaissance Philanthropy team for supporting the broader work of capital markets shaping; Kieron Boyle and the London School of Economics Marshall Institute team for your insights and collaboration.

The fellow travelers I have learned with over the years: Reuben Abraham, Akasha Absher, Kunle Apampa, Sam Bonsey, Ryan Bowers, Amit Bouri, Josh Cohen, Sir Ronald Cohen, Ron Cordes, Bob Dandrew, Soraya Darabi, Stuart Davidson, Michaela Edwards, Christopher Egerton-Warburton, Jed Emerson, David Erickson, Rodney Foxworth, Katherine Fulton, John Goldstein, "Dr. Doug" Jutte, Georgia Levenson Keohane, Peter Knight, Todd Leverette, Dom Mjartan, Nick O'Donohoe, William Orum, Tracy Palandjian, Aunnie Patton Power, Liesel Pritzker, Diana Proper de Callejon, Jenn Pryce, Ida Rademacher, Santhosh Ramdoss, Phil Reeves, Justin Rockefeller, Ommeed Sathe, Jason Scott, Lauren Sercu, Debra Schwartz, Brian Trelstad, Brian Vo, Napoleon Wallace, Caroline Whistler, Adam Wolfensohn, Ion Yadigaroglu, and Lindsay Zizumbo.

Thanks also to the people who provided input on the content of this book and ideas on who to highlight: David Aylward, Beth Bafford, Ross Baird, Cat Berman, Don Chen, Smitha Das, Stacy Faella, Humaira Faiz, Nick Flores, David Foster, Victoria Fram, Tim Freundlich, Elizabeth Garlow, Catherine Godschalk, Harry Guinness, Susan Hammel, Tom Kalil, Margot Kane, Rebecca Kern, Yigal Kerszenbaum, Amy Klement, Zach Knight, Mike Kubzansky, Daniel Lemm, Marcus Martin, Tommy Mercein, Erin Harkless Moore, Elizabeth Moraff, Brian Rajan Nagendra, Charles Oppenheimer, Andi Phillips, Lata Reddy, Alison Rein, Fran Seegull, Jeannie Tarkenton, Catherine Toner, and Jessica Droste Yagan.

Two people whose work and example are quietly reflected in the tone of this book: Jim Sorenson, who has shown so many of us how to describe and conduct this work in a way that can attract bipartisan support; and Trabian Shorters, whose insights and training about asset framing have changed how I see and describe the world.

I would not have been in a position to write this book if not for the people who encouraged me to set out to build an independent advisory business with Bugg-Levine, Inc. and who have provided practical advice, professional support, and camaraderie: The Cone, Jamie Daves, Mary-Ann Etiebet, Christina Leijonhufvud, Rehana Nathoo, Mark Newberg, Chintan Panchal, Tom Scriven, Julie Sherman, Sue Suh, Roy Swan, Ben Thornley, and Maggie Wierzbicki.

Thanks to the team at ImpactAlpha, whose work represents a surprisingly large share of the journalism about the innovations I describe here, and Oscar Abello, our reliably insightful and provocative community finance beat reporter.

Thanks to the team at Wiley: Jesse Wiley for seeing the potential in a book about this new concept called Impact Investing more than 15 years ago, and Brian O'Neill, Julie Kerr, Sangeetha Suresh, and the team for your responsiveness this time around.

I first thought to write what became this book during a fretful, jet-lagged night of insomnia at the Rockefeller Foundation Bellagio Conference Center in early 2025. It was not the first time that remarkable setting provided me with a moment of inspiration and clarity that changed the arc of my career. Thank you to the always-welcoming Bellagio team and to the GIIN team for inviting me to return this time.

This work would not be possible without the support of family, my parents Janet and Sandy Levine, and my in-laws John Bugg, Derek Murphy, and Jacqueline Murphy.

No words could adequately express my gratitude to Ahadi Bugg-Levine for making my life and writing better since the Night of the Red Pen more than 27 years ago.

Finally, Shari Bahrenbach, Reggie Ellison, Lisa Hall, Bim Hundal, Andrew Kassoy, Jonathan Schmidt, Nathan Taft, and Peter Wheeler all helped light the way. Their memory is a blessing and their lives an inspiration for those of us who carry the torch forward.

About the Author

Antony Bugg-Levine has spent 25 years motivated to answer a question that cuts across politics and ideology: How do we put the world's vast investment capital to work solving our deepest problems?

He convened the Rockefeller Foundation meeting that coined the term "impact investing" in 2007, co-founded the Global Impact Investing Network, and co-wrote the field's first book. He also led one of the US's largest community finance institutions for nearly a decade, co-led the community impact team and policy arm of an asset management firm, and advised Fortune 100 CEOs on corporate strategy.

Today, through Bugg-Levine, Inc., he supports foundations and family offices to become more discerning, decisive, and ambitious impact investors.

A third-generation Southern African, he began his professional path in post-apartheid South Africa, where he worked at the Human Rights Commission and wrote speeches for President Nelson Mandela and other African National Congress leaders. He later ran the Kenya and Uganda teams of a global nonprofit, seeing firsthand the promise of expanding access to fair finance.

Antony earned a BA from Yale and a Master's in Public Administration from Princeton and is an adjunct professor at Columbia Business School. He has held fellowships with the Federal Reserve Bank of New York, the London School of Economics, and Renaissance Philanthropy, and was named one of the 50 most influential people in the US nonprofit sector by *Nonprofit Times*.

He lives in New Jersey with his wife and daughter.

Index